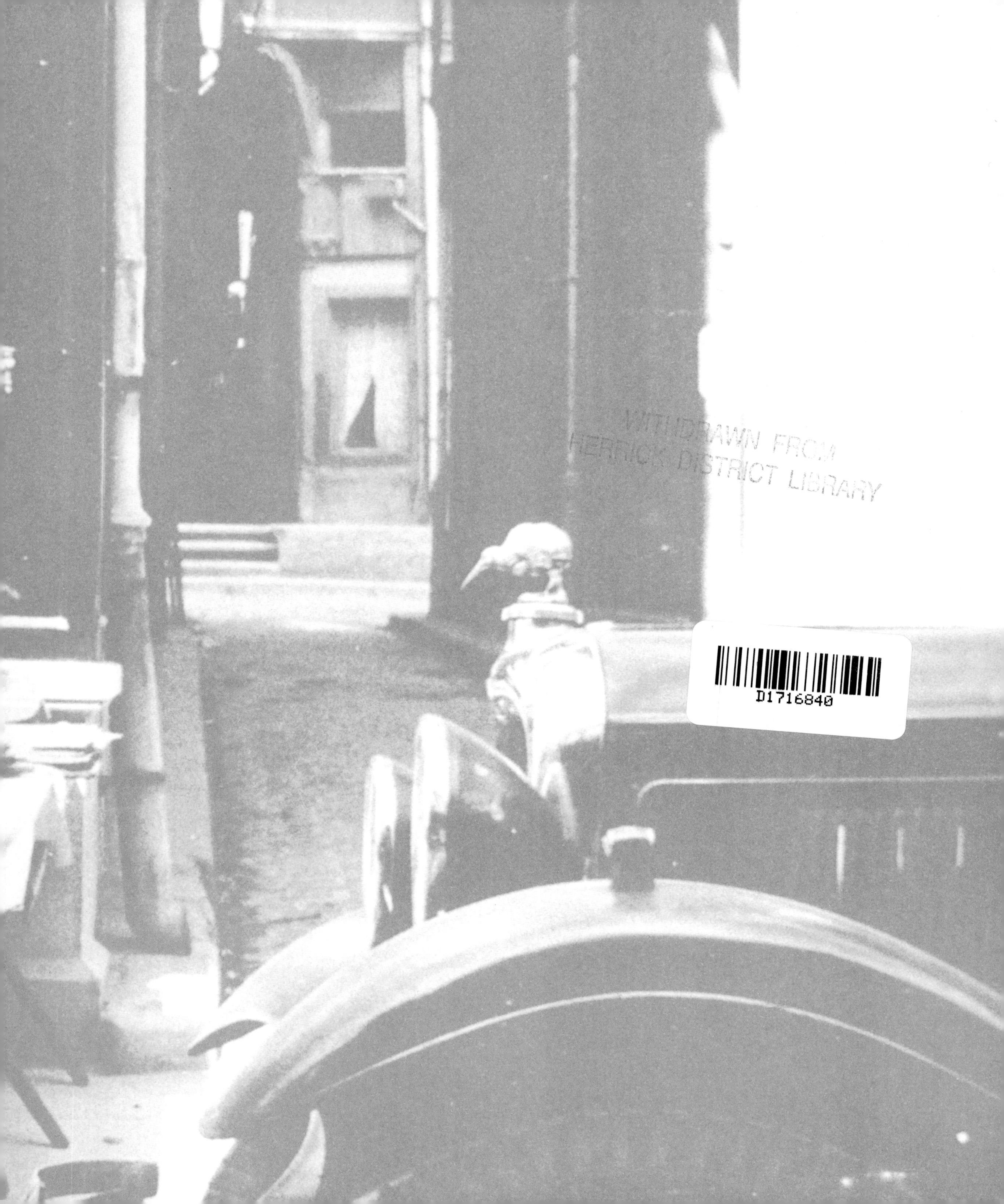

KIWI

KIWI

THE AUSTRALIAN BRAND THAT BROUGHT A SHINE TO THE WORLD

A HISTORY OF THE KIWI POLISH COMPANY

KEITH DUNSTAN

ALLEN&UNWIN
SYDNEY·MELBOURNE·AUCKLAND·LONDON

First published in 2017

Copyright © 2017 Keith Dunstan Estate

Allen & Unwin
83 Alexander Street
Crows Nest NSW 2065
Australia
Phone: (61 2) 8425 0100
Email: info@allenandunwin.com
Web: www.allenandunwin.com

Cataloguing-in-Publication details are available
from the National Library of Australia
www.trove.nla.gov.au

ISBN 978 1 76029 728 2

Project management by Andrew Cunningham
Cover and internal design by Andrew Cunningham
Edited by Neil Conning
Index by Neil Conning
Set in 11/15 pt Scala by Studio Pazzo Pty
Pre-publishing by Splitting Image
Printed by C & C Offset Printing Co., Ltd

10 9 8 7 6 5 4 3 2 1

Peter Morley of Meridian Sculpture Founders, Fitzroy, giving William Ramsay
a new shine. Peter calls the Parade Gloss 'Dr Ramsay's colour enhancer'.
He uses it for restoring bronze sculptures or when finishing new works.

Staff photo at the front of the Kiwi premises, 683 Elizabeth Street, Melbourne, c. 1912

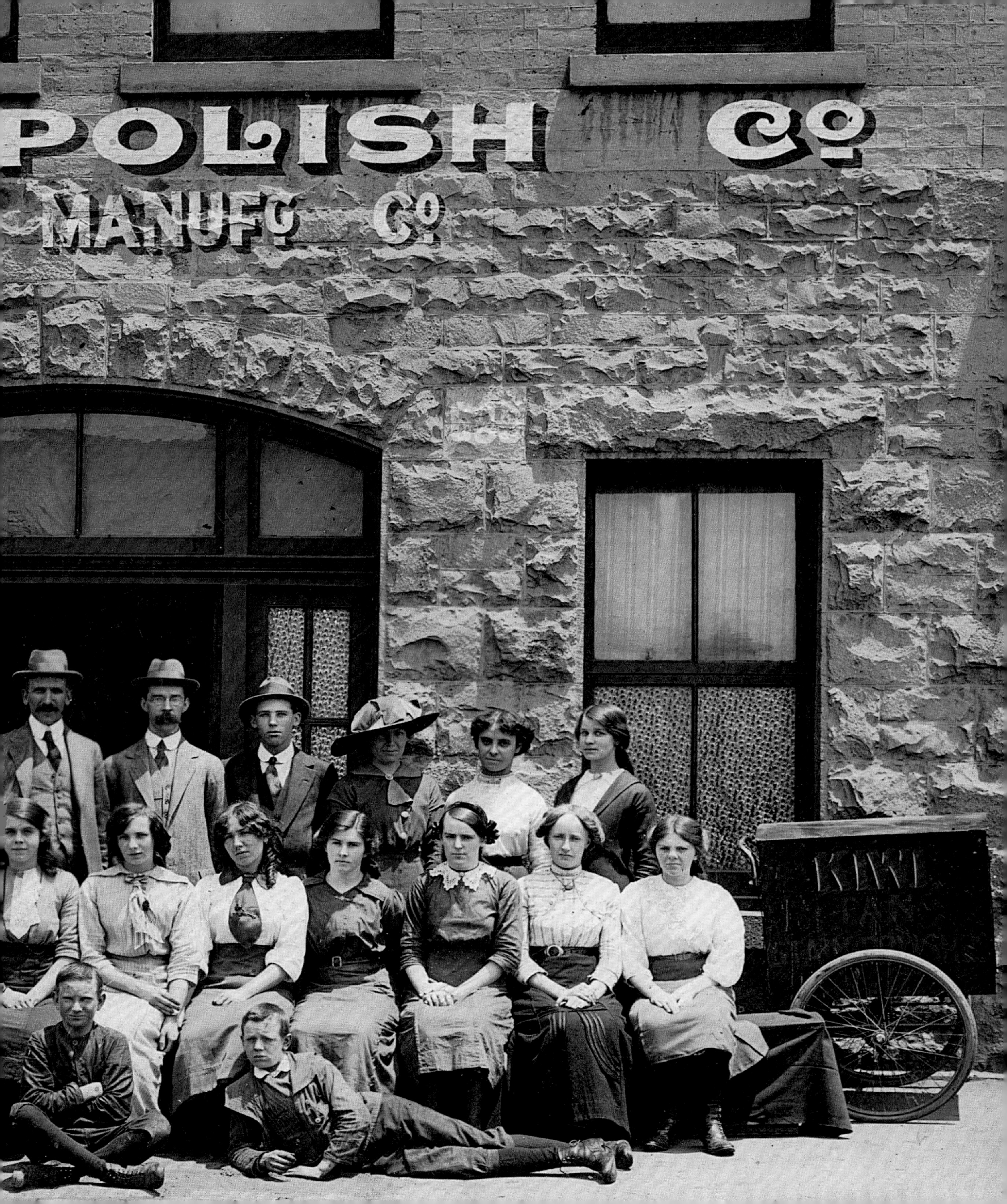
POLISH Co
MANUFG Co
KIWI

ABOUT THIS BOOK

In late 2010, we, the daughter and four sons of Tom Ramsay made a long-awaited decision to commission a history of Kiwi. We were joined by our cousin Patricia Fullerton, who had written a biography of Hugh Ramsay, the painter, and brought an indispensable knowledge of early Ramsay family history.

In asking Keith Dunstan, veteran Melbourne journalist and author, to write the history, we made a fortunate choice. Keith started work on the book in July 2011. In the challenging task of sorting through the archive he had a great deal of help from Angus McDonald, who had started organising the Archive earlier that year. Angus, an author himself and an indomitable traveller is now sadly and untimely deceased. Malcolm Daubney (former senior executive and director with Kiwi) joined our group and brought invaluable help in contacting other former Kiwi executives, fact-checking and in personal knowledge of Kiwi's later years.

Keith himself died in September 2013, but like the veteran journalist he was, not before finishing his final drafts.

The massive task remained of selecting and placing the photos and advertisements and other visual material found in the archive, not to mention all the editing process required to bring the book to its finished form.

Andrew Cunningham of Studio Pazzo has been in charge of the whole book production process; Neil Conning did the editing; both with creative and professional thoroughness and mostly good-tempered patience.

The book is now finished – all those involved in producing it believe that it is a fascinating record of one of the most successful ever Australian companies. This book is our tribute to all the people who made it such a success.

Hamish Ramsay
Anne Folk
Robin Ramsay
Fergus Ramsay
Dougal Ramsay
Melbourne, October 2016

ACKNOWLEDGEMENTS

Many people have contributed information for this book, in particular Ramsay family members Hamish Ramsay, Robin Ramsay, Fergus Ramsay, Dougal Ramsay and Anne Folk. Information and editorial advice was also provided by Patricia Fullerton, great-niece of William Ramsay and author of the splendid biography of the painter Hugh Ramsay. Malcolm Daubney contributed with details of the Kiwi company history. Help was also given by Lee Barr, Lew Bell, Michael Burnett, Tony Carless, Liz Cooper, Lindsay Cuming, Mike Fraser, Brian Healey, Simon Israel, Tony Jamison, Jennifer Jeffries, Russell Martin, Hugh McKelland, Ivan McLaws, Bill Lipsman, John Murphy, Kath O'Connor, Geoff Rout, Graeme Samuel, Denis Shelley, Cam Smith, Noelle Smith, Jan-Willem Taminiau, Peter Thomas, Bev Thompson and Andre Van Vuuren. My nephew Peter McIntosh Jnr helped untangle some of the legal matters.

Many of the extraordinary Kiwi posters and photographs came by courtesy of the advertising agency Hunt Lazaris in Durban, and particularly Craig Ferret, who spent many hours sourcing the material.

Then there are two, perhaps three, special people who should be mentioned. When I was a reporter on the Melbourne *Herald* the sub-editors used to call me Chaucer. That was because of the originality of my spelling. This Chaucer is grateful to Spellcheck. How did we exist years ago without this modern computer wonder? I am most grateful to my historian son Dr David Dunstan, who contributed so many ideas to this book and to my dear wife Marie Rose, who read each chapter as it was written and straightened out all sorts of Chaucerian errors.

Keith Dunstan
Melbourne, 2013

RAMSAY FAMILY TREE

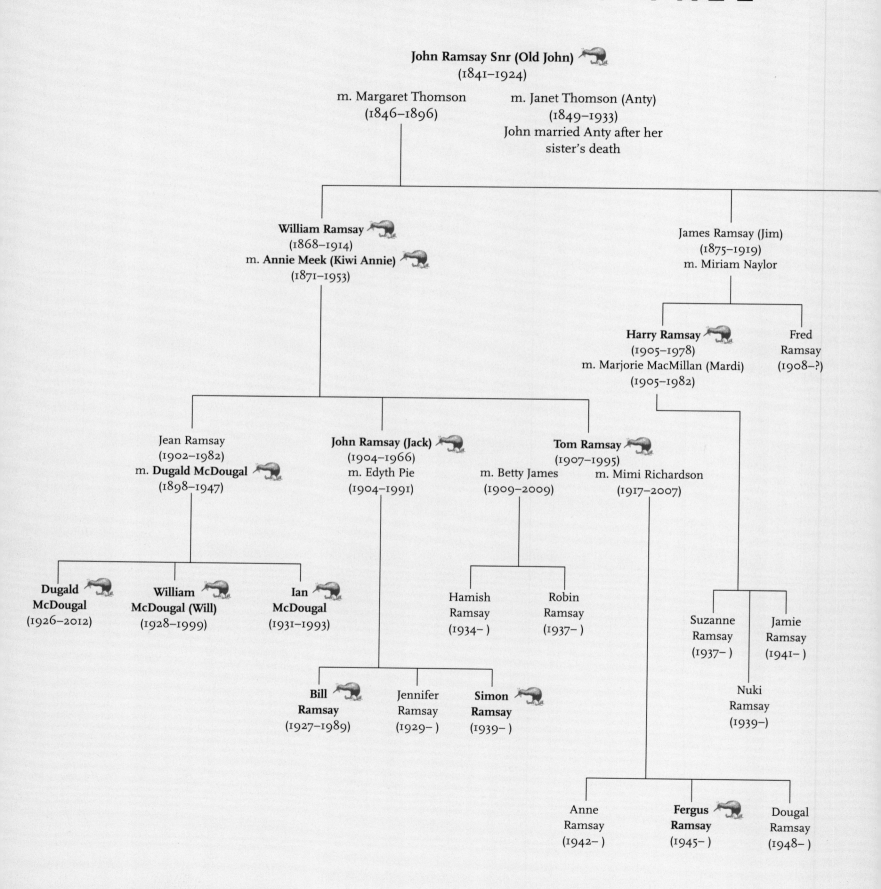

John Ramsay Snr (Old John)
(1841–1924)

m. Margaret Thomson
(1846–1896)

m. Janet Thomson (Anty)
(1849–1933)
John married Anty after her
sister's death

William Ramsay
(1868–1914)
m. **Annie Meek (Kiwi Annie)**
(1871–1953)

James Ramsay (Jim)
(1875–1919)
m. Miriam Naylor

Harry Ramsay
(1905–1978)
m. Marjorie MacMillan (Mardi)
(1905–1982)

Fred
Ramsay
(1908–?)

Jean Ramsay
(1902–1982)
m. **Dugald McDougal**
(1898–1947)

John Ramsay (Jack)
(1904–1966)
m. Edyth Pie
(1904–1991)

Tom Ramsay
(1907–1995)
m. Betty James   m. Mimi Richardson
(1909–2009)   (1917–2007)

Dugald
McDougal
(1926–2012)

**William
McDougal (Will)**
(1928–1999)

**Ian
McDougal**
(1931–1993)

Hamish
Ramsay
(1934–)

Robin
Ramsay
(1937–)

Suzanne
Ramsay
(1937–)

Jamie
Ramsay
(1941–)

Nuki
Ramsay
(1939–)

**Bill
Ramsay**
(1927–1989)

Jennifer
Ramsay
(1929–)

**Simon
Ramsay**
(1939–)

Anne
Ramsay
(1942–)

**Fergus
Ramsay**
(1945–)

Dougal
Ramsay
(1948–)

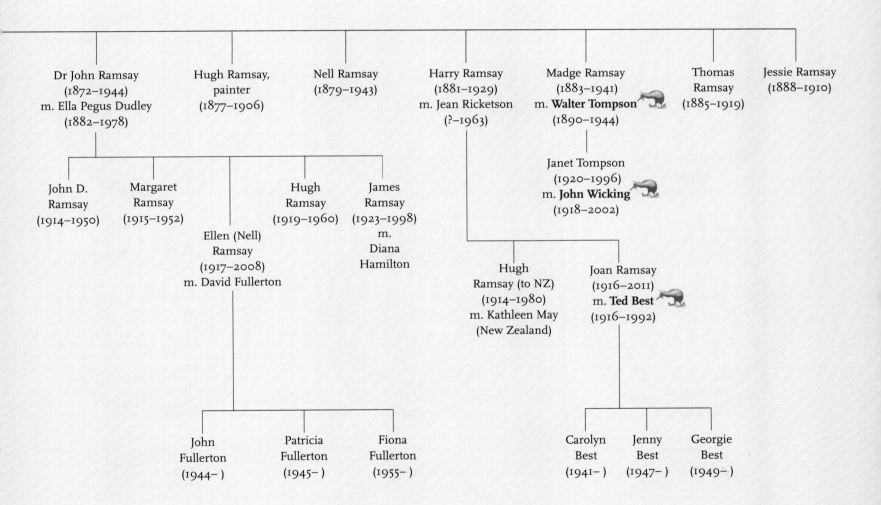

Dr John Ramsay
(1872–1944)
m. Ella Pegus Dudley
(1882–1978)

Hugh Ramsay,
painter
(1877–1906)

Nell Ramsay
(1879–1943)

Harry Ramsay
(1881–1929)
m. Jean Ricketson
(?–1963)

Madge Ramsay
(1883–1941)
m. **Walter Tompson**
(1890–1944)

Thomas
Ramsay
(1885–1919)

Jessie Ramsay
(1888–1910)

John D.
Ramsay
(1914–1950)

Margaret
Ramsay
(1915–1952)

Hugh
Ramsay
(1919–1960)

James
Ramsay
(1923–1998)
m.
Diana
Hamilton

Ellen (Nell)
Ramsay
(1917–2008)
m. David Fullerton

Janet Tompson
(1920–1996)
m. **John Wicking**
(1918–2002)

Hugh
Ramsay (to NZ)
(1914–1980)
m. Kathleen May
(New Zealand)

Joan Ramsay
(1916–2011)
m. **Ted Best**
(1916–1992)

John
Fullerton
(1944–)

Patricia
Fullerton
(1945–)

Fiona
Fullerton
(1955–)

Carolyn
Best
(1941–)

Jenny
Best
(1947–)

Georgie
Best
(1949–)

FOREWORD

This is the story of a remarkable family and a simple recipe that, in their hands, made its way to shops and supermarkets in most countries of the world. The first Ramsays, seven in all, set out from Scotland to Australia in an iron sailing ship in 1878. The father carried a load of bibles which he sold to passengers and a firearm which he used to shoot albatrosses that often followed the ship. In Australia three of his sons made a name: Hugh as a celebrated painter who died young, John as a surgeon and hospital owner in Launceston, and William as a manufacturer and entrepreneur.

William's invention was a shoe polish christened Kiwi. Whether he himself invented the recipe remains a mystery, but the origin of the brand name is easily identified, for he married a girl from Oamaru in New Zealand. An early widow, Annie Ramsay became the chairman of the Kiwi company when her sons took it over and made it global.

Kiwi Dark Tan and Kiwi Black began to woo customers in London before World War One, when the shine on a polished shoe was essential. It was that war which transformed Kiwi: 'There was so much leather, so many boots, so many Sam Browne belts, so many bandoliers, so many leggings, so many bridles and everything to do with horses that had to be preserved and polished.' In the opinion of Keith Dunstan, the author of this book, Kiwi quickly became a worldwide Aussie brand.

OPPOSITE

Kiwi shoe polish, manufactured throughout the world, was available in many colours

In most parts of the world the Ramsays were skilled salesmen and advertisers. One big signboard erected on a busy road in Melbourne was so clever, so diverting to motorists and therefore such a cause of accidents, that Kiwi was told to pull it down.

By the middle of World War Two, the name of Kiwi was such a part of daily speech that Walter Graebner reported in *Time* magazine that 'on a North African battlefield' in 1942 he saw old cans of British-made Kiwi lying side by side with discarded bottles of Chianti; he did not have to explain what Kiwi was. On other battlefields the familiar tins came perhaps from the Ramsay's factory in Warsaw, where the manager and his family were to disappear under Nazi rule, or in the French port of Rouen where the Germans confiscated the factory and made a small mountain of tins of Kiwi to clean and polish the jackboots of Hitler's army. Meanwhile the Allies' soldiers cleaned their webbing equipment with another Kiwi product. The day would come when other Kiwi recipes would sustain the business, the brilliantly shining shoe having dropped a little down the ladder of elegance in the western world.

Part of the fascination of the book is the glimpses of family life – the cars they drove, the intensity with which they travelled ('permanently getting on and off aeroplanes'), the racy and frank letters they wrote, and the web of suicide, marriage, quarrels and deep friendships. Keith Dunstan had almost completed this book when he died in 2013. I have not previously read a business story or family history that is so pithy and observant, and written with such a mix of fun and seriousness.

Geoffrey Blainey
Melbourne, 2016

CONTENTS

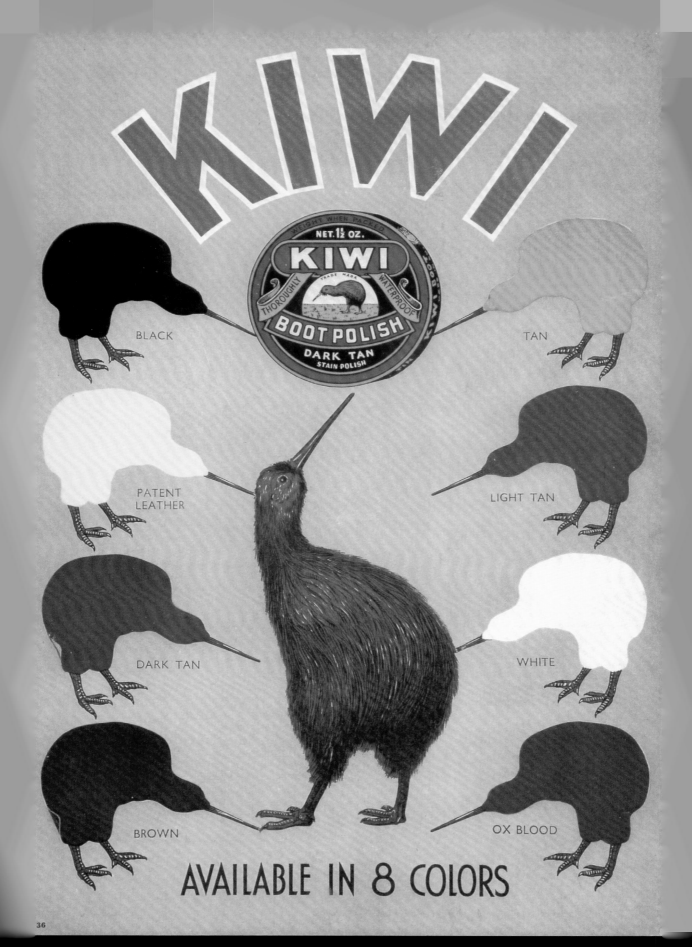

Kiwi poster of eight available colours of polish, 1930s. These colours became part of the foundation of the Kiwi brand across the world. Through the decades, many more colours and other types of polishing waxes were developed and

INTRODUCTION

This book tells the story of Kiwi, an iconic brand and a business founded and developed by some very enterprising individuals. Kiwi at its height had 24 factories around the world and customers in 183 countries.

William Ramsay, the founder, died young and left nothing, except some cables sent from shipboard when he was ill and postcards he wrote to his children on his travels.

His son, Thomas Ramsay, how different he was. He had kept diaries and letters, including those his sons wrote from school when they were at Geelong Grammar. There are filing cabinets in Fitzroy, Melbourne, filled with receipts, newspaper cuttings and orders for Australiana books for his collection. He had a belief in the importance of history. For years, in minute handwriting, he wrote two-line accounts of what he was doing on most days. Interpreting this was not easy. It was like finding the meaning from a tomb in ancient Egypt.

Thomas Ramsay's children saw the importance in Australia's commercial history of Kiwi, which was surely the first worldwide Aussie brand. This book was a joint venture of Ramsay family members Hamish Ramsay, Robin Ramsay, Fergus Ramsay, Dougal Ramsay and Anne Folk. Through their generosity this book has come to be published.

From its beginning in primitive premises in a working-class, factory-filled inner suburb of Melbourne, Kiwi spread around the world. Eventually one could walk into a supermarket almost anywhere on earth and expect to find Kiwi Dark Tan or Kiwi Black on the shelves.

It is the name that has a touch of genius, just four letters. Then there is the instantly recognisable flightless bird on the tin. Why Kiwi for an Australian invention? You see, William Ramsay, the originator of the miracle polish found his bride, Annie Elizabeth Meek, later known as 'Kiwi Annie', in New Zealand. He was inspired to name his polish Kiwi in her honour.

But how good it was, a name so easy to say in any language, so succinct it could fit permanently in memory the next time one was in a store looking for shoe polish. Others thought so too. The company lawyers had a job coping with thefts of the trademark. There were countless imitations, Kimi, Meli, Kuiwy, Twokuiwy, Mimi and others sporting a different bird like ostrich, crane, penguin, cock, and, of course, a kookaburra. That polish was called Jacko.

Nugget, a fierce competitor in Australia, had a large slice of the market, and Tom Ramsay could be driven to rage by hearing someone ask for a 'tin of Kiwi Nugget'.

Kiwi was everywhere in two world wars. It put a brilliant shine on the saddles and harnesses of the Australian Light Horse, on their boots, leggings, belts and bandoliers. Kiwi was also a vital part of the equipment of the Americans in both wars.

When the Anzacs arrived in England during World War I, showing off their shiny leather gear, there was a great marketing opportunity, and there was Kiwi, setting up a factory in London, the first of many around the world outside Australia.

Kiwi went well beyond simply making shoe polish. By the 1960s it was making many different household cleaning products and it had a short foray into the wine industry. It appeared to have no inhibitions about acquiring or making new products or venturing into new markets.

It is almost a game finding the strangest places where Kiwi has appeared. One member of the Ramsay family was visiting Machu Picchu, that strange lost city of the Peruvian Incas. There, working 2,430 metres above sea level was a shoeshine boy putting a mirror shine on the boots and shoes of the tourists. Of course he was using Kiwi.

Along the way, Kiwi acquired a number of smaller businesses, and in 1982 merged with Nicholas to become Nicholas Kiwi Limited, which in 1984 was purchased by Consolidated Foods Corporation, later to adopt the Sara Lee name.

In 2011 Sara Lee announced that it sold its global shoe care business. A press release read: 'S. C. Johnson is pleased to announce it has reached an agreement to acquire Sara Lee's global shoe care business including the beloved Kiwi brand that has been caring for families' shoes around the world for more than one hundred years.'

Created due to the hard work and ingenuity of the Ramsay family, Kiwi products featuring the little New Zealand bird have been prominent around the globe for more than a century. Kiwi was one of the first Australian businesses to export and manufacture its products internationally, and Kiwi could perhaps claim to be the longest lasting and most iconic international brand to have come from Australia.

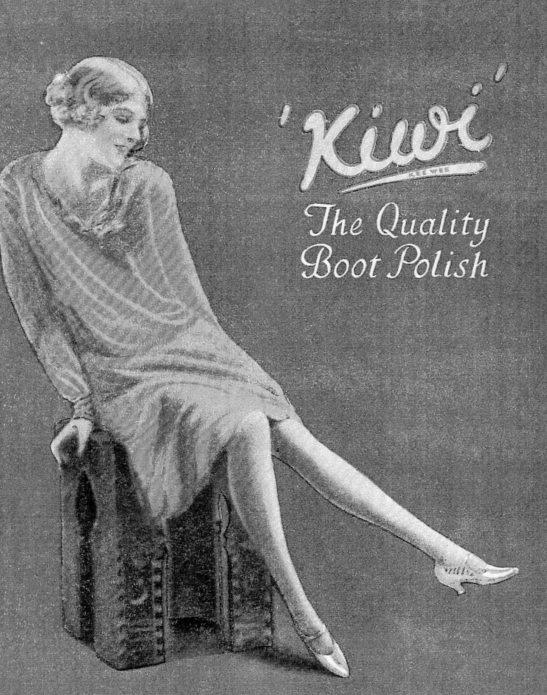

KIWI WORLD MAP

At the height of production in the 1970s and 1980s Kiwi distributed shoe polish from these centres to over 156 countries.

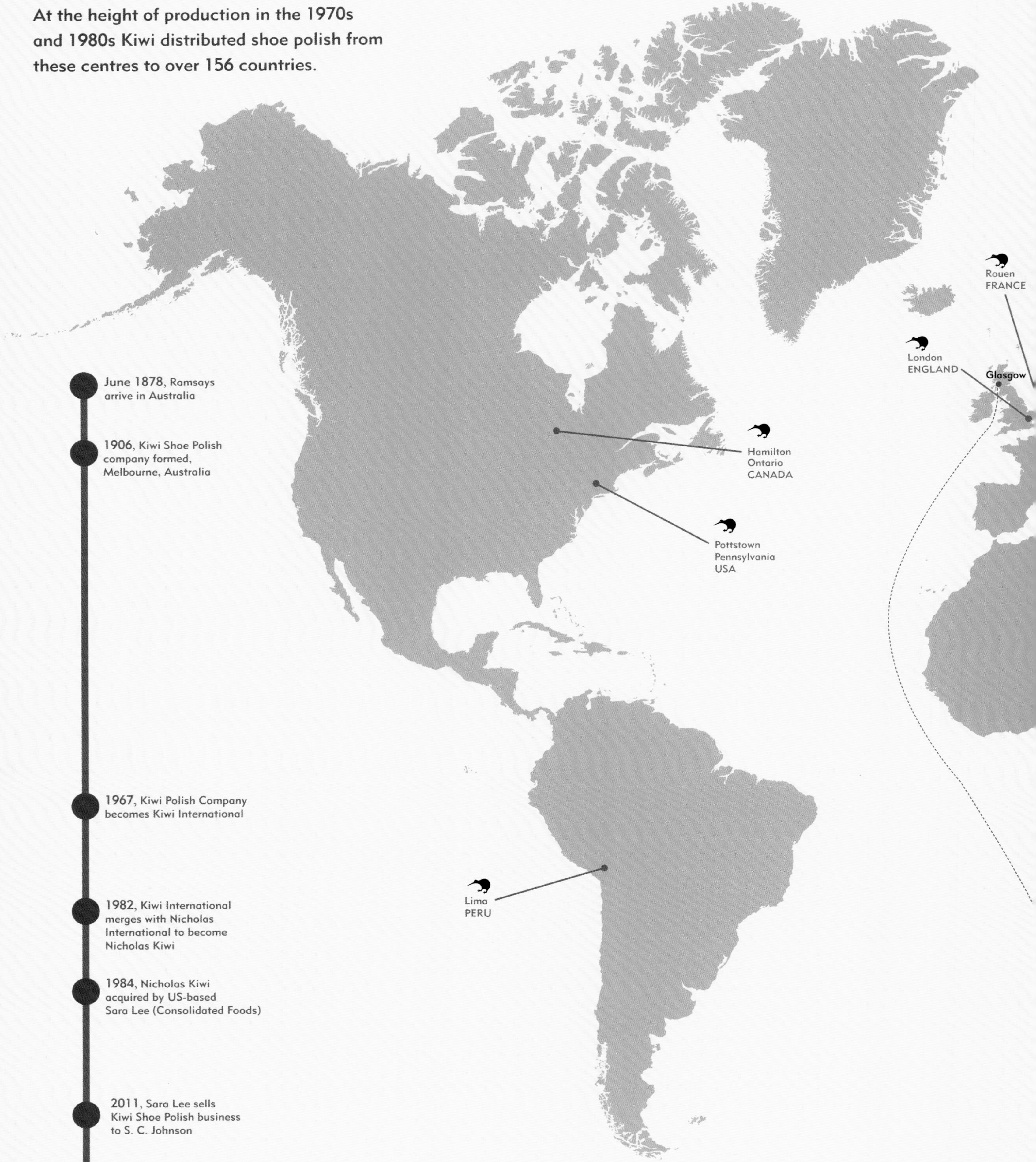

June 1878, Ramsays arrive in Australia

1906, Kiwi Shoe Polish company formed, Melbourne, Australia

1967, Kiwi Polish Company becomes Kiwi International

1982, Kiwi International merges with Nicholas International to become Nicholas Kiwi

1984, Nicholas Kiwi acquired by US-based Sara Lee (Consolidated Foods)

2011, Sara Lee sells Kiwi Shoe Polish business to S. C. Johnson

Rouen
FRANCE

London
ENGLAND

Glasgow

Hamilton
Ontario
CANADA

Pottstown
Pennsylvania
USA

Lima
PERU

Warsaw
POLAND

Rome
ITALY

Tianjin
CHINA

Tokyo
JAPAN

Taipei
TAIWAN

Manila
PHILIPPINES

Karachi
PAKISTAN

Madras
INDIA

Bangkok
THAILAND

SINGAPORE

Colombo
SRI LANKA

Johor
MALAYSIA

Nairobi
KENYA

Jakarta
INDONESIA

Blantyre
MALAWI

Auckland
NEW ZEALAND

Heilbron
SOUTH AFRICA

Melbourne
AUSTRALIA

John Ramsay and his family travelled from Glasgow,
Scotland to Melbourne, Australia in 1878. The journey took three
months and they survived on a ration of lime juice mixed with water, a
relentless diet of soups, salt beef, salt pork, preserved potatoes and rice.

A VOYAGE FROM FROM HUMBLE BEGINNINGS

There are Ramsays and Ramseys, those with an 'a' and those with an 'e'. Legend has it that the Ramseys with an 'e' were a troublesome lot, Highlander Scots, inclined to mischief like cattle stealing and even the consumption of alcohol. On the other hand the Ramsays with an 'a' were Lowlanders, sober, well behaved and infinitely God fearing.

Nobody was more sober, God fearing and respectful of his maker than John Ramsay. He was a small man with a precisely clipped moustache, shaped like a half moon. Above his nose were spectacles like full moons, and there were the eyes, wide open – one sensed John Ramsay missed nothing. According to *Melbourne Punch*, one had only to pick a subject and John Ramsay had the exact piece of scripture to match it, chapter and verse. Challenge him and back he would come with his rich Scottish burr: 'Man, ye're wrong entirely.' No man had the Bible so much on his tongue's end.[1]

John Ramsay was born in 1841 at Forth, a little village in Lanarkshire, Scotland, near Shotts, on the road between Glasgow and Edinburgh. The Ramsays claim to have in their ancestry bishops, musicians, painters and poets. That could be possible, but the solid fact remains: John's father, William, was of humble origins. He married Elinora (Ella) Donaldson and his occupation was flesher and general storekeeper. Flesher was a Scottish term for butcher, and William Ramsay did his fleshing in Shotts.

Young John rejected his father's trade. He was apprenticed to a carpenter and cabinetmaker and he worked in Shotts for 10 years. Some years later he was to make beautiful pieces for the Melbourne family mansion 'Clydebank' in Essendon.

His devotion to religion began early. His Sunday school teacher was Ebenezer Loudon, who, according to the YMCA, had an extraordinary knowledge of the scriptures. It was Loudon who helped John 'decide for Christ'.[2]

The SS *Loch Sunart*, on which John Ramsay
and family travelled, was a sister ship to this
one, the *Loch Etive*.

Margaret Ramsay, c. 1895

He was still a carpenter at Shotts when he married Margaret Thomson on 11 June 1867. In total they produced 11 children, and you could say they had many reasons to call on God for help. William was the first child, born on 6 June 1868, but the next two died soon after birth, James on 1 October 1869, and John on 12 May 1871. John Ramsay the second was born on 26 December 1874 and James (Jim) Ramsay the second was born on 21 February 1875.[3] This was not unusual. So many children died that it was not uncommon to give the healthy child the same name in an attempt to forget the former tragedy.

After their marriage the Ramsays moved to Glasgow, where John was busy indeed. His brother-in-law John Darling invented a fountain pen, one of the first. Next he invented a gyroscopic spinning top, then other gadgets, including metal dyes. Ramsay helped with these ideas and became the agent for the Glasgow publisher James Semple. A canny Scot, John Ramsay was making money.[4]

In 1877 he made a huge decision: he would take his whole family to Melbourne in far-away Australia. This meant three months of hardship in a sailing ship with the possibility they might never make it. Shipping disasters were frequent; between 1797 and modern times 800 ships were wrecked on Australia's Victorian coast.[5]

If Melbourne was as remote as the Moon, it had much allure. The population was nigh on 300,000 and building faster than almost any place on earth. Gold had made it one of the richest cities. The poet and adventurer Richard Hengist 'Orion' Horne predicted Melbourne would become the New York of the Southern Hemisphere. Stories flowed back to London of the wonders of this new city, of its wide streets, its splendid churches, its grand public buildings constructed of stone. Here was a classless society where the working man earned good wages and the inspired eight hours movement set the standard for the world: eight hours work, eight hours rest, eight hours recreation. There was a national gallery, a museum, a great library, and botanic gardens, which were already famous. The Duke of Edinburgh visited in 1867, and there had been two visits by England cricket sides, including the first Test match on 15 March 1877.

Melbourne seethed with confidence and bluster, which inspired British travel writer Anthony Trollope to coin the lines: 'When a gentleman sounds his own trumpet he 'blows' ... They blow a good deal in Queensland, a good deal in South Australia. They blow even in poor Tasmania. They blow loudly in New South Wales, and very loudly in New Zealand. But the sound of the trumpet as heard in Victoria is louder than all the blasts – and the Melbourne blast beats all the other blowing of that proud colony.'[6]

Undoubtedly the blasts of the trumpet reached the ears of John Ramsay. Many of his fellow countrymen, and indeed some of his entrepreneurial relatives, had already migrated to the antipodes in search of a better life. It was as much for his wife Margaret's health as his own desire for advancement that he left Scotland to seek his fortune in the sunshine of a prospering Australian colony.

On 5 March 1878, aged 36, John Ramsay was farewelled from the Glasgow Railway Station by his faithful congregation from the Dundas Street Evangelical Church, with a silver coffee pot inscribed for his 'untiring service to the church'.[7]

The Ramsays:
(back) Margaret, Jessie, John, James,
(seated) Nell, William, Tom, John Ramsay Senior,
Harry, Madge and Hugh, c. 1895

The Ramsays arrived at Hobsons Bay Railway Pier (now Station Pier, Port Melbourne) in 1878

Three days later he sailed on the SS *Loch Sunart* from Greenock on the Firth of Clyde. He took with him Margaret, her unmarried sister Janet, plus his four sons: William, John, James and baby Hugh. His luggage included a large quantity of bibles, which he wrote in his detailed journal of the voyage he was 'gratified to sell' to seasick and otherwise ailing passengers during the trying three months at sea. He also delivered sermons on the wretched state of mankind, taking advantage of saving a few souls while, at the same time, capitalising on whatever commercial interest lay at hand. He found that money could be made from the albatrosses that followed the ship, and he shot them, heedless of the fate of the Ancient Mariner. His approach was pragmatic:

> The mode of skinning is to cut them about the neck a few inches from the head, and slit the skin down the back and peel it off. I am preserving the skin for a muff. I am also stuffing the head to keep, and the small bones from each wing are in high demand on board for pipe shanks. I am also skinning the feet to make a purse or tobacco pouch from each foot. The carcass is thrown overboard.[8]

Despite his commercial interest in shooting albatrosses (and dolphins) with a revolver, Sunday was sacrosanct. He was outraged when a steward killed and dressed a pig, which was 'a wanton desecration of the Sabbath'.[9]

The horrors of the three-month voyage are vividly recounted in his journal – the stifling cabin conditions, seasickness, the pitching and tossing of the ship, a sea burial of a young baby committed to the waves. They survived on a ration of lime juice mixed with water, a relentless diet of soups (pea, kidney and brown soup) salt beef, salt pork, preserved potatoes and rice. Plum pudding on Sundays, Tuesdays and Thursdays was the favourite.

When the long voyage came to an end on 8 June 1878, John Ramsay announced: 'It becomes us to lift our hearts to God and praise him with our lips'[10] (Little did he realise how blessed he was, for on her return voyage the *Sunart* hit a reef off the coast of Ireland and was totally wrecked).[11]

Once ashore Ramsay enjoyed 'a fine breakfast of mutton chops, which was the sweetest morsel . . . for a long time'.[12]

· · ·

Had John Ramsay been able to predict the future he may have thought differently about sailing on the *Loch Sunart*. The two Loch ships had the same owners, and both sank. There were 25 clippers in the Loch line, all named after lochs in Scotland. Clippers were all the rage after the 1850s. They were famed for their grace and beauty, their slim line of hull, sharp bows and high masts with an enormous spread of sail. Built for speed, they were the greyhounds of the sea. Even so, a round trip to Adelaide, Melbourne and Sydney, then back to Glasgow took almost a year. Of the 25 Loch ships 17 sank, crashed on to reefs or just disappeared never to be heard of again.

2

MARVELLOUS MELBOURNE

OPPOSITE

William Ramsay (1868–1914),
Kiwi founder

A new life had started for John Ramsay. This enterprising little Scotsman had thought a great deal about how he could prosper when he landed in Melbourne. He brought with him a trunk full of bibles thinking he would continue in the bookselling business he had left back in Glasgow. Apparently Melbourne's passion for bibles was not quite what he hoped for, so he tried all sorts of things, including the import of pianos and even jewellery. He became such an expert with diamonds that the prestigious Melbourne jewellers Catanach's offered him a position as a diamond buyer.[1]

The family lived in rented accommodation, first in West Melbourne, then Prahran, Windsor and Ascot Vale. The family increased by another five: Nell, Harry, Madge, Jessie and Tom. In his exhaustive memoirs John Ramsay rarely spoke about his wife Margaret. We see her in one photograph in her finery, complete with jewellery, hair pulled back severely into a bun. She had given birth to 11 children and she died in 1896 aged 50.

Two years later in 1898, Ramsay married Margaret's sister Janet, who had come to Melbourne to help with the household. 'Anty', as she was called in the Scottish brogue, was integral to the large family: feeding, washing and tending to the needs of the children. After the marriage she continued to address her new husband as 'Father', and she remained 'Anty' to him and the family.[2]

By the 1880s Melbourne's population had risen to half a million and the 'gold city' seemed awash with money. The great Melbourne International Exhibition opened on 1 October 1880, with a grand building with annexes that covered 9 acres. The first telephone exchange opened in June 1880, just four years after Alexander Graham Bell announced his invention. With the introduction of the hydraulic lift, Melbourne now boasted a building seven storeys high. The Melbourne Cricket Club had its first night football match lit by electricity. Visibility was not good but electric light was there just the same. The first cable tram ran to Richmond in 1887, and now with railway trains, new suburbs, no matter how remote, became accessible to the working man.

New houses spread round the bayside beyond Brighton to Black Rock, out to Malvern, Essendon, Heidelberg … No matter where you bought land, no matter where you built, prices had to go up. This was the new paradise, make the most of it, borrow, borrow, borrow. And the banks were only too happy to lend at 5 per cent.

John Ramsay along with his son William stepped into the real estate business, John Ramsay & Son, Real Estate Merchants, 318 Collins Street, Melbourne. The Ramsays were offering fine shops made of brick in Pelham Street, Carlton; factory sites in Canning Street, North Melbourne and Stanton Street, Collingwood; and a splendid building site in Warrington Road, Surrey Hills. They had a subdivision plan for the Red Bluff Township, '10 minutes walk from Sandringham Station. The most magnificent position and the highest bluff around Port Phillip Bay'.[3]

In 1888 John Ramsay built 'Clydebank', a mansion on the Aberfeldie Estate at Buckley Street, Essendon. It was a classic land boomer style building, which could perhaps fetch $6 million today. Towers on buildings were all the rage in the 1880s. Ramsay would climb the tower with his telescope and he could see the You Yangs, Mount Macedon, the Dandenongs and also Port Phillip.

The plan of the house tells the glory of the Victorian era. On the ground floor there was a drawing room, a parlour, dining room, breakfast room, sitting room, cellar, kitchen, wash house, scullery, boot room and ironing room, John Ramsay's study, plus a 'low bedroom' – a piece of Scottish whimsy, meaning a spare bedroom for visitors. Upstairs there were six bedrooms plus a billiard room. There was also a studio for the young painter Hugh Ramsay, who was to become one of Australia's most celebrated artists.[4]

The house had stained glass windows, elegant tiles, onyx and marble mantels over the fireplaces, and a gracious staircase with banisters. There was a pump organ for entertainment and carefully chosen hymns.

'Clydebank' (see page 13) consisted of 15 acres between Vida Street and Fawkner Street with a frontage to Buckley Street. The Ramsays had a complete range of servants, plus stables, a coach house, orchards and vegetable gardens. The house looked down towards the Maribyrnong River, but Ramsay had another river in mind when he called his mansion 'Clydebank'.

Camelot, and glowing titles like 'Marvellous Melbourne' and 'The Metropolis of the Southern Hemisphere' could not last. The economy was like a beautiful tower built with no foundations. Suddenly it collapsed. There were a number of factors. Wool and wheat almost halved in price, and London became fearful of what was happening in the colony. Perhaps the chief factor was greed, with fraudulent banks, crooked land dealers, shonky building societies and wild borrowing with no fear of the future. In December 1891 four banks closed their doors and suspended payments. In his controversial book *The Pleasant Career of a Spendthrift and His Later Reflections* (published 1929), George Meudell named every wicked land boomer, and also pinned down famous politicians who had been revered as upright members of the community. The book was eventually withdrawn from circulation. Meudell said the loss to the people of Victoria in securities and property was £200 million, a lot of money in the 1890s. Suicides were everywhere, people blowing their brains out, drowning in the Yarra, and one banker killed himself horribly taking prussic acid. Over 50,000 people deserted Melbourne hoping for a better life elsewhere. Many went to the Western Australian goldfields.

John Ramsay lost almost everything, yet somehow he managed to hang on to 'Clydebank', albeit with a heavy mortgage. That mortgage lasted until after 1918, when he threw a dinner party at 'Clydebank'. Sitting at his regular spot, at the head of the dinner table, he held up the old mortgage, paid off at last and proudly announced: 'Look, at last, after all these years I've got it back and 'Clydebank' is mine again.'[5]

But the early years were hard. There were stories of recycling cast-off clothes, of Anty and Margaret refashioning dustcoats into pinafores for the girls to wear to school. Neither Anty nor Margaret were skilled in dressmaking and there were tears before going to school and complaints that other girls had pretty lace dresses.

Ramsay and his eldest son William survived by putting things in reverse. They worked as valuers and liquidators for the Essendon Council and the State Savings Bank Credit Department. Religion continued to play a large part in Ramsay's life. Prayers were held every morning before breakfast and scarcely anything was permitted on Sunday except going to church and reading the Bible. Hymns were the main form of music played on the family organ.

For over 20 years Ramsay gave lessons at the YMCA. Back in Scotland he used to preach at the Glasgow Green. First he was a Presbyterian, but then he became a fierce anti-Calvinist and later, as a Congregationalist in Melbourne he attended the Collins Street Independent Church. Soon after his arrival he went down to the Yarra Bank, the famous 'speakers corner' where every hot-headed firebrand evangelist or wild-eyed socialist could have their say. Briefly he listened to the other speakers, but soon he was shouting, expressing strong disagreement and told the listeners he would come back next Sunday to refute everything he had heard. From then on he was a regular at the Yarra Bank and they called him 'Young Scottie'.[6]

'Clydebank', Vida Street, Essendon, *c.* 1930

3

KIWI ANNIE

OPPOSITE

Annie Elizabeth Ramsay (nee Meek),
'Kiwi Annie' (1871–1933), was a true pioneer,
a woman in charge of an international company
close on a century ahead of her time.

*"It's a
pleasure
to me
KIWI"*

uring the 1890s depression, 'Marvellous Melbourne' suffered a huge lack of confidence, but a new spirit and excitement came with the federation of the colonies. In 1901 the Duke and Duchess of York visited Melbourne for the opening of the first Parliament of Australia. Only a few years before, Melbourne was starved of money; now it flowed without question, all to welcome the future King George V.

For the route of the royal procession, the city built galleries to accommodate 30,000 people, plus eight splendid triumphal arches. The mightiest of them all was at the entrance to the city by Princes Bridge, which served to hide the squalid railway station, yet to become the iconic pink-domed hub of the city.[1] The grand Exhibition Building, built in 1880 for the Melbourne International Exhibition, 1880–81, was the scene for the opening, and it had to be as beautiful as a royal palace. A whole new interior scheme was initiated for the ceremonial opening of the Federal Parliament. Workmen had been on the job, painting the inside in gorgeous azure cream and gold requiring 3,000 scaffold poles and many miles of rope. There was a specially constructed vestibule, and the royal couple were able to tread all the way on a sumptuous crimson carpet. The building was so large it was able to accommodate 15,000 guests from all over the new Commonwealth.[2]

The timing was unfortunate. Queen Victoria had died only three weeks before, so that Her Majesty's entire realm was in a state of mourning. Guests were required to wear either black or grey. The ceremony took place on 9 May 1901. The Duke read a message from his father, King Edward VII pronouncing: 'I now, in his name, and on his behalf, declare this Parliament open.' Then with the sound of trumpets and the booming outside of a royal salute, he pressed an electric button and a message shot off to Buckingham Palace that a new parliament was in action, with the first prime minister, Edmund Barton.[3] Mr and Mrs John Ramsay received a beautifully illuminated card:

> His Majesty's Ministers of State for the Commonwealth of Australia request the honour of the presence of Mr and Mrs Ramsay in the Exhibition Building Melbourne on Thursday the 9th of May 1901 to witness the Opening of the Parliament of the Commonwealth.
>
> *Edmund Barton, Prime Minister*

Tom Roberts (1856–1931) *Opening of the First Parliament of the Commonwealth of Australia by H.R.H. The Duke of Cornwall and York (Later King George V), May 9, 1901* (1903). On permanent loan to the Parliament of Australia from the British Royal Collection. Image courtesy of the Parliament House Art Collection, Canberra, ACT and the Royal Collection Trust. © Her Majesty Queen Elizabeth II 2016

The Parliament of the Commonwealth

His Majesty's Ministers of State for the Commonwealth of Australia

request the honor of the presence of

Mr & Mrs Ramsay

in the Exhibition Building, Melbourne, on Thursday the 9th of May, 1901, to witness the Opening of the Parliament of the Commonwealth.

Edmund Barton,
Prime Minister.

An immediate reply is requested, addressed to—
George H. Jenkins Esquire, Parliament House, Melbourne.
If this Invitation is accepted an Entrée Card will be forwarded to you.

NOTE- THE ILLUMINATED OFFICIAL CARD OF INVITATION WILL BE POSTED TO YOU AS SOON AS IT IS READY FOR ISSUE.

Invitation sent to Mr and Mrs John Ramsay for the official opening of the First Parliament of the Commonwealth, 1901

Self-portrait in white jacket
by Hugh Ramsay, Paris 1902
(National Gallery of Victoria)

Portrait sketch of Nellie Melba
by Hugh Ramsay, Paris, 1902
(National Portrait Gallery)

The Ramsays received another invitation to meet 'Their Royal Highnesses' at an evening reception in the Exhibition Building on the same day at 8 p.m.

There was triumph yet so much tragedy in the lives of John Ramsay's family. Their belief in the will of God kept them going. Ramsay married twice and had nine children. Five died before him. Tuberculosis was very likely the scourge that took them down, except for James, who died unexpectedly in London.

Three of John Ramsay's children had careers that brought them international fame. Hugh Ramsay was an outstanding painter of his time, and his fame continued to grow long after his death. His story is told in a fine biography by his great-niece, Patricia Fullerton: *Hugh Ramsay: His Life and Work*.[4]

Hugh was the handsome one of the family, with extraordinary good looks. He painted a number of self-portraits, including the most striking, *Self-Portrait in White Jacket* (featured on the cover of Patricia Fullerton's biography). The year is 1901, no beard, no moustache, unusual for the time. His dark hair is parted in the middle, his chin is forceful and his lower lip just slightly protruding. A hand with long fingers holds a painter's brush, and one gets the impression, as Milton once wrote, that here is a man who is master of his fate.

Dux of Essendon Grammar School, he was also a talented musician, a profession he could easily have taken up. He played the organ, piano, violin and flute, but even at the age of 14 it was obvious he was determined to be an artist. Naturally his father disapproved, claiming it was 'not only a precarious means of livelihood but also of a distinctly questionable nature'.[5] His passion was not to be denied and in 1894 he enrolled at the National Gallery School under the guidance of Bernard Hall and Frederick McCubbin.

In September 1900 he sailed for Europe, with fellow passengers George and Amy Lambert, who were also heading for Paris. There he shared rooms with other artists in a ramshackle building in Montparnasse. Rarely did he have a brush out of his hand. Working from dawn till late at night, in April 1902 he had an amazing breakthrough. He submitted five paintings to the New Salon. Four were accepted. This was an honour usually only granted to members of the Société Nationale des Beaux-Arts, let alone a 24-year-old Australian exhibiting for the first time.

In Paris he was introduced to Nellie Melba. In an era when the word 'celebrity' had acquired none of its present majesty, Melba was almost the most famous woman in the world. She invited Ramsay to paint her portrait in fashionable Edwardian London. Soon after embarking on her portrait his doctor diagnosed him with incipient tuberculosis. For one who appeared so strong and resolute this was a tragedy. He could only blame Paris, where he had over-worked and neglected his diet in the bohemian world of the Latin quarter. The truth was that pulmonary tuberculosis could be contracted as easily in Australia as it could be on the Left Bank of Paris.

Immediately he returned to Melbourne, where his association with Nellie Melba continued. She staged an exhibition of his works at 'Myoora', her rented house in Toorak.

John Ramsay Snr and his sons Harry, John,
Hugh, William, James and Tom, *c.* 1900

Annie and William Ramsay with their three children:
John (foreground), Tom and Jean, *c.*1913

The next generation of Ramsays, 'Clydebank', 1917
(back) John (Will's son), Margaret (Dr John's daughter),
Fred (James's son), Tom (Will's son),
(middle) John (Dr John's son), Jean (Will's daughter, later
McDougall), babe in arms Nell (Dr John's daughter, later
Fullerton, then Turnbull), Joan (Harry's daughter, later Best),
Hugh (Harry's son)
(front, added later): Hugh (Dr John's son) & Janet (Madge
Tompson's daughter, later Wicking)

RIGHT

(back) John and Edith Ramsay holding Bill
(front) Tom and Annie Ramsay

John, Annie (nee Meek), Jean
and Tom Ramsay

RIGHT

Postcard photo of James,
William and John Ramsay

Vandyck
Studios

BOURKE ST
NEXT GEN. POST OFFICE
AND
274 COLLINS ST E.

MELBOURNE

Despite his illness and against doctor's warnings, Hugh continued painting large canvases between 1903 and 1904. For six months he spent time in the countryside near Barnawatha in an attempt to improve his health but retuned to 'Clydebank' where he died in the arms of Jessie on 5 March 1906. He was 28, and only six years had passed since he set out for Paris. Jessie, four years later at the age of 22, also died of tuberculosis. Jessie and Hugh were buried beside each other in the St Kilda Cemetery.[6]

Hugh's brother John was five years his senior. Born in Glasgow on 26 December 1872, John Ramsay was a brilliant student. Dux of the Prahran State School, he won a scholarship to Wesley College and then studied medicine at Melbourne University, where he won the Beaney Scholarship in Pathology, aged 21. John started his career doing locum tenens at the Alfred Hospital before working at the Auckland Hospital in New Zealand, where no doubt he caught up with the Meek family. Three months later he went to Tasmania, where he became the superintendent of the Launceston General Hospital. In 1912 he married an English nurse, Ella Pegus Dudley. In 1924 he borrowed £11,178 from the Kiwi Polish Company to buy St Margaret's Private Hospital in Launceston, and it was here that he virtually put Launceston medically on the map. The *Burnie Advocate* described him as one of the most notable surgeons in the Commonwealth. A pioneer in the surgery of hydatids and the use of local anaesthesia for operations, he was also the first surgeon in Australia to restart the human heart after it had stopped beating. In 1924 he was made a Commander of the British Empire and in 1939 he was knighted. With many other business interests, he was on the board of Kiwi, but was not one of those board members who just came for the good lunch. He was an outstanding golfer, a great billiards player, competent at tennis, and so good at cricket that he played for Tasmania against Victoria and for Northern Tasmania against South Tasmania. He was a feisty character with strong opinions and relationships with his Kiwi Ramsay relatives were often far from easy.

William Ramsay, the founder of Kiwi, was different from his other famous brothers. He did not keep a diary and was not a prolific letter writer, so many of his activities remain a mystery. Maybe he did not have the good looks of Hugh. He was more angular and wore a Lord Kitchener style, 'Your country needs you' moustache. He was born on 6 June 1868, and the first part of the mystery is why he went to New Zealand and married a New Zealand girl, and how it happened that the most famous leather polish in the world came to be known as 'Kiwi'.

The New Zealand girl was Annie Elizabeth Meek, later nicknamed 'Kiwi Annie', and the connections between the Meeks and the Ramsays go back to Lanarkshire in Scotland and to the little town of Shotts. Annie's father, Thomas Meek, was born on 18 October 1842 in the rural town of Shotts, midway between Glasgow and Edinburgh, where he did his apprenticeship as a joiner and cabinetmaker. John Ramsay Snr, born in 1841 was also apprenticed as a joiner and cabinetmaker in Shotts, so not only did Meek and Ramsay train together, but they already shared kinship by the marriage of their grandparents, William Meek and Mary Wallace, who had married in 1828.

Sir John Ramsay (Dr John) receiving his knighthood at Buckingham Palace, 1939

Annie's father Thomas Meek had migrated to New Zealand in the 1870s, settling in Oamaru on the South Island where sheep and wheat were the main products. Initially working as a contractor, he began to prosper when he invested in a threshing machine with his brother John. Together they started up a small flour mill in Severn Street, Oamaru, expanded production, acquired the Red Lion Mill and then acquired T. Evans & Co. By the 1880s they were the largest flour millers in Australasia with a building five storeys high. They had the first telephone system in 1881 and in 1888 they lit their mill with 34 incandescent lamps.

In 1901 William Ramsay described himself as an estate agent, and the day after the formal federation of the Australian colonies, he married Annie in New Zealand on 2 January 1902 at the Meek mansion 'Holly Bank', Oamaru. With its elegant cast-iron balconies, 'Holly Bank' looked surprisingly like 'Clydebank'. In much the same way as 'Clydebank' was bought in 1943 by the Roman Catholic Church, in 1926 the Meeks sold 'Holly Bank' to the Catholic Dominican Sisters. Used as a training school for novitiates, it became St Thomas's Girls High Schools until 1935. Unlike, 'Clydebank's ongoing occupancy by the Catholic Church, in 1935 'Holly Bank' was sold to developers.

Hamilton McKellan formed a partnership with William Ramsay in 1901.

Just three months after the wedding William Ramsay started a business partnership with Hamilton McKellan. The capital of the manufacturing and importing business at 62–64 Bouverie Street, Carlton, consisted of £60. The partners were entitled to profits in equal proportions. The recipes used in the manufacture of goods traded became the property of both partners and were not to be divulged by either of them.

Hamilton McKellan and William Ramsay met in the 1890s when Ramsay was evaluating properties. McKellan was born on 4 August in the late 1860s in Ballymena Northern Ireland, migrated to Australia in the 1880s and married Elizabeth Williams in Melbourne. Their first little factory at 62 Bouverie Street, Carlton, was near the grand old bluestone Carlton Brewery. Their partnership lasted less than two years. The cancellation was witnessed by W. H. Roddick, who was later to become the accountant and secretary of the Kiwi Polish Company.

One wonders why the agreement was cancelled. According to a note in the Kiwi files, Roddick said Percy William Shackell, a former partner of McKellan, served him with a writ. According to company records the Anderson Manufacturing Company Pty Ltd was registered at 9 Queen Street Melbourne. Blanche Henrietta Anderson was one director with 40 shares and Elizabeth Louisa McKellan was the other director also with 40 shares. Elizabeth McKellan was Hamilton McKellan's wife. H. McKellan, J. C. Anderson and F. R. Boyce also were listed as shareholders. In another document dated 1902, the directors listed were William Davenport and Percy William Shackell.

The Anderson Manufacturing Company manufactured 'disinfectants, inks, machine oil, sheep dip, fire kindlers, fuller's earth and other articles'. This meant the Anderson company was making exactly the items that interested McKellan and Ramsay. Almost certainly Percy William Shackell did not believe McKellan could swim in two pools at the one time. According to McKellan he won the case before the Supreme Court with costs.[7]

First Kiwi factory,
62 Bouverie Street, Carlton

The Anderson company was short-lived. On 6 October 1911 Tuckett & Styles of 359 Collins Street held an auction and William Ramsay bought it for the sum of £29 19 shillings, and that included 13 dozen sanitary blocks, two and a half dozen drums of carbolic, two bags of compound, nine bags of sawdust, plus all goodwill, trademarks, labels and formulae.

The McKellan & Ramsay letterhead announced they were chemical manufacturers, 62 and 64 Bouverie Street, Telephone 2274, and listed a large number of products:

Phenyl, disinfectant powder, lightning stove polish, lightning clothes cleaner, boot creams, fat black for harness, asbestos fire kindlers, linoleum polish, furniture polish, eucalyptus oil, petroleum jelly, sewing machine oil, carbolic oil, cycle lubricant, marking ink, anilines for ink and brushwork, 'Dead Black' and 'Snow White' for rifle shooting, 'Sanacutis' salve for eczema and all skin troubles, 'Wash-Eesie' powder for washing clothes – no rubbing required.

This was a time of wonder cures, elixirs, potions and Dr Morse's Indian Root Pills. The magic of chemicals could do anything. The world was prospering again after the depression of the 1890s and society was looking for new inventions. Ramsay was indefatigable; he searched the world for ideas. His files were loaded with recipes. The bicycle was all the rage, so William collected a recipe for repairing the strained and aching limbs of ladies and gentlemen who had tortured themselves pedalling up hills. There was also a polish for putting a brilliant finish on pianos.

There was an ingenious idea for stopping one's hair from going grey: two ounces of coconut oil, an ounce of bay rum and few drops of bergamot; rub well into the roots. There was an excellent plan for a hair restorer: a mixture of rose water, glycerine, milk of sulphur and sugar.

There were recipes for treating consumption and pneumonia, and for curing 'inebriates' – one would not want to use a harsh word like drunkards. There was a cough mixture that was very interesting. If it did not cure the patient it would certainly put the poor creature out of his or her misery. This was the recipe: 3 ounces of peppermint, 3 ounces of aniseed, 3 ounces of paregoric, 3 ounces of laudanum, 1 pound of treacle and 1 pint of boiling water. Both paregoric and laudanum are derivatives of opium.

William hunted all over for exclusive recipes. He paid £2 10s for a marking ink formula and £1 5s for spice and worm powders for horses, cattle and poultry. He went to London for metal polish and white shoe cleaners. There was £5 to a Carlton firm for a white cloth cleaner, and for polish that would clean white buckskin boots. He paid 3 guineas for a recipe for a silverware polish.

He had a number of recipes for boot polish, including two in that critical year, 1905. One came from H. C. Standage of Aston Manor, Birmingham. He described this as 'nugget' polish, with a charge 2 guineas for the recipe and exclusive use in the colonies.

The second recipe, perhaps more interesting, appeared to come from Germany. The recipe warns that the mixture must not be heated over 212 degrees and then to gain a 'mirror like' surface for the polish the cooling had to take place slowly after the filling of the tins. This sounds very like the polish McKellan & Ramsay sold in 1905 under the Mirror brand.

On 20 October 1901 McKellan wrote a letter:

I propose

1. That a proper deed of partnership be drawn up.
2. That I draw three pounds weekly.
3. That you (W. Ramsay) be paid a reasonable amount for keeping the books and taking an interest in the business generally.
4. That at the end of the year a balance sheet be drawn up, and that the profits (if any) be decided or left in the business just as we see fit to determine.

I think this is a just and reasonable proposal.

Clearly it was an uneasy partnership, but it left the question as to who actually was the inventor of the leather polish that was to make Kiwi such a success story. The patent office in Australia was established in 1904. Before that patents could only be registered in England. A search by patent lawyers could find none for Kiwi Black or Kiwi Dark Tan. One reason could be the patent office does not accept a new patent if the product already has been on the market. However, there's another more likely reason. Once a patent, like boot polish, has been registered, then the recipe is in the public domain. Anyone can look it up and maybe copy something like it. The recipe for Kiwi always was a better kept secret than the atom bomb. There was never a patent for Coca-Cola. That too was top secret, closely guarded against all rivals.

In his income tax return for 1911 William Ramsay listed £31 5s 6d for patents. This was a lot of money for that time, and it did go to the patent office. However, it was for the registration of the Kiwi trademark. William thought the name 'Kiwi' was almost perfect. It would register in the mind in any language. Even in Moscow they would look at that flightless bird, know it was a kiwi and think of boot polish.

However, this does not solve who invented the recipe. The McKellan grandchildren insist that Ramsay was just the businessman, and that their grandfather Hamilton McKellan, who had no head for figures, was the inventor. He and his wife Elizabeth, or Bessie as she was often called, had five children. They lived in various rented houses in Malvern. Hamilton was always experimenting with chemicals either in the kitchen or the garage and one time he set the kitchen on fire. He was told to move on by his landlord.[8] Noelle Smith's cousin Hugh McClelland[9] remembers his grandfather at 23 Kinross Avenue, Balaclava. He was an industrial chemist and he had a shed in the backyard where he experimented with shoe dyes and polishes. McClelland said: 'I knew him as a very warm person with great faith in God and fellow mankind. I heard my first radio broadcast on a crystal set that he made in the 1920s. It was a magical moment I always remembered. It was about that time I had a number of warts on my face and he said, 'I would like to buy them from you for a penny.' I took the coin and the warts completely disappeared within a fortnight. Why would I not have total faith in him after that?'[10] Hamilton McKellan died in August 1934, in his early eighties.

The mystery deepens, because after the break-up of the partnership Hamilton McKellan became an employee of McKellan & Ramsay. He was on a salary of £3 a week, plus commission. In January 1912 Ramsay wrote a letter to McKellan (undated). It was far from friendly. He pointed out that in addition to his salary McKellan had received £171 in commission since 1 April 1911. Actually he had been overpaid. He added: 'I would also mention that you left my employ on the 15th last month without giving me any notice whatever. I am informed that you have stated in the City that you asked for a half share in

Articles of Agreement made the *eleventh*

day of *April* One thousand *nine* hundred and ~~ninety~~ *one*

Between *Hamilton McKellan*

of *95 Davies Street Brunswick* in the ~~Colony~~ *State* of Victoria *Manufacturer*

of the *first* part and *William Ramsay*

of *317 Collins Street Melbourne* in the said ~~Colony~~ *State* *Estate agent* of the

second part **Whereas** the parties hereto have agreed to enter into Partnership in the trade or business of

Manufacturers and Importers at *62 and 64 Bouverie Street Carlton*

for the terms and subject to the stipulations hereinafter contained **Now these Presents Witness**

that each of them the said *Hamilton McKellan*

and *William Ramsay* for him self h *is* heirs executors

and administrators **Doth** hereby covenant and agree with the other of them h *is* executors and administrators in

manner following that is to say—

1. **THAT** they the said parties hereto will henceforth become and remain partners in the trade or business

of *Manufacturers and Importers* for the term of *two* years

from the date of these presents if *either* of them shall so long live ~~and with the option of either~~
~~of the said parties having of the partnership continued for a further term of three years~~

2. **THE** business of the said Partnership shall be carried on under the style or firm of *McKellan*

and Ramsay at *Nos 62 & 64 Bouverie Street Carlton* or at such

other place or places as the said partners shall from time to time mutually agree on

3. **THE** capital of the said Partnership shall consist of the sum of *Sixty*

pounds which shall be forthwith ~~contributed by the said partners in equal proportions~~ *advanced to the partnership by the said William Ramsay*
The said Hamilton McKellan

4. ~~EACH~~ partners will at all times diligently employ him~~self~~ in the business of the said partnership and carry

on the same for the greatest advantage and ~~neither of them~~ *he not* will directly or indirectly engage in any other trade

or business either alone or in partnership with any other person

5. **NEITHER** partner shall take any apprentice or hire or dismiss any clerk traveller workman or servant without

the consent of the other partner

6. **THE** partners shall be entitled to the capital stock in trade effects and profits of the partnership in equal

proportions. ~~subject to the said William Ramsay having, in the event of the~~
~~partnership being dissolved, a prior claim on the assets of the~~
~~firm for the amount of the Capital he has advanced as aforesaid~~

7. **THE** capital and all other monies of or belonging to the said partnership shall be paid as soon as possible after

the same be received into such Bank to the credit of the said firm of *McKellan and Ramsay*

as the partners shall from time to time agree on

8. **THE** rent of the shops stores houses and buildings where the partnership business shall be carried on or which

may be used by the partnership and the cost of repairs and alterations and all rates taxes payments for insurance and

other outgoings whatsoever in respect of the same and the wages and remuneration of all persons employed in the

partnership business and all other monies to become payable upon account of the partnership and all losses which shall

happen in the same shall be paid out of the capital of the said partnership and the profits arising therefrom or if the

same shall be deficient by the partners in equal shares

9. **WHEREVER** there shall be occasion to give any security or undertaking for the payment of money on account

of the partnership (except when the contrary shall in the common course of business be unavoidable) the same shall be

signed by both of the said partners and if (except in the case aforesaid) either partner shall give any such security or

undertaking which shall not be signed by the other of them the same shall be deemed to be given on the separate

account of the partner so giving it and he shall satisfy the same out of h *is* separate estate and shall indemnify the

other partner and the partnership from all liability and expenses on account thereof

10. **IF** either of the said partners shall lend any of the monies or deliver upon credit any of the goods of the

partnership to any person or persons whom the other partner shall previously in writing have forbidden h~~im~~ to trust the

indifferent persons one to be chosen by each partner or the representatives of each partner in the usual way and whose decision or the decision of the umpire to be named by the said two arbitrators shall be final and conclusive on

the said partners and their representatives provided the same be made within thirty days after reference of the matters in dispute with power to the arbitrator of one party to proceed alone after refusal or neglect of the other of the said parties for seven days after notice so to do to name an arbitrator on his behalf and such decision may be made a Rule of the Supreme Court of the Colony of Victoria on application of either of the parties to the reference.

~~In Witness whereof the said parties to these presents have hereunto set their hands and seals the day and year first above written~~

~~Signed Sealed and Delivered by the said~~

19. That cheques drawn for the business of the partnership shall be signed by both partners. —

20. That the Recipes used in the manufacture of goods traded in by the aforesaid firm shall become the property of both the saids partners and shall not be divulged by either of them. —

21. That in the event of dissolution if either of the said partners make use of the Eucalyptine Disinfectant for commercial purposes it is hereby agreed that each shall pay to the other at least one third share in the profits of the sale of same. —

22. That it is agreed notwithstanding the first clause that the said partnership may be dissolved at any time by mutual agreement of the said partners —

In Witness whereof the said parties to these presents have hereunto set their hands and seals the day and year first above written. —

Signed Sealed and Delivered by the said Hamilton McKellan and the said William Ramsay in the presence of

Hamilton McKellan

William Ramsay

W. H. Roddick
15 St John's Road
Toorak.

The aforesaid Agreement is hereby cancelled as and from 15th March 1902

H. McKellan

William Ramsay

Witness. — W H Roddick.

the business. You know that this statement is not true and that you only asked for a third share which I offered you without prejudice as far as the Australian business was concerned. A cheque for above amount of £12 6s 6d is requested.'

It is doubtful whether the requested cheque ever arrived.

The following month Hamilton McKellan was sending out letters on a McKellan & Co. letterhead, 529 Sydney Road, Brunswick. This one was to Mr Middleton, c/o Messrs Johnson & Sons, Castlereagh Street, Sydney.

> Dear Sir,
>
> I have left McKellan & Ramsay and have joined the firm of McKellan & Co. and we are manufacturing Black and Tan Boot Polishes at the above address. As you are aware I was the sole originator and manufacturer of the 'Kiwi' and what I am making now will be a superior article and the price will not be any more. When I left, the Assistants left also and are now associated with me ...
>
> Yours faithfully
>
> H. McKellan

The story did not finish there. On 24 September 1919, McKellan wrote to William Ramsay's father, John Ramsay. Less than a month earlier his son Thomas Ramsay had died of tuberculosis at 32. Another son, James, had died in London on 4 July, aged 34.

> Dear Sir
>
> I have noticed with regret your heavy recent family losses and it makes it more difficult for me to say what I propose, but as I cannot allow the matter to remain over any longer, I must lay before you the following.
>
> It will be within your recollection that your son William, and I joined together years ago in partnership and that in consequence of legal proceedings which were not justified, being taken against me, I put your son in a satisfactory position, so that in the event of the worst happening, as the result of the law suit, he would not in any way suffer. He and I were to have a half interest in the business, but when the legal proceedings came to an end, and I was vindicated your son William, for reasons probably best known to himself put off from time to time the carrying out of an arrangement that was definitely made between us, although he promised over and over again that such would be done. In the meantime Kiwi developed, and circumstances arose in which I was asked to go to England, which I agreed to do when my proper position in the business was made right.
>
> Such treatment of myself would be described in business circles in very strong language and how he answered his conscience I cannot tell.

McKellan attached three pages, which listed '14 facts' Fact number seven stated:

> The business made slow progress for some years principally because I had to do all the work, that is to say, I did the manufacturing and the selling as well, Mr Ramsay only keeping the books. He might show himself at the factory once or twice a week. Everything else was left to me.

McKellan finished his letter saying he understood the control of Kiwi was in John Ramsay's hands, so as man to man he was now asking that he be restored to his rightful position in Kiwi. He wanted an answer within seven days and if the reply was not satisfactory he proposed to enter a suit in equity in the Supreme Court. Win or lose, his position as an honourable man would be vindicated.

There is no record in the files that John Ramsay answered the letter, so only the dead know who actually invented Kiwi Polish. The question remains unanswered. Who did invent the recipe for Kiwi? Was it William Ramsay or Hamilton McKellan? Maybe, it was neither. Was it a recipe purchased overseas? However, another query remains: why did McKellan allow himself to be an employee and leave Ramsay as the dominant force in the partnership?

4

MUD, MANURE AND SHINY SHOES

OPPOSITE

Kiwi stand, Melbourne Royal
Agricultural Show, 1930s

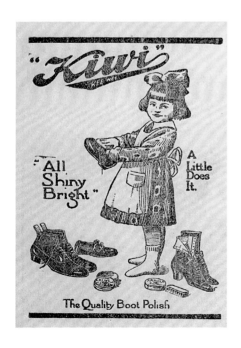

"Kiwi"
KEE-WEE
"All Shiny Bright"
A Little Does It.

The Quality Boot Polish

Shiny shoes are a modern phenomenon. The 19th century was the era of the hansom cab, horses, rough old roads and mud in the streets. Shoes were the first victims. The story goes that on every street corner in London there was a bootblack. He had a large old tin kettle and a pigskin filled with blacking made of ivory black, coarse moist sugar, water and vinegar. They had brushes, but also they had a knife, which they used to carve off the dried mud, and they applied their deadly mixture with a rag tied on the end of the stick. No shine.

Right back to medieval times dubbin was popular. This was a waxy mixture, made from tallow, oil and soda ash, and it was used to soften and waterproof the leather, but no shine. Eventually shiny shoes did become popular and fashionable. Households with lots of servants used lanolin, beeswax and tallow. One didn't buy 'shoe polish'. The usual term was 'blacking', and that was because it often contained lamp black.

Towards the end of the 19th century factories were making boots and shoes at a price the masses could afford, and all that leather was crying out for something better. In England Cherry Blossom came on the market and in Australia we had Nugget, Kiwi and Cobra. Manufactured in England, Nugget was imported to the Australian market in the late 1890s and then manufactured in Victoria from about 1910. Kiwi and Cobra polishes appeared in 1906.

Legend has it that the Kiwi brand first appeared in Melbourne in 1906, but it was earlier than that. The first appearance of the Kiwi trademark appeared in the *Victorian Government Gazette* for 24 June 1903. It was for Kiwi Brand Wash-Eesie, and according to the *Gazette* it was a washing and cleaning compound, submitted by William Ramsay of 317 Collins Street, Melbourne, trading as McKellan & Ramsay.

The choice of the Kiwi for a washing powder was intriguing. Not only is the Kiwi a native of New Zealand, but it is one of the most curious of birds. It is slightly smaller than a domestic hen, round and podgy with soft brown feathers that look like hair. It has no tail, and its wings, if you can find them, are under the feathers. The Kiwi does not fly, and those wings have not been used for maybe a million years. Unbearably shy, it sleeps in hollow logs or safe little gullies, and comes out at night to fossick for food.

The little creature is almost blind and can see only a few inches ahead. But the kiwi has other advantages a long bill with nostrils almost at the tip, which makes it unique.

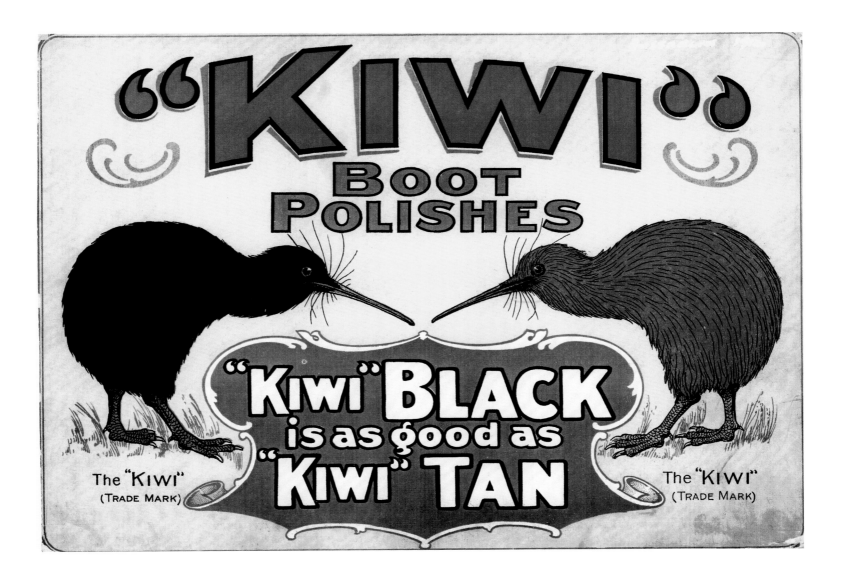

Other birds have their nostrils either at the roof or in the middle of the beak. So the Kiwi beak has the sensitivity of a radar beacon and, combined with exceptional hearing, sight is barely necessary. The kiwi uses its own effective methods in its nocturnal hunt for seeds, grubs, worms or even little crayfish.

No creature can lay an egg like a Kiwi. They are huge up to six times the size of a hen's egg. The female kiwi leaves the nest as soon as she produces the egg. Then it is up to the male to oversee the incubation. The unfortunate male sits on the egg for maybe 75 days and he loses up to a kilo in weight. Once the female kiwi finds a mate or vice versa, they are bonded, monogamous, like a happy married couple. If they survive the environment they can live for 25 years. Of course, the environment is tough. The Maoris used to hunt the kiwi for meat. They were a delicacy and their feathers were used to make beautiful coats. Kiwis were not easy to find, and the hunters used dogs with rattles on their collars so that they could be followed in the dark. Don't be misled. It does not mean they are easy to catch. The Kiwi is fierce when trying to defend itself, and it can move like a top sprinter.

Come the white invasion of Europeans and forest lands being turned into sheep and cattle farms, the kiwis lost their natural habitat, driving them almost to extinction. Since

1908 law has protected the kiwi. It cannot be hunted, trapped or even wilfully disturbed in its natural habitat. A kiwi cannot be kept as a pet and its export is prohibited, except in the case of a few zoos like the San Diego Zoo in California or London and Edinburgh. There are five varieties of kiwi. The largest species, the Spotted Kiwi, is doing well and there is an estimated 20,000 on the mountainous parts north-west of Nelson and the Southern Alps. On the other hand the Haast Southern Brown Kiwi has become rare with only 300 in a restricted area of the Haast Range of the Southern Alps.

There was always the theory that the kiwi was a close relative of the moa, which like the kiwi was a flightless bird. They were almost four metres in height, but through hunting became extinct around 1400 AD. Recent DNA studies by British scientists have a different theory. The kiwi DNA is more closely related to the emu and the cassowary, so it is very likely the kiwi was an ancient import from Australia.

So how clever was William Ramsay. In Annie Meek he found a Kiwi wife, and the name for his company had both Australian and New Zealand ancestry. How did the little bird get its name? The male kiwi had the household job of sitting on the egg. The female kiwi would be out foraging for food. They would keep in touch by calling each other. The sound was a long 'ki' and short 'wi'. The Maoris called them kiwis for that reason. They became a national New Zealand emblem, and any New Zealander soldier, civilian or Olympic athlete just has to go by the name Kiwi. Ramsay thought it a superb name for a shoe polish.

Wash-Eesie fell as easy prey, just like the kiwi. However, Ramsay had faith in his little bird, the symbol, the trademark that looked so good. Shoe stores were appearing all over Melbourne, and Collingwood was already well known for its shoe and boot manufacturing. In 1906 McKellan & Ramsay produced a black shoe polish. The kiwi looked marvellous on the round tin and there was the theory that even if you couldn't read or write you would always recognise that bird. The launch date was 13 October 1906, and by the year's end the small company had sold 86 gross. All sales figures were by the gross (12 dozen). So in three months, in modern terms, they sold 12,384 tins.[1]

McKellan & Ramsay could hardly boast having a factory. Their quarters were incredibly cramped. They had two rooms, each about the size of a normal living room, plus a shed out the back. Here they were supposed to do all their manufacturing, packaging and research development for new products. On Fridays and Saturdays they hawked their Kiwi polish on the streets and at show time they took it out to the showgrounds. Competition was fierce, and for a time the future looked bleak. In the whole of 1907 and 1908 they sold only 46 gross.

Yet 1908 was the key year. Until that time polishes were just polishes. They would produce a shine, but they would do nothing for the leather. Shoes that had gone through a hard time in the ferocious heat of a Melbourne summer and endured the mud and slush in Collins and Bourke Streets in the winter needed revival; they needed their colour back. In that year McKellan & Ramsay produced their Kiwi Dark Tan, the polish that has become so famous. Until then

William Ramsay and Hamilton McKellan in the first Kiwi
outlet with a Nugget poster nearby (top left), *c.* 1905

black was the thing, carbon black, soot black and the old dubbin were used to rub into anything brown. But Kiwi Dark Tan was new. It restored that rich dark tan to leather and it sold instantly.

In 1909 William Ramsay took it to Sydney and sold 100 gross. This was a splendid breakthrough. A menu for the trip remains in the Ramsay file. Ramsay was aboard the SS *Bombala*, 3,540 tons, a steamer that did the run from Melbourne to North Queensland. The menu for breakfast on 2 May 1909 was impressive.

Iced pears and cream
Grilled Yarmouth bloaters
Grilled loin chops and tomatoes
Veal cutlets and lemon sauce
Braised ham and port wine sauce
Crumbed calves liver and oysters
Curried giblets
Roast beef
Snow and Lyonnaise potatoes
Pikelet and honey

John, Annie and Madge in possibly the family Itala, mid-1920s

OPPOSITE

The new Kiwi premises, 683 Elizabeth Street, Melbourne, c. 1912

Everyone wanted the new Kiwi polish. This was how its popularity soared. In 1911 they sold 5,479 gross; in 1912, 9,459 gross; in 1913, 13,522 gross; in 1914, 27,711 gross; in 1915, 34,540 gross, in 1916, 45,271 gross.[2] Progressively, they had to move to larger premises. In 1909 they found 576–578 Elizabeth Street, Carlton. That was not big enough so in 1911 William Ramsay leased 683 Elizabeth Street, Carlton. The firm was no longer called McKellan & Ramsay. An old photograph shows the full team standing outside the front door. It is a two-storey building, bluestone down below, brick above and a lofty pediment. Nobody was left in doubt regarding what went on inside. There were signs from top to bottom. This was the Kiwi Polish Co.

In his income tax return for 1912 William listed 18 employees with wages of £1,149. Then in 1913 his costs included a motor car. Repairs and petrol came to £66 13s and he paid his chauffeur £43 12s. The chauffeur could have been Ramsay's younger sister, Madge, who was one of the Melbourne's first car drivers.

Madge drove everybody, including her father John Ramsay. Ramsay liked to sit in the front alongside the driver. With a stopwatch in his hand he would cry out 'Faster, faster.' Nicknamed 'Bayonet', the car was a Ballot, an early French automobile. It was sadly lacking in power and it had dire problems getting uphill in the centre of Melbourne from Flinders Street to Exhibition Street. The only way Madge could make it was to put the car in reverse and go up backwards. There was an acetylene generator for the headlights, which sat on the running board. It was a fine looking machine; both headlights and

acetylene generators were brass, which the young Ramsays remembered vividly. The brass required frequent polishing.[3]

The Ballot factory made engines before World War I, but did not produce a touring car until 1920. The Ramsays had an earlier car: a 9.5 horsepower Standard. This could have been the motor car that struggled up Exhibition Street.

Kiwi was now moving into every state, even way out west to Perth. William Ramsay's big ambition was London. The first idea was to send Hamilton McKellan, but the two men could not agree on terms, and when they put an end to their association in 1911 William asked his father to go there instead.

John Ramsay arrived in London with his second wife Janet (Anty) in March 1912. It was a poor time for his debut. There was much industrial unrest, including a national coal strike. How was it possible to set up a factory when there was no coal and the city was at a standstill? The miners were striking for a wage of 10 shillings a week. They stopped work for 18 days and the Archbishop of Canterbury made an appeal for God's help in all the churches. A month later the *Titanic* sank with a dreadful loss of life. Amidst all this there were the passionate suffragettes smashing windows, which seemed to John Ramsay a strange way for acquiring the vote. However, he was pleased to get a telephone, which cost him £5 a year plus 3 shillings for 360 calls. Beyond that there was a fee of a penny a call. The hotels were expensive, but he did find a boarding house: bed, breakfast and dinner for 30 shillings a week, dinner at 6.30 p.m., a shilling extra for lunch.[4]

In a letter dated 27 March 1912 he described their sightseeing: Westminster Abbey, Buckingham Palace, the House of Commons, and the House of Lords. He also went to Downing Street and looked at the residence of Mr Asquith and Lloyd George, noting the windows the suffragettes had smashed. Nor did he miss the statues of the Duke of Wellington and Queen Victoria.

A few weeks later they went to Scotland to see his brother James. John Ramsay also made a sentimental journey to Shotts. It had grown 10 times the size since he left, and he visited Stevenson's workshop where he worked for more than 10 years. 'I heard the sound of hammers going and I went in and found a tall young man and another man and two apprentices at work.'[5]

John Ramsay found a factory at 18 Verulam Street in the inner London district of Holborn, off Gray's Inn Road, a halfpenny tram ride from their boarding house. Ramsay wrote home almost every week, but it seemed he received few letters in return. He did hear that William had been to the Melbourne Cup, won by Piastre in 1912, which outrageously beat the favourite Duke Foote before a crowd of 54,203; prize money £8,676.[6]

John Ramsay bought a second-hand typewriter for 11 guineas and hired a typist for 15 shillings a week. He was paying himself and Anty 25 shillings a week. But Anty did have a job: the meals at the boarding house were so bad she came in to cook lunch every day.

John Ramsay was optimistic, glorying in the future one week, but almost in despair weeks later. On 8 November 1912 he was at the Shoe and Leather Fair and he reported

William Ramsay, the founder, in attendance at the 1913 London Exhibition.

REALIZATION.

C. W. Faulkner & Co. Ltd. London, E.C.   British Production (Copyright).
Series 1338.

POST CARD

C.W FAULKNER & CO LTD

London
23rd Jany '14

The C.W.F Series

Dear Jack,

In, about a week after getting this, Mother & father should both be back in Melbourne. Won't it be nice when we are all together once more Jack? Are you having a good time at Clydebank? I think you all will be? Have you been out in Grandpa's motor car. How do you like it? Just bonsar eh? Dad is looking forward to seeing you all again before very long. Hope you are good children while mother is away. Lots of love & kisses from Dad.

that he was having a great time. He had samples of boots on display with shades of tan and ox blood, which were delighting the trade. He wrote: 'The boot done up with black on the stand is good, you can hardly tell it from patent leather two yards away. We have got lessons how to put on the polish. They rub the polish on with a finger until the surface is quite smooth putting on as little as possible . . . as soon as it feels dry, stop rubbing and polish with a soft cloth called Velvet. It is something between a fine velvet and a chamois.'

In other letters he would show his disappointment. A traveller resigned after three days, disheartened because he failed to get a single order. 'Our orders are small, miserably small, compared with yours. We have a good factory . . . with every appliance. It would be cowardly to run away.'[7] Another time he wrote, 'Orders are beginning to drop in. We have sent out over six gross this week, chiefly black.' He always ended his letters: 'With devotion . . . May a sweet sense of the divine presence be ever with you is the daily prayer of your loving father.'

On 13 November he received a shock. A cable arrived which 'suggested' that he and Anty should book their passages and leave London for Melbourne in early January. Then 'if convenient' leave Tom in charge until William's arrival in early March.

Tom was William's youngest brother and in 1913 he was 28 years old. He was on the staff as John Ramsay's assistant at 10 shillings a week. John Snr wrote: 'My Dear Son . . . It came like a bombshell into our midst, and set me thinking after a good solid talk over the situation, both Tom and I came to the decision that this step would simply wreck all that we have done and there would be only one thing to do when you arrived, viz, to wind up, pack up and return which would be no easy job unless at a tremendous sacrifice . . . God bless you my dear son, I feel your cable was meant to benefit us, but having put my hand to the plough it would be the humiliation of my life to leave here before you reach London.'

John Ramsay had no faith that young Tom could manage affairs on his own. 'Tom,' he said, 'is good at his own work but he knows nothing of the business side of affairs.' So he decided to send Anty home at the required time and remain in London until William arrived. On 10 January 1913, a cold, raw and foggy morning they arrived at Tilbury Docks, where he said goodbye to his wife for the next four months. He wrote: 'I hope Anty will have a good passage and God will bring her safely through the dangers of the deep.'[8]

He need not have worried. Anty arrived home safely and Tom's brother William arrived in England at the end of March aboard the P & O Liner SS *Marmora*. The London business did not go to ruin. Sales in Britain and on the Continent soared to 6,000 gross, which was equal to all Australian sales. While William was in London, Annie and the children went to stay at 'Holly Bank', Oamaru with her parents.

OPPOSITE

Postcard sent by William from London to his son Jack (John). This card was written eight months before William's death in September 1914.

SS *Medina*

Cable from Annie and James (Jim) to William awaiting William's return, February 1914.

The man who did not write many letters sent home a small mountain of postcards. William's letters to his sons Tom and John still exist: colour reproductions of Hampton Court Palace, the Life Guards on parade, Marble Arch, the Eiffel Tower, Blériot aircraft in full flight, and he sent a beautiful souvenir of the laying of the foundation of the new Australian Commonwealth building (Australia House) at Aldwych by King George V and Queen Mary on 24 July 1913 in the presence of the Australian High Commissioner Sir George Reid.

William Ramsay kept writing to his children about how he would see them all in London and what fun they would have together. When clearly that was impossible, he told them what good times they would have together in Melbourne. He was not telling the truth. The doctors had already told him he was suffering from cancer. First he sent a cable advising he was leaving on the SS *Medina* and he was dreadfully sorry for Annie and the children. Their trip to London was off.

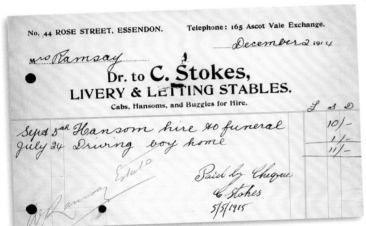

On 21 January 1914 he cabled Annie: 'Doctor says growth stomach advises immediate return. Leaving Marseilles 30th. Could you and, Tom, if advisable, and Jim meet me Colombo. Leaving 2nd class. Much love, Will.'

On 26 January he made a new will in which he said: 'If the London business is continued I devise that it be formed into a company of 120 shares apportioned as follows; my estate sixty-five shares, my father forty shares, my brother Thomas nine shares, my brother James four shares, William Henry Roddick two shares total one hundred and twenty shares.'

On 28 March 1913 he received a cable to the SS *Medina* from Colombo from his wife Annie and his brother, James Ramsay: 'Patiently awaiting tomorrow. Love, Anne.'

William Ramsay returned home and died at 'Clydebank' on 4 September 1914 aged 46. He was buried in the Melbourne General Cemetery. A. A. Sleight Funeral Directors and Embalmers sent in their account for £48 12s 6d. This covered:

Inner coffin, covered with white embossed cloth, lined and padded with best satin.
Outer casket in solid oak, French polished mounted solid brass handles and ornaments,
name & age engraved on brass plate.
Hire of hearse and pair (Sunday)
Six mourning carriages and pairs
Velvet and gold pall
Attendance of bearers, funeral directors

C. Stokes Livery & Letting Stables sent in an account: Hansom hire to funeral. Eleven shillings.

Souvenir in Commemoration

OF THE

Laying

OF THE

Foundation

Stone

OF THE

Australian

Common-

wealth

Offices,

AT

Aldwych

BY

THE
KING
AND
QUEEN,

Thursday,
July
24,
1913.

The foundation-stone of the new Australian Commonwealth building on the Aldwych site will be laid by the King to-day at noon.

His Majesty will ride from Buckingham Palace by way of the Mall, the Admiralty Arch, and the Strand, returning by the same route.

The King and Queen and Princess Mary will be received by Sir George Reid, High Commissioner for Australia, who will be accompanied by the Agents-General for New South Wales, Victoria, Queensland, South Australia, Western Australia, and Tasmania, Captain R. Muirhead Collins (Official Secretary of the Commonwealth in London), Lady Reid and Miss Reid.

A grand stand to accommodate 1,200 has been erected at the left-hand corner of the land marked "The Site" on the illustration above, and it is arranged that the ceremonial shall be witnessed by the High Commissioner, the Agents-General of the Australian States, and by all the prominent resident and visiting Australians in London.

The foundation-stone is known as trachyte stone and has been bought from the Commonwealth to be incorporated in the building, in the construction of which Australian marble and timber will be largely used.

Earl Grey's scheme for an Empirorium in Aldwych, to be a London centre for all the Oversea Dominion Goverments and a permanent exhibition of the products of the Empire, for the promotion of inter-Imperial trade, has advanced a step further.

A full account of the scheme and its objects has been issued by the sponsors of the movement, who state the establishment of the Dominion House on the Aldwych site would enable:—

1. The Goverments of the self governing Dominions and of their various States and Provinces, to concentrate on one central site their offices, now widely distributed in parts of London.

2. The attention of the home consumer to be fixed exclusively on the products of the Dominions oversea.

3. The manufacturers of the United Kingdom to assist to meet the requirements of Greater Britain.

Earl Grey is the chairman of the directors of a company, the Dominion Site, Limited, which has been formed to carry out the scheme, and the other directors include:—

The Earl of Plymouth.
Sir Leander Starr Jameson (South Africa).
Sir J. Henniker Heaton (Australia).
Mr. George McLaren Brown (Canada).
Mr. George Beetham (New Zealand).
Mr. Harry E. Brittain.

S. Burgess, Print, 'o' Place, Strand, W.C.

KIWI AT WAR

OPPOSITE

Trooper Alexander Gibson Forsyth,
4th Light Horse Regiment. Kiwi was highly
valued for maintenance of leather in
both world wars.

T he year was 1916, and Kiwi had shed all doubts that it could take on any competitors, whether in Australia, England and even all Europe. The time had come to show extra muscle by combining the Australian and British companies under the title of the Kiwi Polish Company Pty Ltd. The first meeting was held at the Modern Chambers, 317 Collins Street, Melbourne on Friday 7 January.

Annie Elizabeth Ramsay was one of the first directors. She couldn't be there because she was on holidays at Peterborough on the Victorian coast. There was John Ramsay Snr, Dr John Ramsay from Launceston, James Ramsay, son of John Snr, who was still working in London and William Henry Roddick. John Ramsay Snr was appointed chairman, W. H. Roddick managing director and John Ramsay Snr became temporary company secretary, without salary. Only two directors had to be present to provide a quorum.

The appointment of W. H. Roddick was interesting. He had been there right from the beginning as the accountant with William Ramsay and Hamilton McKellan. He was the eldest of a family of five boys and two girls. His father had arrived from Scotland in 1852 and worked for the firm of Groves & McVitty, wholesale grocers. No one ever called WHR 'Bill'. In the Scottish style he was always 'Will'. In the 1930s he lived in style in Heyington Place, Toorak and drove a Packard motorcar. His nephew, Max Roddick, remembers that when guests dined at his house a maid would serve them in starched collar and cuffs. For many years he was president of Prince Henry's Hospital in St Kilda Road and he received a CBE for his service. After his wife Annie died in the 1950s Roddick sold his house to St Catherine's School next door.

The first issue of share capital for the Kiwi Polish Company was 8,360 ordinary shares and 5,490 employees shares fully paid up to £1. Shareholders included Annie Elizabeth Ramsay, John Ramsay of Launceston, John Ramsay of Essendon, James Ramsay, Thomas Meek Ramsay and Henry Danford Charters.

How did those shareholders fare? There is no doubt that the Great War of 1914–18 was the making of Kiwi. There was so much leather, so many boots, so many Sam Browne belts, so many bandoliers, so many leggings so many bridles and everything to do with horses that had to be preserved and polished.

Sergeant Francis Wesley Tyler,
11th Machine Gun Company, at
Chermside army camp, Queensland

The success of the business in London began slowly. In 1912 John Ramsay sent samples and circulars to Indian princes. He sent samples to the army, and in 1914 he went round to boarding houses all over the United Kingdom.[1] He sent letters to all British Army districts. A copy of one went back to Australia.

The Brigadier General in Charge of Administration,
Scottish Command,
Edinburgh

Dear Sir,

Enclosed circular will bring under your notice a new polish for
brown or tan leatherwork – military belts, puttees, etc.

It is very much appreciated by military men in Australia.
Captain H. G. Vaux, ADC to Governor Carmichael, says: 'It is far
the best brown polish I have ever used.'

It is equally good for boots and shoes. I would be pleased if you would permit
me to forward examples for your experts to test and if they find them superior
to what they are now using, I shall be delighted to supply your Command with
whatever colour you instruct me to obtain. You will see by my price list that we
make the tans in four shades.

Awaiting your commands, I am, Dear Sir,

Yours respectfully,

John Ramsay,

Manager.[2]

In 1914 James Ramsay wrote to his brother William saying that the business would not grow unless they spent a large amount of money on advertising. This the company did. At times there were complaints from the board in Melbourne, and strict limits were fixed.

One wonders whether the London office took matters into its own hands. After the outbreak of war in 1914 Kiwi commissioned a film, which was extraordinary for the time. There had been earlier company films. Bird's Custard made one in 1902 and there was another for Dewar's Whisky. These films no longer exist and they were 50 feet in length. The Kiwi film is eight times as long and it was made as a promotion for the product. There are good copies in archives both in Melbourne's Latrobe Library and the Australian National Library in Canberra. It runs for nearly nine minutes and presents a

AUSTRALIA
1919

KIWI AND HIS PALS.

KIWI

BOOT POLISHES
BLACK & TANS
PRESERVE ALL LEATHERS

charming story, dating back to those halcyon days when it was the custom for guests to leave their shoes outside the bedroom door, then find them brilliantly shined when they awakened next morning. The film is titled *Shine Sir*. No sound, of course. But the words are presented in classic silent movie frames.

The opening scene is in the manager's office at the Hotel Imperial in London. The manager is a stern gentleman with a large Edwardian moustache. He is talking earnestly with a worker from the boot room. He is about to join the army. He is a volunteer destined to fight in France.

'Good luck!' says the manager, 'I only wish I were young enough to shoulder a rifle myself!'

The worker goes off and hardly a minute goes by before another man comes in. He too is off to France. 'Sorry Sir! I've just got to go . . . won't you wish me luck?'

The manager is aghast and wonders what he is going to do. 'Only one man left and 200 bedrooms – 400 boots to clean! Heavens!!' In the next scene the manager is putting out a sign: 'Wanted Boot Boys'. It is close to another, which reads: 'King and Country Needs You'.

Two grubby little boys, maybe 10 to 12 years, read the sign. One says: 'I can't clean shoes for nuts – can you, Jim?'

The camera moves to an Aussie Digger in a slouch hat. He is leaning against a wall and he overhears what the boys are saying. 'Can't clean boots? I'll show you something that will clean them for you! Come along and I'll introduce you to Kiwi.'

They go to a shop and come away with Kiwi. They call on the manager. He looks at these grubby infants with contempt. How could they solve his problem?

'Give us a chance, Guv'nor,' they cry. He ponders, then with no choice gives in. 'Show me what you can do . . . If you make a good job of it – the job's yours!'

The boys bounce into a gleeful jig. In the next scene they are at the back of the hotel. There is a pile of boots of all shapes and sizes. They are polishing with such speed that you can hardly see their hands move. The manager returns and the silent movie pronounces: 'The surprise of his life'.

'Boys, you and Kiwi are the goods! I'll give you a pound a week each!'

Next the movies pronounces: 'Pay Day.'

The boys are in the manager's office. They are spruced and shiny like Kiwi itself, their hair plastered down, and they are wearing uniforms with brass buttons up to the neck. Politely they receive their money. The commercial ends: 'Kiwi ("Kee-Wee") is the Australian polish that came over to help.'[3]

Shine Sir went into cinemas all over Britain and Australia. This was probably one of the earliest commercial movies ever made. There were other forms of advertising. In an era long before radio and television, posters were an art form. Carlton Ale, Saunders Malt Extract, Beecham's Pills, Hutton's Hams and Raleigh Bicycles all produced posters of such quality they became collectors' items. The Kiwi posters were outstanding. A World War I poster has an Aussie Digger showing a tin of Kiwi to three other servicemen. It is

OPPOSITE

A selection of frames from the *Shine Sir* film commissioned by Kiwi in 1916. Apart from its commercial value, this is a gem of the silent era. *Shine Sir* can be viewed at the National Film and Sound Archive

FRAMES FROM 'SHINE SIR'

August 1914
The Boot-Room staff at
the Hotel Imperial
joins up

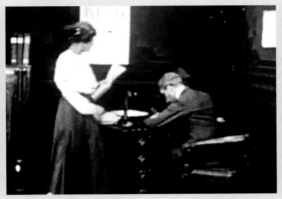

"Good-luck! I only wish
I were young enough
to shoulder a rifle
myself!"

"Shine, Sir!"

Produced by
THE LONDON PRESS EXCHANGE LTD

"Can't clean boots? I'll
show you something that
will clean them for you!
Come along and I'll
introduce you to 'KIWI'!"

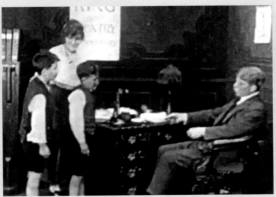

"Give us a chance, Guvnor?"

titled 'Kiwi and his Pals'. The pals are splendidly international. One is an English Tommy, behind him is an Indian in a crimson turban, and the third is a French matelot. Their Kiwied boots are very shiny.

Another cunning advertising method was the purchase in August 1916 of 40,000 rulers, emblazoned with the wonders of Kiwi. They cost 68 shillings a thousand, and no doubt went to schools everywhere to sit beside the inkwells at classroom desks.

As the war progressed, millions of men were under arms. The demand in England had mainly been for black boot polish, but now the demand for tan became huge. The Australian Light Horse, with their splendid shiny bandoliers and leggings were walking advertisements for Kiwi. Furthermore, every boot shop in London was stocking Kiwi. Kiwi sales in Melbourne were 45,271 gross and in London 22,291 gross. The factory in Verulam Street, Holborn, was too small, so the company moved to 715–719 Fulham Road SW, which had four times the floor space at rent of £5 a week.[4]

In the early days of European settlement a range of symbols were in use in New Zealand: the silver fern, the moa, the Southern Cross as well as the kiwi. The silver fern and the Southern Cross received official recognition but the word 'kiwi' had a lovely ring about it and troops around the world were beginning to recognise the name. The people of the Long White Cloud have been called 'Kiwis' ever since the war.[5] However, there was a weird irony. The New Zealand Government would not accept the brand name of Kiwi Shoe Polish. New Zealand was the one place where it could not be used. So if one wanted to buy a tin of Kiwi in Auckland, Wellington or Christchurch, it had to be Mirror Polish, the first name McKellan & Ramsay had used back in 1905.

There were many stories about Kiwi from the front, including a particularly colourful tale from a Digger who signed himself 'Dickie'.

> Just before Christmas 1917 our ammunition parks were along the
> Baillieul-Armentieres road and as our O.C. wanted us to have a spread,
> a few scouts were sent out to procure young pigs and poultry, and ordered
> to buy them where other means failed. Bricks were carried as back loading
> from Armentieres, and we built a brick oven – rough but honest.
>
> A few days before Christmas, a squadron of Fritz planes, escorted by a
> circus of fighters, emerged from the low-lying clouds, and started sending
> down Christmas presents.
>
> Bill, the Greasy, and myself made for the oven only to see the Sergeant
> Major's highly Kiwied leggings disappearing in the door, so we nose-dived
> into a nearby ditch.
>
> When Fritz had gone, and the S.M. had reversed out of his possie,
> Bill exclaimed 'We made that oven to roast the little pigs in not as a sty,
> to roast one big pig.'
>
> And for once the S.M. took it lying down. – Dickie.[6]

A poem put to music under the direction of Mr Laurence Richardson includes the following verses:

Members of the 1st Australian
Divisional Signal Company, Mena
Camp, Egypt,1915. Inside the tent
is a box bearing the Kiwi trademark.

I'm sending him my photo
It was framed by Harry Peake
As a token to remind him
That news of him I seek;

And a tin of Kiwi Polish
To give his shoes a shine,
So that when he visits Blighty
His south end will look fine.
Our brave boys in the Trenches
A gallant lot and true;

We love to read of each brave deed,
By the lads we so well knew.
'Tis our duty and our pleasure
To aid them all we can,
And to help in some small measure
Each soldier and each man.[7]

Then there was an undated letter from Mark Block in France to his father H. Block at 9 Queen Street, Melbourne.

> You ask if there is anything I particularly want, there is only one thing that I can think of, that is Dark Tan Kiwi Boot Polish. There is nothing in the world to touch it. It is practically unprocurable out here. The man with a tin of Kiwi is envied by all his pals. It is a wonder that the people who boost Australian Manufactures in the papers have not got hold of this fact. If there is one thing an Australian soldier admires it is 'Kiwi'.

In 1915 the board appointed William Ramsay (known as Willie) as the London manager. William Ramsay, the Kiwi founder had died in 1914. Willie was a cousin, and to add to the confusion his wife was Annie Ramsay, same name as the wife of the founder

William. The new manager, Willie, came from Motherwell in Lanarkshire, Scotland, South-East of Glasgow. His cousin, James Ramsay (UK managing director), was keen to appoint him, but John Ramsay Snr, now chairman of Kiwi, was not. Eventually 'he came round' and, as Tom Ramsay recorded in his personal notes, 'So many people adore Willie.' James was the prime mover in the appointment of Willie, and to make matters even more complicated, soon after Willie brought in his Scottish brother James Ramsay to be his assistant.

James Ramsay, born in Scotland in 1875 and educated in Australia, was almost eight years younger than his brother William, the founder of Kiwi. James's promotion was swift: On 16 July 1918 the board appointed him joint managing director with W. H. Roddick. After holding this position for less than four months in Melbourne the board despatched him to London for a year. No doubt having a managing director, or ex managing director, in London was a good idea. The London factory was booming. It was sending Kiwi all over Europe, to the Middle East and even South Africa. It was clear London, not Melbourne, was the real future. James wanted to go to London to take Willie Ramsay's place.[8] Willie, who was thoroughly convinced that London was his personal castle, was not pleased. The board told James he was to be in London for at least three years and that he was to be very thrifty and indulge in no unnecessary expenses.

Regardless of this, in June 1919 James contacted the board saying he was short of staff and he wanted to appoint a Mr Howieson. The entry for board minutes on 6 June 1919 was: 'Board resolved to notify Mr James Ramsay that the Board did not desire any further appointment to be made and therefore were against the appointment of Mr Howieson on the London Staff.'

According to notes made by Tom Ramsay, on 4 July 1919, just a few weeks later, James Ramsay took his own life. According to hearsay he jumped out of a window. Whether he was upset by the high-handed actions of the board or whether he could not get on with his cousin Willie Ramsay, we do not know.

After his death there was a strange silence on the matter of James. Suicide at this time was a shameful thing, particularly for a devout Presbyterian family. On 30 July 1919 the board met again. James's father, John Ramsay Snr, was in the chair. The minutes state: 'The Board placed on record its deep regret at the sudden death of the director, Mr James Ramsay and appreciation of the excellent work he had done in the service of the company as joint managing director.'

James Ramsay was 34 years old at the time of his death. His youngest brother, Thomas Ramsay, died of consumption two months later on 13 August 1919. He was 32. This time the board did not comment.

The will of 'The Late Mr James Ramsay' was produced, and the board gave its approval to advance Mrs James Ramsay £50 a month for three months. Three months later the board approved the £50 for another three months, and again three months after that. Finally the board showed its generosity and made the £50 a month a continuing item. However, on 10 October 1926 the board increased the payment to £100 a month, but two months later it made another decision: 'Payments to Mrs James Ramsay to be discontinued.' Her name was Miriam and she had two children to support: Harry and Fred.

Meanwhile, the factory in Elizabeth Street, Carlton was proving so small it was like working in a cupboard. In April 1916 Kiwi bought land at 188 Burnley Street, Richmond for £1,800. Richmond was a thriving industrial area. It was the home for Bedggood's boot factory; Bryant & May, the celebrated makers of matches; the Wertheim Piano factory in Bendigo Street; H. J. Heinz and Rosella, tomato sauce makers; Alcock & Co. billiard table makers; and Burnley Street brickworks, founded by the well-known builder of the Exhibition Buildings, David Mitchell, father of Nellie Melba. However, the war was on, so any thought of building was out of the question. In February 1919 a tender was let to W. C. Burns for £9,000 with provision that any excavation of rock would be at 10 shillings a yard. In February 1920 the board decided Mr Burns was a failure and it gave the contract to A. P. Crow, this time for £12,000, and he had to complete the job in five months. In 1922 Kiwi Polish Co Pty Ltd was up and running at 188 Burnley Street. Its telephone number, in the combination of letters and numbers of those days, was J1101.[9]

It occupied a two-storey building, with the Australia office downstairs and the international office upstairs. It had no resemblance to the old grubby establishment, and the floors were polished so that they shone like mirrors, perfect for a company that prided itself on shine.[10]

On the top of the landing in a glass case was a stuffed kiwi. As kiwis became an endangered species, it became politically incorrect to give such treatment to the dear creatures. But they were the company's symbol of success, and at one time there was a total of nine stuffed kiwis in its offices around the world. There are still a few stuffed kiwis in private hands. These are now rare items.

KIWI
The Quality
BOOT POLISH
BLACK AND TANS

RAMSAY FAMILY CARS

1 Renault, 1904
2 Chrysler, 1928, Tom's 21st birthday present
3 Itala Tipo 50b Tourer 1923, with John, Jean and Annie
4 Sunbeam, bought in England and imported to Australia 1926
5 Lanchester 10 Open Sports coupe 1933, England

6

LOOKING AFTER BUSINESS

fter his son William's early death in 1914, John Ramsay Snr took over as chairman of the Kiwi Polish Company. It had been a long haul for him since 1878 when he migrated from Scotland with his young family aboard the clipper *Loch Sunart*. In the early 1920s his appearances at board meetings began to lapse, and he died on 3 March 1924. He was religious to the end.

There were many tributes. Shortly after his death a little book containing his writings was published, revealing his lifetime dedication to the church. William Howat wrote: 'My memory of the late Mr John Ramsay goes back to 1894, when the disastrous failure of many banks and building societies brought us together in common sympathy. I was deeply impressed with the calm confidence he had that his Heavenly Father was still Love.'.

D. Christie wrote: 'He had his full share of business difficulties and domestic sorrows, yet through it all he always bore a cheerful spirit. Each Sabbath found him in his accustomed place preaching the gospel from some pulpit. Sunday was no idle day for him. We often wondered how he stood the strain. His addresses, all committed to paper, were usually prepared when the rest of his household had retired. His "den" at 'Clydebank' held an accumulation of years of toil.'[1]

William Ramsay's widow, Annie, took over as chairman of the company. Later, from the 1960s, feminists were talking of a glass ceiling and how few women had control of large companies, but 'Kiwi Annie' was a true pioneer, a woman in charge of an international company close on a century ahead of her time. However, ambitious young men were on their way. Her son John Ramsay Jnr was appointed to the board on 11 February 1925. He joined the company on 26 April 1926 at £2 a week. His rise was rapid. On 7 October he became acting secretary. He received a bonus of £250 and a wedding present of 50 guineas when he married Edyth Mary Pie. A year later he was acting chairman on a salary of £1,000 a year, big money and big responsibility for a man who was 22 years old.[2]

Thomas Meek Ramsay, better known as Tom, three years John's junior, went to Scotch College. He was a clever student and he could have enrolled at Ormond College on a scholarship, but his mother Annie wouldn't allow this, as scholarships were for those who needed them, so she paid for Tom's course at the University of Melbourne. He studied chemistry, philosophy and pure mathematics before he started at Kiwi. His mother gave him a Chevrolet coupe for his 21st birthday.[3]

John and Tom looked incredibly alike, particularly when they wore the fashionable Ronald Coleman moustaches. They could have been twins. The resemblance ended there. John was more of an introvert, not such a good mixer. By contrast, Tom loved parties, a good time and smart hotels. They both liked expensive automobiles.

In 1923 Lady Elizabeth Bowes-Lyon married the Duke of York and the BBC broadcast Big Ben for the first time, but employment was bad in Britain. The London Kiwi office dismissed four girls before Christmas and trade was down. Yet over the longer period Kiwi was booming. Between 1914 and 1924 Kiwi built its distribution to over 50 countries, including Germany, Belgium, France, Switzerland, Austria, China, Russia and South America. In 1925 the company was spending money on advertising in South Africa, Rhodesia, and west and north Africa. Agents were appointed in Barbados, Trinidad, Demerara, Belgian Congo, Mauritius, Malta and Palestine.

Although business was good, expectations were high. William Ramsay felt increasingly isolated in London. His cousin William Ramsay (Willie) had appointed him as manager, and he considered the office entirely his baby, even calling himself managing director even though James was actually the managing director. Unless they made use of expensive cables it took a long time to get replies from Melbourne.

Willie employed his brother James as his deputy. On 28 April James wrote to the Kiwi directors: 'I wish to raise a point which has always been on my mind since the creating of the agreement, namely the relative difference between Mr William Ramsay's salary and mine ... the difference in my salary being in my case a third less.'

Willie Ramsay's salary was £1,350 plus 5 per cent when net profits of the London office exceeded £5,000. Salary for James was £500 plus 2.5 per cent when profits went over £5,000. James finished his letter with a P.S.: 'My suggestion regarding salary is that it should be augmented to £1,000 either immediately or during the period of the agreement.'[4]

The board was horrified. Lesser employees had no right to contact the board direct. That was Willie's job. But Willie wasn't happy either. He had been offered only a three-year contract, and never for a moment did he think he would be called upon to accept so short an agreement. 'May I ask,' he wrote, 'if it is necessary for me again to come with my hat in hand and beg for reasonable recognition of my services? My directors surely know me sufficiently well enough to appreciate that such a procedure is most painful to me.'[5]

The 'easy opening' Kiwi tin opened by twisting a coin in the slot – simple to make, but Kiwi endlessly searched for an alternative that was easier to use.

Letters were going back and forth to Walter Tompson. Now Walter's full name was impressive. He was Walter Henry John Griffiths Tompson, more commonly known as Wally. On 17 December 1918 he had married Madge Ramsay, the lively daughter of John Ramsay Snr and famed for being one of Melbourne's first female automobile drivers, who made history when she drove her car in reverse up Exhibition Street, the city's steepest hill. Walter was a skilled accountant, and no doubt family connections helped to get him into Kiwi. On 14 February 1921 he was appointed secretary manager with a salary of £750 a year.

On 17 February 1928 he arrived in London to investigate the company's problems. He was there for over a year, and this could have been the start of the problems that beset the Ramsay family through the 1930s. Criticisms came thick and fast. He criticised the lack of communication between Melbourne and London. He did not like the distribution arrangements in Melbourne. He could not go to Norway because of the slowness of installation of machines. He thought the easy-opening cans of polish were not easy-opening. He was critical of the slow manner in which everything was done.

Kiwi maypole team, Eight-Hour Day, 1928: V. Halford, Q. Chenery, A. McLeod, A. Belzer, R. Smythe, V. Murphy, B. Lasseter, M. Simpson, M. Meguiness

He said he was sorry he had ever agreed to take the trip. He had rather a rotten time in England. He cabled his resignation on 16 October 1929 and he wanted it to take effect on 9 February 1930. ('This gives him time to get all his fares and expenses paid up to that date,' Tom Ramsay commented drily.) The board accepted Tompson's resignation, and he received a cheque for £3,537 14s 9d.[6]

His replacement at Kiwi was another family member, Fred Ramsay. Fred was the younger son of James Ramsay, the former managing director who had suicided in London in 1919. Fred's appointment was as 'Acting Secretary', and he was present at board meetings for the next three years. Walter wanted to know what Fred was paid, and the answer was £450 a year.

This was far from being the end of Walter Tompson's relations with Kiwi. He was not a director. Tom Ramsay was terrified that opposing forces on the board might make Tompson a director, and he was appalled at the idea. Walter did not become a director, but as a shareholder he could attend annual meetings, where he was a busy bee with a powerful sting. He averaged 10 to 15 difficult questions at every meeting. To his credit, many of his queries were justified and made the board stick to the exact rules under the Companies Act. However, all this was the exact opposite to the happy days of the 1920s when board meetings were like amiable family gatherings. There was another factor that horrified Tom Ramsay: the presence of lawyers. Mr J. Turnbull from Blake & Riggall, represented Mrs E. M. (Edith) Ramsay, wife of John Ramsay Jnr, and Mr J. Rhoden of Malleson & Co. attended for Mrs John Ramsay (Anty), widow of John Ramsay Snr.

At one meeting Walter Tompson was making so many objections that Mr Turnbull said, perhaps rather tiredly: 'The objections have been made and noted.'

THE QUALITY POLISH

MAKES A SHOE SHOW

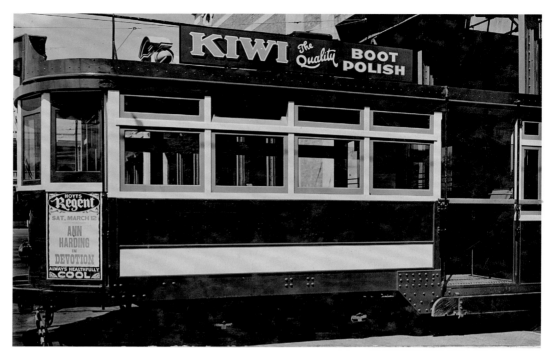

Adelaide tram, 1932

Tompson fired back: 'Mr Turnbull has no interest in the affairs of the company and he is only acting on behalf of someone.'

John Ramsay Jnr had a neat reply for that one: 'Neither is Mr Rhoden.'[7]

Walter had another problem regarding his bête noir, Mr Turnbull. John Ramsay made it possible for him to be present by giving his wife Edith one share in the company. As a shareholder, she could be represented by her own attorney. A regular line of attack for Walter was the huge amount of cash reserve held by the Kiwi Polish Company. This ranged from £93,000 to over £100,000. The excuse was the Depression, with the board believing that at times of severe financial hardship spare cash was necessary. Anything could happen. Walter said if the money wasn't handed out to shareholders, then why keep it in shaky local banks; it should be held in English banks.

At the meeting on 20 January 1932 he asked what the directors intended to do with the surplus. Mr Turnbull replied: 'The shareholder I represent (Mrs E. M. Ramsay) thinks the question of the reserves is a matter for the directors and they would have gone thoroughly into the matter taking into account the extraordinary position of business at this time and she is quite prepared to follow the guidance of the directors.'

Mr Tompson: 'How many shares does your client hold?'

Mr Turnbull: 'One share.'

Mr Tompson: 'And she is the wife of the managing director.'

At the annual meeting on 20 January 1932 Kiwi Annie was in the chair, nervous indeed about conducting such a difficult meeting. She had been ill, suffering from goitre, and

Billboard advertising, Victoria, c.1925

she had lost weight, but she was determined to be present in case she was overwhelmed by what Tom Ramsay described as the opposition. There were complaints on that day about the travelling expenses of John Ramsay Jnr (Edith's husband) containing items that should only have been personal. Walter Tompson complained too about £1,200 listed as 'shareholders balance'.

'That amount,' said Annie, 'is my personal drawing.'

Tompson: 'Everybody is having a dip into the pie.'

Walter asked for a formal meeting so that he could get answers to a number of questions. There were actually two meetings: one on 29 January 1932 and another on 8 February 1932. The meetings were with Tom Ramsay, and there must have been a stenographer present because every word was recorded. There was a note attached to the second interview: 'The appointment was for 10.15 and Mr Tompson arrived 17 minutes late.'

Tom Ramsay told Walter there had been too much unpleasantness and insinuations made like 'dipping in the pie'. There were suggestions that bonuses had been handed out that were not warranted. Tom asked Walter whether he thought he was well paid. Walter replied he was quite satisfied by the way he had been paid, 'but when a person says that you are a coward and like other people in Kiwi he'd gone wrong he did not consider that was good treatment'.

Tom Ramsay replied: 'If your conscience was clear it should not matter what people call you.'

Why Walter Tompson was called a coward we do not know, unless it had something to do with the 1914–18 war. Dr John Ramsay referred to it in a letter to his nephew John: 'Wally never forgets that he considers he was called a coward, and he has set out to disprove this statement practically. How far he will go, I do not profess to know! But men who consider that they have a grievance will often go to extreme lengths.'[8]

'Coward' was one thing. Tompson claimed that Fred Ramsay had called him a liar. According to John Ramsay, Tompson put in the transfers for William Ramsay's estate. Then he asked Fred Ramsay, acting company secretary, if he would give him a letter stating that probate had been produced to the company. Fred refused. He said he did not know whether probate had been produced or not. Tompson insisted it had been produced and Fred replied that the board had no record of it. Tompson then claimed that during this altercation Fred Ramsay called him a liar. John Ramsay was called in to calm things down. Next morning, according to John, Tompson went for him again and it was two hours before 'everything was alright'.[9]

Such behaviour seems out of character for Fred Ramsay. His niece Nuki Monahan says he was a most kindly man. She remembers him coming to their house and amusing them with all sorts of conjuring tricks. He never married, and spent the later years of his life in North Queensland.

In another letter Dr John Ramsay wrote: 'My only regret is family estrangement. I had hoped time would mellow the bitterness and soreness that has existed and that some sort of reunion would be possible to make Christmas and the New Year happier for the family.

OPPOSITE

Kiwi developed a range of colours for women's footwear. This poster by James Northfield captures the intent perfectly.

ABOVE

Hoarding for Kiwi White Cleaner, Punt Road
railway bridge, Richmond, Victoria, 1925. This is where
a Kiwi advertisement caused a traffic problem in
the 1960s (see page 130).

OPPOSITE TOP

Railway advertising hoardings,
Malvern, Victoria, 1925

OPPOSITE BOTTOM

Railway advertising hoardings,
Victoria, 1925

It is a rotten spirit in which to develop the rising generation. If anything can be done I would gladly help. But so far there has appeared to be no possibility of a rapprochement. The Ramsays are a stubborn folk, but surely there is some way out.'[10]

There was a way out. In 1934 Tom Ramsay had a private meeting with Walter Tompson. He commented to his Uncle Jack (Dr John Ramsay): 'Don't tell Annie what I am doing.' Peace came to the family, and little more was heard of Walter Tompson. He reported that he was offered a job with Dunlop Rubber,[11] and later worked as a chartered accountant in Collins Street. On 16 August 1942 Tompson enlisted in the army with the rank of lieutenant colonel. He died on 14 November 1944 aged 54.

During the 1930s the world was in a state of depression. Australia was one of the worst affected countries, and Melbourne fared more badly than other cities. Factories all around Kiwi at 188 Burnley Street were either laying off staff or going out of business. The census of 1933 showed that 28.9 per cent of the male work force and 13.5 per cent of the women in Richmond were unemployed. Many were starving and children were coming to school with only a cup of tea or a plate of soup to sustain them for the whole day. In 1930 the mayor of Richmond stated that in his council area 4,000 were out of work.[12]

Kiwi staff, Burnley Street, Richmond, 1929

Some, like the well-known retailer and philanthropist Sidney Myer made generous donations. Annie Ramsay donated £1,000 to the Children's Hospital Endowment in 1927 and in following years she made many large donations to hospitals. In June 1937 she endowed a bed at Prince Henry's Hospital in the name of her grandson Hamish. Kiwi made donations to at least 13 hospitals in Melbourne every year all through the 1930s as well as hospitals in Sydney, London and provincial Victoria. There were also small donations to cricket clubs, football clubs, rifle clubs and various benevolent societies.

Maybe sales were down a little, but Kiwi fared extraordinarily well during the Depression. There were lots of new slogans. For example: 'No detail is missed when success is at stake'. Obviously a gentleman could not be a success unless his shoes shone like the sun: 'There's no shoe like an old shoe'. Shoes could not survive to be old unless they had a daily lather of Kiwi. But 1933 saw the arrival of the best slogan of all: 'They're well worn but they've worn well', and this was the inspiration for dozens of posters. One of them showed a picture of a pair of golf shoes, beautifully polished. The caption in small words read: 'This illustration was taken from a pair of golf shoes 5½ years old . . . in regular use. Soled twice. Kiwi tan used. Owner J.R., Toorak.'

The J.R. had to be John Ramsay. Oh yes, well worn and worn well. (This early advertising slogan was well known in Australia and the UK prior to World War II.)

It was good to be with Kiwi, but it was hard work. In 1933 the workers were allowed two 10-minute breaks and half an hour for lunch. There was a bell to announce these breaks, and later a buzzer was controlled from the switchboard. The labellers were paid at the rate of fourpence a gross. Any rejects had to be relabelled by the girl who caused the rejects. A good girl could average 3.5 gross tins an hour. Lidders were paid a one penny

They're well worn ... but they've worn well ...

thanks to **KIWI**

BLACK POLISH . . . TAN POLISHES

Polishes, Protects and Preserves . . .

... White Cleaner and Shoe Creams

Advertisement published in the *Australian Grocer*, 1937

TOP
Tom and John Ramsay (left) stand proudly in front of the latest concepts on show at the Kiwi Sales Conference, 1937.

BOTTOM
Billboard in Elizabeth Street, Sydney featuring a face that bears a striking resemblance to Franklin D. Roosevelt

 76 KIWI: THE AUSTRALIAN BRAND THAT BROUGHT A SHINE TO THE WORLD

a tray, which held 66 tins. The lid had to go down very carefully on to the tin; any error would let air in and cause cracking of the polish. A good lidder could do 6.7 gross an hour, which meant over £6 a week. In April 1935 a new conveyor system was installed. This meant staff could be reduced by eight girls and five boys.[13]

Kiwi paid good dividends all through the 1930s plus two returns of funds, so undoubtedly Walter Tompson's recommendations had an effect. Late in 1933 the board agreed to hand back part of the reserves to shareholders, leaving £60,000 for emergencies. Tom Ramsay said his account that day was credited with £3,550.

There were two significant changes. Annie Ramsay decided she would step down as chairman, but remain on the board. Then Dr John Ramsay decided to quit his position as trustee of the William Ramsay Estate. He told his lawyers that as payment for this task he would accept 1 per cent from the dividends of the estate. Seeing that the dividends amounted to £480,000, he was asking for £4,800. Mr Turnbull of Blake & Riggall thought this was far too much. He recommended a payment of £1,000. Annie was prepared to go to £2,000. Tom Ramsay wasn't happy. He wrote: 'Uncle Jack is claiming responsibility for the success of the business. He had nothing to do with the management and Dad paid for his education at the university. There's no reason to recompense him because the business has been successful. He received honorariums for all meetings up to £275. Finally Uncle Jack was awarded £1,500.'[14]

The board decided it would be wise to have one of its top men, either John or Tom Ramsay in London full-time. In March 1932 the decision was made to send Tom to London for two to three years. This meant he would have to resign as a director. But what would be his title in London? Willie Ramsay considered himself managing director in London. It was a problem not easily solved.

The board decided further tariffs were making trade so difficult both in France and New Zealand that the only alternative was to manufacture in those countries. Harry Ramsay, the younger son of James and brother of Fred, was the choice for New Zealand. In 1934 he went to Auckland to open a true Kiwi branch in the land of the kiwis.

KIWI PUBLICATIONS

Kiwi used a wide range of advertising techniques beyond point of sale and billboards.

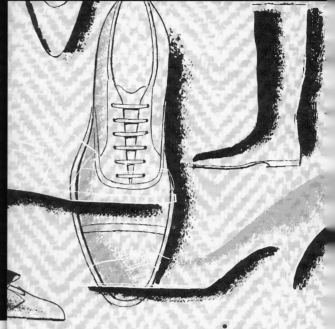

GOOD GROOMING TIPS *from* KIWI

QUICK AND EASY

Two centuries ago, polishing shoes was a major project. On the following pages of this booklet you will discover that bootblacks of that era included among their tools a kettle, pigskin, knife, two or three brushes and an old wig.

Today, superior KIWI polishes make shoeshining quick and easy —a few minutes once a week for a polish, ten seconds a day for a quick brush-up. And what results KIWI gives! Shiny shoes that keep their like-new look longer.

This minor investment in time and effort pays off in good shoe grooming — so important in personal and business relationships, for shoes make the first impression.

To help you with your good shoe grooming, we offer the following quick and easy hints that will keep your shoes *looking new.*

Polishing new leathers (KIWI Neutral Polish for first shines) builds up a protective coating that prevents scuffing and forms an invisible shield against water and stain. An easy application of KIWI polish helps "break-in" new shoes because it has a softening effect on the leather.

Do not, however, apply a dressing to new suede or canvas shoes until they need it.

REGULAR POLISHING TIME

It takes only seconds to attend to your shoes after each wearing. A daily buff-up will bring back the handsome gloss to shoes that are shined once a week with KIWI. (NOTE): KIWI *polish is better for leather because it works into the pores, lubricates the leather to keep it supple.*

brown polish.

Neutral KIWI is the perfect dressing and cleaner for such high-fashion colors as greens, greys, off-whites and pastels.

Do not, however, try to change black shoes to brown by applying brown polish. If you should want to change the color of a pair of shoes the best way is to see your neighborhood shoe repair man. Quite expert at dyeing shoes, they do a fine job at reasonable prices.

Paste Polish-Colors

BLACK	OXBLOOD
BROWN	MAHOGANY
NEUTRAL	CORDOVAN
TAN	DARK BROWN
MID TAN	RED
DARK TAN	BLUE

Removing old polish

It's wise to watch for light and dark patches [in] leather. If you detect patches, it is time [to] clean off old polish, dust and dirt. Apply [KI]WI Neutral Polish which will dissolve the [o]ld polish. Turn the cloth continually, us[in]g a clean surface at all times. The cloth [wi]ll absorb the excess polish. Then apply [re]gular KIWI polish as suggested on the following pages.

It is unwise to use soap and water to remove old polish. The tender leather will harden and spot.

First aid for injuries

Take prompt action with spots. Use a mild household cleaning fluid to remove grease, oil or tar stains. Try to get rid of mud before it cakes, since scraping may damage the leather.

If you detect cuts in shoe leather, it is possible to fade them out. Use an emery board to clean the cut. Apply the proper shade of KIWI polish. When the surface dries, you'll need a magnifying glass to find the cut, even if it is a fairly deep one.

Allow wet shoes to dry naturally at room temperature before shining them. Do not try to dry them near direct heat (and NEVER in the oven!). Use shoe trees or stuff with paper to maintain the shape.

THE TALES OF KIWI

"Rise and shine!" the Sergeant bawled,
  "Come, shake a leg, my men.
We're due for our inspection,
  And we've lots to do 'fore then."

The camp was all commotion,
  The men with might and main
Brushed their clothes and polished
  To bring their unit fame.

With pride they marched out to parade
  Before their Colonel keen,
He gave one look and then exclaimed,
  "Such boots I've never seen!"

A brief respite when Private Jones
  Came marching into view,
His rifle held quite carelessly,
  In his hand a flower or two.

He went up to the Colonel,
  And dropped down on one knee;
"I'm sorry I am late, sir,
  Let these flowers plead for me."

The Colonel was astounded,
  He gave an angry roar,
Until he looked at Jones's feet
  And saw the boots he wore.

"How came you, Private Jones," said he,
  "To shine your boots like that?"
"Why, Kiwi was the magic, sir,"
  The answer came quite pat.

His troop was filled with proper pride,
  Their mascot he became;
His life's a bed of roses
  Since Kiwi brought him fame.

The court was dull,
The King was cold,
The jesters were infirm and old,
The Maids-in-Waiting had grown fat,
The music left the old King flat.

He sat and grizzled at his gout,
And prayed that he would soon "pass out."
And then a knock upon the door—
A Courtier—a message bore:
A deputation waits without,
Who claim that they can cure your gout:

The King's face brightened with a grin.
He begged him bring the party in.
They entered, first the Teddy Bear
The Kiwi borne upon a chair,
The Emu and the Kangaroo,
The Major Mitchell Cockatoo.

When introductions were complete,
The King bade each one take a seat.
The time has come, the Kiwi said,
To talk of many things—
Of shoes and wax and turpentine,
And polishes for Kings—

And as you turn the pages of this book,
          we will unfold ——
Each story that brought pleasure
          to the King as they were told.

THE
FRENCH
CONNECTION

OPPOSITE

Kiwi products manufactured
in France were sold
throughout Europe.

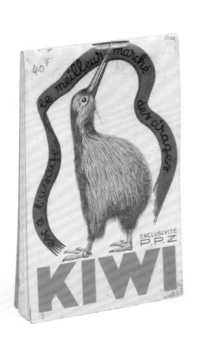

n the 1930s horses were giving way to automobiles. This meant less leather, with fewer harnesses and saddles. Proper roads and footpaths were taking the place of dusty tracks, shoes were replacing boots, and all this meant a lessening need for shoe polish. The Depression had many effects. Kiwi, dating back to 1906, had always loved agricultural and trade shows. At Sydney, Melbourne, Brisbane, and yes, London too, there was a splendid Kiwi stand, girls in uniform, displays of shoes and boots, some of them old that had been polished to look better than patent leather.

The Kiwi Stand at the annual Melbourne Show was something to behold. Built in rich cedar wood, it resembled the bar at one of Melbourne's most expensive hotels. It could have been the bar at Menzies Hotel. The uniformed girls handed out free samples, fans, rulers, blotters, clackers and picture books. There were several stuffed kiwis. One reporter wrote:

> A pair of leggings on one of the stands was so well polished that they should
> have delighted the most fastidious person. Kiwi patent leather polish was
> also exhibited. This polish is colourless, and is claimed not to soil dresses. It
> is most suitable for using on delicate shades of kid or calf, and also two-tone
> shoes, but the manufacturers claim it can be used on any kind of shoes.[1]

The board eventually decided that the time for exhibiting at shows was over. As an advertising venture it wasn't worth the money. Board members decided they would sell all the Kiwi stands. The Sydney Show stand fetched £25.[2]

However, Kiwi was still advertising heavily elsewhere. In *Chop Sticks* magazine for September 1932, there was a picture of a gentleman carrying his cane, shoes brilliant with the message: 'To the well-groomed man, no detail is too small to escape his notice. And that's why he insists on Kiwi for his shoes.'

There were times when Kiwi got into trouble. On 1 June 1937 Kiwi made a special offer. An advertisement appeared in Australian newspapers. Buy two tins of Black and

one tube of White Cleaner, value one shilling and sixpence – we will give it to you for a shilling. Then came the slogan: 'The morning routine: shave shower and Kiwi'.

The slogan was banned as obscene. Later there was a saying that even the repressive Victorian Premier Sir Henry Bolte was said to have used in his more eloquent moments. The morning's routine was: Shave Shower Shit and Shampoo. Of course, nice people would not have questioned that Kiwi simply meant polish, but Kiwi's Morning Routine was too much for some family newspapers.

These were difficult times and the United Kingdom, Europe and even Asia was the hope for better sales. Tom Ramsay and his wife Betty sailed for London in 1932 for a three-year stay. His thoughts were never far from Melbourne. He complained he had to return home at least once a year. How difficult that was. Every trip there and back took him three months. One trip was aboard the Orient Line SS *Otranto*, 20,000 tons. He said trips on overseas ships meant tips for most of the stewards. This was the bill on the *Otranto*: cabin steward, £5, table steward £2, wine steward £3, head waiter £2 1s, bar steward £4, stewardess £1 pound, and deckhand 10 shillings.

But in London relatives were never far away. In 1925 Tom Ramsay's sister Jean visited Singapore. There she met Captain Dugald McDougall, who was both dashing and handsome. In his full dress, captain's gear with Sam Browne belt and kilt he looked magnificent. After several meetings they decided to get married. Legend has it they were dining at the legendary Raffles, a hotel well known to Somerset Maugham. Captain Dugald wrote across the menu: 'Will you marry me?' The menu is now in the hotel museum. Jean's older brother John went to Singapore to be best man. Dugald and his bride went to Malaya, where they operated a rubber plantation. Perhaps it was bad economic times, for Captain Dugald left his plantation and moved to London to be assistant manager for Kiwi.

There were complications in London. Who was running the place? Neither John Ramsay nor the board could think of an appropriate title for his younger brother Tom, who, after all, was now the second most powerful figure in Kiwi.

The board invited Willie, Manager UK, and his wife Anne to visit the Melbourne office. When his boat, the *Nairana*, arrived in Tasmania on 3 October 1934 he gave an interview to the *Hobart Mercury*. He told the reporter this was his first trip back to Australia in 50 years. Although he was born in Scotland, he was educated in Australia, and between 1882 and 1884 he had attended the Prahran State School with his cousin, William Ramsay, founder of Kiwi.

The world economy may have been depressed, but Willie Ramsay said he found more confidence in trade prospects in England than anywhere else in the world. He noted that Melbourne was having a tram strike. 'Such a thing,' he said, 'would never have occurred in England. The trams would have been run by some means or other.'

Willie claimed that he had control of the export of Kiwi products to 58 countries, all parts of the world except the Far East. France was the latest problem. The French had introduced a quota system, which allowed only 25 per cent of the previous year's exports into the country. The only answer was to manufacture in France.

It was never easy. On 4 January 1934 Tom Ramsay and Captain Dugald McDougall visited Pierre Zecchini, who had a factory at Bagnolet on the Seine 5 kilometres from the centre of Paris. The locals were known as Bagnoletais. Zecchini manufactured shoes and household paint under the Les Specialites PPZ brand and became the licensed manufacturer of Kiwi polish in France.

Everything had to come from London: the blended waxes, the colour range, containers, labels and cartons. Tom Ramsay in a colourful interview on his retirement recalled the situation. He said when he first started at Kiwi he didn't want to be just an airy-fairy chemist. He believed he had to do everything. At the time everything at Kiwi was done by hand – from filling the tins to putting on the paper labels. So he became a fully trained factory hand. He even volunteered to drive a truck and make the deliveries.

At the age of 24, in a strange factory in suburban Paris, Tom became a factory hand again. 'I remember it well,' he said. 'We had to leave our hotel at 5 a.m. to get the factory going by six. The Metro was freezing at that time of the morning. Our only luxury was coming home to the hotel at night for a steaming hot bath. My brother-in-law Dugald

French Kiwi poster and advertising graphics, including wooden pencil case and ruler

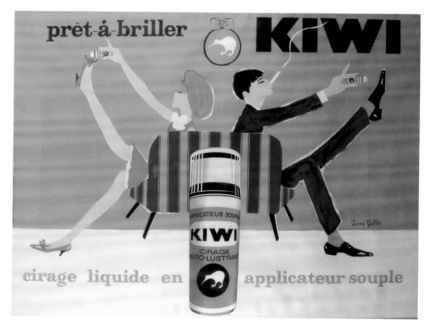

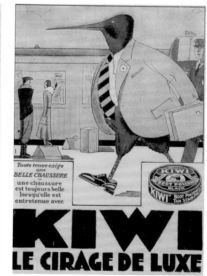

PUBLICITE INTERDITE !..*

L.BERCHADSKY

* Regarde bien toutes les marques de cirage qui existent sur le marché.

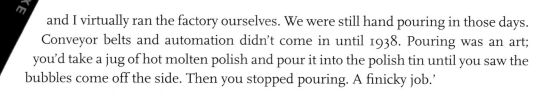

and I virtually ran the factory ourselves. We were still hand pouring in those days. Conveyor belts and automation didn't come in until 1938. Pouring was an art; you'd take a jug of hot molten polish and pour it into the polish tin until you saw the bubbles come off the side. Then you stopped pouring. A finicky job.'

Tom remembered a funny incident when he and Dugald had to get back to London in a hurry. 'The weather was so bad all shipping had been stopped. So I suggested we take a plane. My brother-in-law was very enthusiastic, he hadn't been in one. I'm talking about the days of the rattly old biplanes and triplanes. Even in good weather you couldn't talk to your fellow passengers – there was so much noise you had to pass notes. We got up in the air and it was the roughest flight I have had, a nightmare. I asked Dugald – by note – how he felt. And he replied: "It's terrific! Why haven't we done this before?"'

The French authorities became even more difficult. A tax inspector called, and Pierre Zecchini showed him the distribution agency agreement he had with Kiwi, which went back to 1925. The French wanted to impose retrospective taxes right back to that date. Relations with Zecchini were often heated and strained. He believed he was the owner of the Kiwi mark in France. To avoid a ruinous dividends tax, Kiwi had to form a French company. It had the impressive title Société Rouennaise de Cirages, and came into being on 17 March 1938. There was an issue of 450 shares, of which Captain McDougall held 150. Kiwi had to establish its own French company with a factory at Rouen. R. D. (Randy) Mann was appointed to run the factory and he began hand pouring shoe polish on 24 May 1937 and machine pouring on 27 July the same year. Randy had quite a history. During the last years of World War I (1917–1918), he was a pilot with the Royal Flying Corps. His rank was second lieutenant. After the war he held various posts. He was in Sumatra between 1920 and 1928, Siam between 1929 and 1932, then in the Gold Coast, Africa for two more years. In 1934 he joined the Kiwi Polish Company, and Tom Ramsay sent him to France that year.

Mann settled in Rouen, a beautiful medieval city, at one time the capital of Normandy, with a Notre Dame Cathedral to rival the one in Paris. Joan of Arc, one of Rouen's more famous daughters, was burnt at the stake there in 1431.

After some tense negotiations, Kiwi struck a new agreement with PPZ on 6 July 1939. Meanwhile, in 1934 John Ramsay opened a factory in Auckland, New Zealand, where his cousin Harry became the factory manager. In 1937 Kiwi opened yet another factory in Warsaw, Poland.

Tom Ramsay was happy with life in London. He was keen on squash, having played C grade pennant at the South Yarra Club back in Melbourne. In London he joined the Princes Club, one of the oldest sporting clubs in England, and played twice a week.

However, Tom was missed in Melbourne. His brother John, the Kiwi managing director, thought it not practical for Tom to be in London, and that he should return to take his rightful place on the board in Melbourne. Tom commented: 'John thinks the Board at present is useless, decisions are left to him and he has to make them

before the Board meets. Candidly he is fed up with it. He has carried the company and accepted responsibility for the past six years. He would rather resign and get out of it. He wants me back at headquarters and the only solution is for someone to visit overseas once a year.'

John Ramsay lived in a large two-storey mansion in Whernside Avenue, Toorak. In 1938, through Agg & Duff Shipping Agents, he imported a Rolls-Royce chassis, valued at £500 and engaged Martin & King body builders to complete the car.

Tom lived in a large Tudor-style mansion in Struan Street, Toorak. Tom's wife Alice Bettine, known as Betty, had been in partnership with Zara Dickens (later Dame Zara Holt) in a fashion business in Little Collins Street, Melbourne. In 1936 Betty engaged a brilliant young architect, Roy Grounds, to design a nursery and a swimming pool. She had meant to call his partner Geoffrey Mewton, but Roy answered the telephone and was around quickly for a consultation. He must have made an impression, because soon after Tom and Betty went for a holiday to Southport, Queensland Roy followed. According to Tom, that is when the trouble started.

Tom took Betty, Hamish, aged four, and Robin, 15 months on a trip to England in the hope that Betty would forget Roy, but it did not work. On 11 September 1938 Betty and Roy moved into a London hotel, then went off together and lived in a little cottage in the South of France, where they stayed until the coming war forced them back to Melbourne.[3]

As for Tom, he left with Hamish, baby Robin and a hired nurse and returned to Melbourne. Immediately, he started divorce proceedings on the grounds of separation. On 4 October 1941 at Mount Lofty House, Crafers, South Australia, he married Catherine Anne Richardson, better known as Mimi. That was the start of a long and very happy

Kiwi was manufactured in France and sold throughout Europe. Note the Kiwi dispenser similar to that in the picture opposite and the 'coincidence' of the Kiwi radiator emblem.

marriage. As for Roy Grounds, his divorce came through on 24 October 1941, and on the same day he and Betty married.

On 4 April 1946 Betty Grounds sought access to the children in a custody case before Mr Justice Wilfred Fullagar in the Practice Court. It did not go well for Betty. The judge was told that in the 13 months after Betty left her husband she spent the time travelling Europe with Grounds and did not communicate with Tom Ramsay or the nurse except for an occasional postcard sent to Hamish and one or two small presents. Judge Fullagar found in favour of 'the innocent father'. He said it was natural, reasonable and proper for an innocent father to object to his children being brought into contact with a man who had taken their mother and his wife away. Judge Fullagar said the Act required him to regard the welfare of the children as the paramount consideration. The mother's adultery was a factor counting against her having access. What could she do for them now except disturb and confuse them?[4]

Bottle of French Kiwi
'Champagne'

Betty Grounds returned to Melbourne and went back into partnership with Zara Dickens. Zara, had recently married Harold Holt, the future prime minister of Australia, and was now Zara Holt. Zara and Betty continued to run 'Magg', the haute couture fashion house of Melbourne.

Tom was very upset at the loss of Betty, but there were compensations. In late 1939, looking for a holiday house, he found a place that was so beautiful he couldn't resist it. 'Hascombe' in Alton Road, Upper Macedon, was up for auction on 21 October 1939. He was prepared to pay £3,750 and put down £100 on deposit. This was to be a much loved happy retreat for so many Ramsays for the next three decades. A 1952 brochure described it as a 'charming painted timber home'. It had two reception rooms; a large sun room; cocktail bar; large games room, six main bedrooms, two colour-tiled bathrooms; self-contained wing of five bedrooms and bathroom; a separate wing of three bedrooms and bathroom; manager's cottage with five rooms and bathroom; stables; four-car garage; glorious gardens; lake; delightful log cabin; two tennis courts; 26 acres; and pine plantation with approximately 1,000 pines. Mimi made the garden her passion, and it became one of Victoria's finest gardens. The garden is listed on the National Trust Heritage Register. Most of the original house no longer exists.

With her own team of gardeners, Mimi made it something of great beauty, with terraced levels, pathways and flower gardens that responded to the deep, rich mountain soil. There were also rare trees like a century-old horizontal elm, a Himalayan fir and Cappadocian maple, all of which were placed on the Heritage List. According to her son Fergus, Mimi had a gardener who was trained at Burnley Horticultural College. This gardener told him: 'Being with your mother is like doing the ultimate exam in horticulture. She knows the botanical name of every plant in the garden. I think she was testing me.'

When war broke out 'Hascombe' was a perfect retreat for many members of the family.

KIWI

LE CIRAGE DE LUXE

 MARRON CLAIR (4)

 SANG DE BŒUF (8)

 NOIR (1)

 ACAJOU SÉLECT (6)

 MARRON ROUGE (5)

 ROUGE ROYAL (9)

 BRUN PARISIEN (7)

BLEU MARINE (10)

NEUTRE (3)

 JAUNE CIRE (2)

EXCLUSIVITÉ
PPZ

KIWI IN THE 1930s

TOP

Children joined the Kiwi Club as
part of a loyalty program. 4RO is still
a Rockhampton Queensland Radio Station.

BOTTOM

Kiwi promotional truck

Kiwi staff, Burnley: V. Griffin, G. Parry,
J. Ley, B. Aird, P. Russell, c. 1939.
Jessie Ley was Tom Ramsay's private
secretary for many years.

WORLD WAR TWO

In 1942 Walter Graebner reported in *Time* magazine that on a North African battlefield he saw old cans of British-made Kiwi side by side with bottles of Chianti.

Surely there couldn't be another war. It was only 20 years since the First World War, when there were 20 million men in uniform, with half of them killed, wounded or becoming prisoners of war. The Russians were estimated to have lost six million. Eleven per cent of the population of France were either killed or wounded. At the Somme, on 1 July 1916, 60,000 died or suffered terrible injuries all in one day.[1] In September 1938 Tom Ramsay wrote from London to his brother John:

I still don't think there will be a war for various reasons, mainly that I think Hitler is bluffing, but things look so ominous that one must take all precautions possible. There is nothing else talked about here but war. We are commencing digging in the spare ground an air raid shelter to house all workers. These shelters are not great resistance against a direct hit. Gas masks are being issued as quickly as possible to all workers and I heard only in the last 20 minutes that trenches are being dug in every park.

A few days later he wrote again:

Well it looks as though the war has blown over. The Czechs have accepted the four-power pact and since then there has been a message that Hitler and Chamberlain have got together and there is every possibility of some agreement between Germany and England which should ensure world peace … I have sent the kids away this morning to Devon where they should be comparatively safe.[2]

Of course, Neville Chamberlain was duped. He signed the Munich agreement, which conceded the Sudetenland of Czechoslovakia to Germany. Hitler invaded Poland on 1 September 1939, and two days later Britain was at war, together with its Allies and the British dominions. The first Kiwi casualty was the factory in Warsaw. The German Army overran Poland and the factory was completely destroyed. The Kiwi factory manager Rudolf Kulik and his family were trapped, and the factory bombed. In 1940 there was one desperate letter from Kulik, but then silence. In 1946 there was confirmation that the whole Kulik family had died during the occupation.[3]

Neville Chamberlain shortly after meeting Hitler, Munich 1938. Germany invaded Poland on 1 September 1939.

The London office was quickly on a war footing. Willie Ramsay wrote that petrol rationing was now on. Ten-horsepower cars were allowed 6 gallons a month; 14-horsepower 8 gallons and 20-horsepower 10 gallons. He had a 31-horsepower Buick and he used 15 gallons a week just to get to work. There was only one solution: he would have to get a room close to the factory. Willie's brother James was now working full-time for the Auxiliary Fire Service (AFS) and at the same time trying to do his job for Kiwi.

Tom Ramsay wrote:

> If you saw the factory now you would hardly recognise it, sand bags right up and closing in the front door. All windows right round are boarded up and fitted with shutters which can be opened during the day and closed when necessary. Also petrol pumps and all turpentine pipes are sandbagged. The tarpaulins for the glass roofs have not yet been delivered and these are to keep rain out in the event of windows being broken by shrapnel and it is anticipated it will not be possible to get glass for their immediate repair.[4]

In 1940 the war began in earnest. The German blitzkrieg swept through Holland and Belgium into France. The situation was becoming increasingly uncomfortable for the Kiwi staff at Rouen. Randy Mann, the manager of the Rouen factory, lived on what he called 'the unhealthy side of the Seine'. Pierre Zecchini offered him his house at La Baule, a fashionable seaside resort in Southern Brittany, which seemed well away from hostilities. On 24 May Mann evacuated his family to La Baule, then returned to Rouen on his own, where he slept in the factory in case of emergency. On 4 June Rouen was severely bombed and eventually a fire between the cathedral and the Seine burned out of control for 48 hours. Germans aircraft activity prevented firemen having access to the area.

Advertisement for Kiwi shoe polish from RNZAF *Contact* magazine in which the kiwi becomes a bomber pilot, 1943

On 7 June Mann gathered all the account books and documents and left again for La Baule. He put all the Société Rouennaise de Cirages (SRC) share certificates and vital company documents in a locked box. He intended to return on 10 June, but this proved to be impossible. He told John Ramsay that he had left 8,000 francs in the office safe, and he was very sorry, but he had no idea the enemy was so close. At La Baule he thought he was in no immediate danger, but on 16 June he received word from the French Commissariat that there was not a day to be lost, and that he should leave immediately.

Mann explained: 'I was able to get my family on to a troopship with one small suitcase, which left on the night of 16 June. By good fortune, I met some military friends, who secured my departure on another troopship, which left on the morning of the 18 June. Enemy aircraft attacked us while we lay in the harbour, but we had no casualties. I had

UNITED STATES MARINE CORPS
REGIMENTAL EXCHANGE
4th MARINES, M.C.E.F.

26 May, 1937.

Dodwell & Co. Ltd.,
P.O. Box 410,
Shanghai. China.

Dear Sirs:

Fourth Marine personnel have used KIWI polish almost exclusively for a number of years and have found that it gives complete satisfaction in every respect. Members of the command would now be very skeptical of any product placed in the Regimental Exchange to replace KIWI. The undersigned has no hesitation whatever in recommending KIWI to other branches of the American Service.

Very truly yours,

REGIMENTAL EXCHANGE, FOURTH MARINES,

(Signed) JAMES C. BIGLER

JAMES C. BIGLER,
First Lieutenant, U.S. Marine Corps,
Regimental Exchange Officer

U. S. S. LOUISVILLE
MARINE DETACHMENT

Melbourne, Australia
18 February, 1938.

The Kiwi Polish Co. Pty. Ltd.
Burnley Street
Richmond E-1

Dear Sirs:

The Marine Detachment on the Louisville has used Kiwi Dark Tan polish throughout my tour of duty on the ship. It has been found much superior to other polishes and I fully recommend its use for polishing and as a preservative for leather.

Yours very truly,

(Signed) A. T. MASON

A. T. Mason
Captain, USMC.

ATM/dl

LEFT

Testimonial letters extolling the virtues of Kiwi polish among the ranks of the US marines and recommendation for its use to 'other branches of the American Services'

only a gas mask and two slabs of chocolate in a small haversack; all our other personal effects have been lost, we abandoned the car on the quayside. I have also lost £500 standing to my credit in the bank.'

Mann was very distressed that all operations in France had come to nought within a few weeks. He 'sincerely hoped' the girls in the office, the factory staff and the boiler man would come through the present ordeal unharmed. He reached an English port on 20 June with no possessions apart from what he stood up in. He and his family received a warm welcome from Willie Ramsay and staff. He thanked them for making the Manns so comfortable.[5]

Mann told John Ramsay about the documents in the locked trunk at La Baule, and said he was sure Pierre Zecchini would do his best to look after them. There is a comment across the letter, and it looks remarkably like the handwriting of Tom Ramsay: 'Like hell, he pinched the lot.'

And did he? Madame Y. Marinier, an employee of the Kiwi France company, SRC, wrote a sympathetic letter to Mann, including:

> I must tell you that the first time Mr Zecchini came in 1940, as he had his car,
> he took quite a lot of files, among others, all the correspondence which was
> on top of the wardrobe in the lavatories, but I could not oppose it because you
> know what he is and he had told me that it was in agreement with you. I do
> not know whether this is true.[6]

Relations with Pierre Zecchini had always been strained, and proved later to be extremely bitter. France was defeated and an armistice was declared with Germany. Zecchini caved in quickly. He saw no immediate future for his country and he thought it obvious that Britain too would fall to Hitler. He put out a memo to his staff.

Voluntary Departure for Germany

To our Personnel
Certain factories have received the order to close.
Able-bodied personnel are invited to leave voluntarily for Germany.

The forced closing of factories has put and will put in unemployment a large number of workers, men and women, and this is just the beginning of winter. Amongst them there are those who could, at this moment, avoid this alternative by accepting a contract to work in Germany.[7]

Next Zecchini set about reopening the factory. At first the Germans considered using the factory for storing vehicles. He obtained 'authorisation', presumably from the Vichy Government, and received a priority despatch of 10 tons of turpentine. By September 1941 the factory was producing between 950 and 1,100 dozen tins of Kiwi daily. Where did it go? Undoubtedly it was for the jackboots of the German Army.

In September 1942 the RAF carried out a series of raids, and seven bombs fell within 50 metres of the Rouen factory, causing severe damage. Destruction of railways and rolling stock committed to the Russian front caused production to slow to a trickle. In 1944 the Allies were closing in. Bombardments destroyed quays, bridges and factories. On Sunday 27 August there was a major raid by the RAF, and a bomb fell in the factory yard, badly damaging the works and the office.[8] The leader of the raid was Squadron Leader Bill Edrich DFC, who later played 35 Test matches for England. In 1947 in an amazing golden summer he scored 3,539 runs. On his many tours to Australia he became a close friend of Tom Ramsay.

Nor did the factory at Ealing in London go unscathed. On Saturday 19 January 1944 the Luftwaffe attacked. A stick of 17 incendiaries straddled the target. One landed directly on the Kiwi factory, and embedded a metre down into the concrete floor. It did not explode. Two others landed harmlessly at either end of the factory. They did not explode either. A British disposals squad removed the bombs, and why they did not explode remained a mystery. After the war a German pilot admitted that he deliberately unarmed the stick of bombs.[9] He did not explain his reasons, but one can imagine it is easy to develop a conscience when you are dropping bombs and you don't know who you are going to kill.

Back in Melbourne at last, everyone was feeling the effects of the war, clothes rationing, sweet rationing, petrol rationing, and the chairman, John Ramsay had a gas producer fitted to his Buick. Gas producers were inventions of the devil. A horrid large tub was fitted on the back of the car. The gas came from burning charcoal, and if the chairman ever fed the machine himself, he would have finished with charcoal hands and a charcoal face. The Buick would have panted to reach 40 or 50 miles an hour.

Architects Bates, Smart & McCutcheon designed air raid shelters for Kiwi in Richmond and Samuel Birchmell, the company accountant, complained about a meeting at 5.30 p.m. because he did not want to venture through the streets in a blackout. Shades had to be worn on car headlights. The army looked at John Ramsay's mansion in

Australian aircrew members of a North African Coastal Squadron in the Middle East receiving gifts, including Kiwi polish, sent from Australia, July 1943

Whernside Avenue, Toorak with a view to taking it over. In 1942 Annie Ramsay received notice that the army required her Mornington holiday house 'Seaview' to be vacant by 4 May. At the same time Mimi Ramsay had to answer the State Emergency Council request for accommodation available at 'Hascombe', Mount Macedon. She reported that 'Hascombe' had seven living rooms, 18 bedrooms and sleepouts, and two stables suitable for sleeping accommodation. They could take eight boy and eight girl evacuees, and she would require 16 single mattresses and 48 blankets.

Tom Ramsay joined up on 21 August 1940 at the age of 33. He was appointed lieutenant in headquarters of the Fourth Division Petrol Company. He had some experience having served in the Scotch College Cadets, also in the Melbourne University Rifles. He went into training at Balcombe Barracks on the Mornington Peninsula followed by a war administration course with the Department of Defence. At the finish of the course on 2 April 1941 he received a letter signed by Lieutenant Colonel Russell and Major Denvil offering 'most hearty congratulations on having attained the highest points for the course'. But perhaps he believed his talents were not being put to effective use. Three weeks later he applied to go on the Reserve of Officers and he joined the Department of Munitions, where he remained for the rest of the war.

ABOVE

Kiwi sponsored many radio shows. Here we see the winners
of the 4MB Kiwi Radio Eisteddfod, Maryborough, Queensland, *c.* 1940.

BELOW AND RIGHT

The Kiwi Book of Magic, produced for
loyal junior Kiwi Club fans

JUGGLING

Juggling is one of the most exciting shows on the stage, and what's more it is something that cannot be faked. It requires a lot of patience to become a good juggler but if you practice the various steps one by one as they are set out here for you, you will find yourself becoming quite good at it in a short time.

For practice work rubber balls are the best because they are not too big.

When you put on your show what about painting your rubber balls with luminous paint? Halfway through the performance have the stage blacked out . . . you can imagine the wonderful result with luminous balls shooting up in the air from nowhere.

A. This is the first principle of all juggling. Just toss a ball straight up in the air and catch it again. See the illustration here. This is called a *vertical fall.*

That's quite easy you say—

yes—but remember that the ball should fall to the exact position from whence it was thrown. The ball should also go up the same height each time too, say about three feet. Practice this with both hands until you can do it blindfolded and with perfect confidence.

B. *Double vertical fall.* Take a ball in each hand. Toss the right-hand ball. As soon as it begins to

fall, toss up the left one, and so continue, having two balls in motion continuously.

As a variation toss both balls up

together taking care that they both rise to the same height and therefore fall together.

A still further variation is to take two balls in one hand. Toss one up, and as it descends toss the other up. Keep the two balls going in one hand. Practise with

---

You show your audience a glass three-quarters full of ink. In order to show that it is really ink and not, say, milk, you dip the corner of a playing card in the fluid. It comes out really inky.

If there is still someone who doubts you in the audience, offer to pour the ink over that person's head.

The glass is now covered with a handkerchief; the mystic words are said: "Bazooka, Bazunnions, Stewed Steak and Onions!"

The handkerchief is whipped away. Behold! The ink has changed to lemonade which you can offer to one of the audience to drink.

THE EXPLANATION

How's it done? Well—the glass was filled with lemonade in the first place, and what the audience imagined was ink was really a piece of black silk wrapped around the inside of the glass. Have a look at the illustration here.

TRICK No. 5.

THE MATCHBOX MINT

The matchbox needed for this trick can be made in a few minutes. In front of the audience tip out the few matches the box should contain, then place a halfpenny in it, shut it and rattle vigorously. Upon opening the box, the halfpenny has changed into a shilling for there is a real shilling in the box and no sign of the halfpenny.

EXPLANATION

The drawing here shows how it is done.

A slot is cut at the bottom of one end of the tray, so that a halfpenny placed in the box can slide out again. Wedged between the top of the other end of the tray and the cover is the shilling. The

box is kept half open and a few matches put in to throw people off the scent.

As soon as the halfpenny is put in it is almost immediately slid out into the palm of the hand, and held underneath the box where it remains for the rest of the trick.

Tom returned all the money he had earned as an army officer: £97 1 2d. He received a thank-you letter dated 14 July 1942 from the Federal Treasurer, Mr J. B. Chifley, which said in part:

> Your generous action in making the amount available for the purchase of armament for the defence of Australia is very much appreciated, and I will be glad if you will accept my thanks and that of the Government for this valuable contribution. 14 July 1942.

Tom Ramsay kept immense files detailing production. For example, the number of cartridge cases produced at Rocklea Munitions plant from 1 June 1940 until production ceased at war's end was 2,421,789. The production of mortar bombs for the week ending 15 March 1944 was 57,392.

Meanwhile, his brother John had his problems. On 19 February 1941 there was a fire at the Kiwi factory in Burnley. Now fires did happen at Kiwi. Not only at Burnley but also at other factories around the world. The formula for Kiwi Boot Polish called for turpentine and other inflammable solvents. The polish had to be poured into cans at high temperatures, which could be dangerous if any flame or spark were nearby.

On the morning of 19 February, according to the newspapers, 2,000 people were gathered in Burnley Street to witness an 'inferno'. Black clouds of smoke were pouring out of every window. 'Dizzy from the fumes, and half blinded by very dense smoke, the firemen performed the remarkable feat in gaining control of the fire in 30 minutes,' reported the *Argus*. Fifty gallons of boot polish were destroyed and machinery was extensively damaged. The *Argus* further reported that after inhaling the fumes for more than half an hour, few of the 25 firemen were able to eat anything but the lightest food for the rest of the day.[10]

John Ramsay had a different story. 'Trousers rolled, I crawled underneath dense smoke to turn on the conveyor and move polish away from the fire. Also I stood on the refrigerator arm and stopped firemen from turning on water instead of foam with much argument, as instructions from Fire Brigade Headquarters were to use water. A few firemen were overcome by turps fumes (Why wasn't I?) The cause of the fire was static discharge from the leather belt to the polish on top of the pouring machine.'[11]

Like World War I, World War II was almost unparalleled in the history of human horror, but for some it had benefits. It was good for the poor; jobs and money were available once again. There was a huge increase in secondary industry, which gave Australia prosperity for the next 30 years. It was remarkably good for Richmond. War meant jobs and money in a whole range of industries, boot factories, tanneries, textiles, clothing, knitting factories, food preservers, and of course, the makers of boot polish. All of these things were located in Richmond.[12]

Kiwi staff at Burnley factory, 1940s:
G. Parry, J. Ley, H. Kent,
W. Webster, V. Griffin, ?. McVeigh,
D. Roberts, E. Downs

Kiwi van making a delivery
to a US warship

The Kiwi factories were at full pressure. The product was sought after by Allied troops everywhere. In 1937 US troops stationed in Shanghai already were using Kiwi, and the brand was never forgotten. On 3 November 1942 Walter Graebner reported in *Time* magazine that on a North African battlefield he saw old cans of British-made Kiwi side by side with bottles of Chianti. The factory in Richmond, Melbourne was working non-stop. On 18 May 1942 the staff had 250,000 crescents for labelling on tins for the army and 850 gross of tan for the Army Canteen Service 'to be delivered by Wednesday'.[13]

A few days later, Captain Heverty of the Canteen Service reordered 520 gross, which also had to be delivered in a hurry. He was prepared to take Dark Tan if he couldn't get Light Tan. But the factory could never get enough supplies. They were constantly short of high-quality turpentine. Then there was a special wax, carnauba, made from the carnauba palm, which only grew in Northern Brazil. John Ramsay went to the government and complained. Kiwi was getting 16 tons a year and this was simply not enough. He said, 'I got heated and that was a mistake.' The government official, a Mr Hall, said he would not grant further licences. However, John Ramsay tried again and he was promised 100 drums of carnauba to cover an American order. Still not enough, said Ramsay. He wanted 320 drums.

There was further trouble. The ship, the *Melbourne Star*, was on its way to Melbourne with a cargo of ICI dye for boot polish. The *Star* had endured an incredible war. In 1940

Luftwaffe aircraft bombed her off the coast of Ireland. In the summer of 1943 at the order of Winston Churchill, a huge naval force set out to relieve and literally save Malta. There were 14 of the fastest merchant vessels afloat and 34 naval ships. The Navy lost an Aircraft Carrier, HMS *Eagle*, three cruisers and a destroyer. Only five of the 14 merchant ships survived, and one of them was the *Melbourne Star*, albeit damaged.

If that wasn't bad enough, on 2 April 1943 a U-boat sunk the *Star* off the coast of Bermuda, and most of the crew went down with her. Apart from ICI dye, she was carrying torpedoes and ammunition. Kiwi had to find substitute materials for the high-quality dye. Naturally there was not enough Kiwi to go round. In March 1942 the *Sun News Pictorial* reported that boot polish was unobtainable in Melbourne stores. There was an appeal to servicemen to buy their boot polish from the military canteens, which were well supplied. They were asked not to make their purchases at city and suburban stores, which had almost no stock.[14]

The troops did buy the polish. The Melbourne *Herald* reported that Australian troops always wanted the high-quality Kiwi Australian polish. Even in dusty Tobruk the troops used the polish, which was among the more popular lines sold by Australian Army Canteen Service. It added: 'In Tobruk's sand and dust it was impossible to retain a shine on boots for more than a pace or two, and at first the polish was a drug on the market at Tobruk. But soon the troops found that without the polish their boots cracked rapidly under the desert conditions.'[15]

Orders never stopped coming. On 19 October 1943 the Australian Comforts Fund wanted 108,000 tins. US forces in Melbourne wanted 500 gross a month. Captain Rich of the army said: 'Kiwi is the polish the men want and they can't get enough of it.' But getting enough was the big problem. The shortages of turpentine and carnauba continued for several years after the war's end.

There was one Ramsay who did not live to see the end of the war. Sir John Ramsay died in Launceston on 6 February 1944. He was the last Ramsay survivor of the family that came out to Australia aboard the clipper *Loch Sunart* in 1878. He was such an important figure the Launceston *Examiner* devoted almost a page to his obituary:

> Probably never in the history of medicine in Australia has one man been so
> outstanding as an administrator, a teacher, and a surgeon. He did pioneer work
> with the surgery of hydatids and the use of local anaesthesia. He was the first to
> perform the operation of restarting the human heart after it had ceased to beat.
> There were tributes from the Governor of Tasmania, Sir Ernest Clark, the Premier,
> Mr Cosgrove and the Lord Mayor of Melbourne, Alderman T. S. Nettlefold.[16]

Sir John's widow, Ella, phoned his nephew John, chairman of Kiwi, and said to him, very directly, 'You are the head of the family now.' He was indeed.

Burnley staff singing for
radio broadcast, 1940s

110

THE ROAMING RAMSAYS

he amazing success of Kiwi was due to the energy of the brothers John and Tom Ramsay. They did not wait for markets to come to them; they seemed to be permanently getting on and off aeroplanes chasing new venues. There was not a year when they were not using their passports combing the world to sell Kiwi.

John started early. He had two amazing trips by car in 1933 and 1934, which illustrated the hazards of motor travel long before the invention of freeways. The first was to Brisbane for a shareholders' meeting. The second trip was out west to check on the Adelaide office.

There was no such thing as a Newell Highway then. John laboriously travelled to Brisbane via Sydney:

> The first night out on the way to Sydney was rather disastrous. It rained all the way from Melbourne to Albury. We were making for Gundagai and when we got to Tarcutta about 7 o'clock we found they were making a new bridge and you had to cross the creek on an open crossing. When we got there a woman was stuck in the creek and when the roadmen pulled her out they told me I could go across at my own risk. The creek was a raging torrent. They had three inches in the previous 36 hours.

John did not risk it. He went to sleep in the car and the workmen woke him at 1 a.m. The creek had gone down two feet and it was safe to cross. However, 24 miles beyond Gundagai he reached the Hillas Creek Bridge.

> To get on the bridge there was a short approach … it held my weight alright but as soon as the car got on it the front wheels went down over the hubs and the bumpers rested on the decking of the bridge. By this time it was 3 o'clock and raining like one thing and the creek started to come up again. I spent some time out on the bridge knocking logs away from the radiator and fell in the creek twice. It was as cold as - - -.'

At daybreak I located a homestead about two miles away on a hill and they were very decent and sent their truck and three men down and we levered up

Cartoon featuring
John Ramsay, 1940s

the front of the car and hooked her out. Although water had been running through the radiator underneath a bonnet full of twigs and straw the car started first try.[1]

On the trip to Adelaide he made it to Bordertown with no trouble. Then he had 100 miles to go along a railway line before stopping at a country property.
He wrote:

> The first sand hill we got stuck in and we were there for about two hours having dug the car out about six times and then got it stuck further up until the differential and the backs of the running boards and the petrol tank were on the ground, when we gave it up as a bad job ... I stayed in the car and it was as hot as - - - and I nearly died of thirst. Assistance arrived in about two hours.[2]

It was another two days before he reached Adelaide. On the way back to Melbourne the car gave trouble with faulty petrol feed. The joys of motoring were over.

It was no wonder that after the end of World War II the brothers insisted on air travel. Tom Ramsay made trips to England even before the war's end. Air travel then was long, noisy and often uncomfortable. The airliners were converted bombers. There was the Lancastrian, which was a remodelled Avro Lancaster. It was the old Lancaster bomber with the gun turrets removed, a streamlined nose and extra fuel tanks in the bomb bays. It was fast. It could average 354 km/h, but there was little space for humans. It was good for mail and cargo, and there was room for just seven passengers, usually VIPs. They flew also in the Avro York, the passenger version of the Lancaster. It had a large square fuselage and it took 53 passengers. The York was reliable but noisy, and when the aircraft flew high the passengers had to wear oxygen masks. Unlike the Lancastrian or other bomber derivatives, the York was a stayer, and flew over 50,000 sorties during the Berlin airlift. The third aircraft for the Ramsays was a converted American Liberator, which hardly had more room than the Lancastrian.

The Avro York was a British transport aircraft derived from the Second World War Lancaster heavy bomber, and used in both military and civilian roles between 1943 and 1964.

The brothers were very different. Tom had a sense of history, particularly his own. He kept a cryptic diary, and kept every letter, even his boys' letters from boarding school; he recorded his itinerary, he noted every person he met, where he went, what he ate, and what he purchased. John Ramsay did none of these things, so his story is much more elusive.

On 6 July 1946 Tom wrote that he was due to fly to London on a Liberator, but he decided against it. The Liberator was too noisy, too cramped, so he went by the Avro York. He said in the York they made up bunks for the passengers, one above the other. The oxygen masks were greasy and the Mae Wests had a nasty smell. Mae West was the name given to the life jackets of the period, named after the American film actress presumably because of their splendid upfront padding. The trip to Colombo by the RAF 'was bloody awful, full of inefficiency and not very comfortable'. The ground staff were not very helpful and there was delay after delay. They spent 29 hours on the ground. They spent five hours over the water getting to London via Madras.[3]

His objective had been to get to France, where the situation was as tricky as ever. In March 1945 there had been a 'strictly personal' despairing letter from manager Paul Letournelle to Randy Mann, who was still in England. Letournelle had been looking after the Rouen factory during the German occupation. He said that following talks with Mr Ramsay, Pierre Zecchini had decided to close the factory in Rouen and suspend all the staff. The company SRC (Kiwi in France) would be dissolved and Mr Mann would not return any more to Rouen. He didn't know what to think or do, and he asked if it was true that Mr Ramsay had agreed to close the factory.[4]

Letournelle gave Mann the good news that he had rescued seven trunks and boxes saved from the Germans. Moths had got into the woollen garments but the household linen was in perfect condition. Mrs Mann wrote back asking if he could find her corsets. Alas, they were not to be found.

A history of the French operations reports that both John and Tom Ramsay visited Rouen in 1946. Mann returned at the same time, but the picture was bleak. It was further complicated by obstruction and misleading information given by Zecchini and his lawyer Devaureix on the company law situation. 'It became quite obvious that they hoped to frighten us [Kiwi] to such an extent to leave them in complete control.' There was also trouble in regaining possession of share certificates. It was only with the help of a new legal adviser, Mr Lechanteur, that Kiwi was able to solve this problem.[5]

Tom Ramsay's diary gives his version of events on a visit in June 1947. He went by train to Rouen and walked around the city. It was tragic, rubble everywhere, the bridge and waterfront wiped out. Yet he found the factory in working order, with much room for expansion. He sat in the sun and had long talks with Letournelle, and on 1 July he tried to meet Zecchini but had no luck. They went into an office and talked with lawyers, and after a stormy session they finally came to an agreement in Kiwi's interests. They walked to Zecchini's office 'to meet the arch rogue', and by 10 o'clock all was calm. They had drinks to cement the friendship. Tom wrote: 'I believe he is much relieved but his conscience is not too good.' As well it might not be for a man who had collaborated with the Germans during the occupation.

John and Tom Ramsay wanted the Rouen factory in full production, but an even greater priority was North America. Tom Ramsay remembered that back in 1936 US marines stationed in Shanghai were crazy about Kiwi. Tom's closest friend in America was Fred Whitney, whose firm, Whitney & Oettler of Savannah, Georgia, produced top-quality red gum turpentine. Turpentine, or 'turps', is the distilled resin of trees, an important ingredient in solvents and cleaning products. It was burned in lamps, and in the 19th century was even added to cheap gin. Its supply was the biggest worry right through the war years. In Australia it was unobtainable.

Kiwi Sales Conference, 1947. Tom (second from left) and John (far right)
head up the sales team. Cousin Harry Ramsay (far left).

Tom wrote to Fred Whitney just before the war's end:

> We have been making strong efforts to obtain permission to return to
> turpentine. We have had so many complaints regarding the time it takes to
> get a polish we will appreciate any alleviation of our solvent problems. The
> trouble here has been worse than in other markets as we have had to use very
> low-grade mineral solvents and have not had an opportunity of using white
> spirit as our more fortunate London branch has been doing. Still all polish
> manufacturers are in the same boat here and the public has just had to
> take it or lump it.[6]

Tom had a close relationship with Fred and Laura Whitney that went back to 1933 and
lasted all their lives. There were presents of nylon stockings to Mimi when they were
scarce, also the latest fashions. Fred made sure Tom had all the latest Vinyl recordings of
musicals. Tom didn't think much of *Oklahoma*, but *My Fair Lady* was a huge hit, and he
told Fred: 'If you were not up with *My Fair Lady* in Melbourne you didn't exist.'

On 22 April 1946 Fred wrote to Tom:

> You will be quite proud when you reach New York to see Kiwi polish all over
> the place. It is becoming very well known and it is very seldom that I speak to
> a friend that he doesn't know of Kiwi!

The Ramsay brothers knew it was vital to move quickly. American troops in Europe
had used Kiwi when fighting against the Germans. Kiwi was part of their issue and
they knew it was better than all the other polishes. How long would
they remember it? There was a rival company called Esquire that was
spending huge sums in advertising, money that Kiwi could never find.
The great problem for Kiwi was getting the dollars. Both the Chifley
and Menzies governments kept a miser's hand on foreign exchange. In
the 1940s it was not fashionable to go into debt, and US dollars were
particularly precious. Companies had to beg for dollars, and travellers
heading for the US were rationed; they were lucky to get US$500 to
take with them.

Tom's daughter Anne tells a story of John and Tom in New York in
1947. Their dollar ration had been spent. They had so little money they
could not eat, yet they were supposed to behave like affluent Australians
setting up a brand new business. Their hotel had many function rooms,
and every day some business was putting on a promotion, public
relations for a new product. They found it easy to join the throng,
pretending they were eager customers. So it was possible to tuck in
to the canapés, the smoked oysters, the chicken sandwiches or whatever was on offer.
Finally they became sick of this and decided to have a proper meal in the hotel dining

US sailors polishing their
boots with Kiwi

Kiwi factory, Pottstown, Pennsylvania

room. They were shocked when the bill arrived. They couldn't pay. Tom offered to go out and wash the dishes. Anne doesn't remember whether he actually lived up to his offer.[7]

The president of the American Kiwi operations in 1977, Michael Burnett, recalls an anecdote recounted by a USA Kiwi executive. Soon after the war Tom Ramsay was flying across America and had an interesting conversation with a man sitting alongside him. It was Larry Emley, an executive with Colgate Palmolive, and his credentials seemed perfect. Tom said, 'Why don't you leave Colgate Palmolive and start a Kiwi company for us in the US?' Tom said he would provide $100,000 to get the job on its way. Soon after this, Larry accepted the challenge and Tom provided the funds. His interest in the American market was probably because of the troops returning after the war with awareness of the Kiwi brand, and the huge size of the market. It was a remarkable act of mutual trust, and Larry soon became Kiwi's top American executive.[8]

First they thought of Baltimore, because it had an excellent port, but Tom did not like the city, preferring Philadelphia, where the port facilities were almost as good. He leased premises on the waterfront, and this became Kiwi's first American factory. But it was only temporary and proved far too small. Towards the end of 1947 the company moved to Pottstown, about 60 kilometres north-west of Philadelphia. They had trouble getting equipment, with none available in the US for two years. Filling equipment had to be sent from London. They also had trouble getting dollars. The battle to get dollars out of the Australian Government took nearly 18 months. And then there was a shortage of tin plate. In March 1947 Tom wrote to Fred Whitney: 'The tin plate position in America has thrown large spanners in the Kiwi works and we are awaiting another letter from the States to give us a starting date which we think cannot be earlier than September. This is a grave disappointment as it means a few more months in which our competitors can be pretty active in trying to hook the business from us.'[9]

Bill Ramsay, Olympic Athlete

There was much travelling at this time. Tom wrote: 'TMR tearing round USA. Mimi has almost given up hope of seeing me again.'[10]

It wasn't only the USA; there was also London and Europe. On 31 August 1946 Willie Ramsay, the Scottish cousin of the original Australian founder, William Ramsay, announced his retirement after 31 years as manager of the London office.

Tom wrote from the London factory at Bramwill Road, Ealing, that he had to think very hard for a present for Willie's long and dedicated service to Kiwi in London. He was presented with a leather suitcase from Swaine & Adeney with a silver plate signed by the family: 'William Ramsay with thanks for a job well done.' It was presented at a dinner party at the Albany Club.[11]

In July 1948 there was a gathering of Ramsays in London for the Summer Olympic Games, the first Olympics to be held since 1936. This Ramsay gathering was because 'Bill' Ramsay, John's son and Tom's nephew, was a member of the Australian team. From an early age Bill had been recognised as an outstanding athlete, triumphing as a boy at Geelong Grammar School in the public school combined sports, and receiving the Steve Bayley Memorial Cup for outstanding sporting ability.

First Kiwi factory in USA, Philadelphia, 1948

Sadly, the Olympics 800 metres was no triumph for Bill. The *Argus* ran a headline: 'Jostling May Have Robbed Ramsay of Place'. The race took place at the Wembley Stadium. Bill was successful in the heats and in the semi-final he drew the outside lane. He finished fifth, not good enough to go into the final.

Bill continued to compete in athletics for several years after the Olympics, but Kiwi changed his life and he rose to become managing director.

Tom kept travelling long circuitous routes throughout the world in search of new markets. As an example of his energy, in May 1952 he drove a Buick from San Francisco, via Los Angeles, a journey of 5,100 miles (8,050 kilometres) to Philadelphia. Actually Los

Examples of
US Kiwi magazine
advertisements, 1950s.

Tom Ramsay presenting
Bill Harratt with his
25-year award, 1954

Angeles was a problem with its freeways. Once he got on to them he didn't know how or where to get off. Eventually he cruised into Pasadena, stopped at San Bernardino for petrol and cake, then he drove through the famous Mojave Desert to Las Vegas, which like many before him, he found 'a wonderment of motels, gambling joints, and neon lights'. Like everything else he did, Tom liked to go fast. So he was driving at 70–80 mph (112–128 km/h). He was so devoted to business he was doing a job that normally would have been handled by a travelling salesman. He claimed he made 200 wholesale and retail calls spreading the message of Kiwi.[12]

By 1955 Tom had been round the world 11 times and had logged up about 800,000 miles (1,287,500 kilometres). He did get to meet Mimi sometimes.

THE SINCEREST FORM OF FLATTERY

OPPOSITE

Tom Ramsay (1907–1995)

nnie Ramsay died on 25 May 1953, the day after her 82nd birthday. Without her the world-famous brand would never have got its catchy name. In 1906 William Ramsay had married 'Kiwi Annie' in Oamaru, New Zealand and as a result dedicated the brand name for the boot polish he invented that year with that remarkable little bird. Annie never forgot her home town, living in style at 2 Harold Avenue, East Malvern, a house originally built for Sir John Monash, the First World War hero, which she called 'Oamaru'.

William Ramsay had died in 1914, leaving Annie a widow for 39 years. She was chairman of the Kiwi Polish Company from 1923 to 1933, which meant she was 50 years ahead of her time. It was rare indeed in the 1920s for a woman to be in the chair of a large successful company. This was a time when family members were involved in legal battles, when board meetings could at times be filled with acrimony.

Annie collected jewellery and fine antiques, and made regular visits to London to see her daughter Jean. At 'Oamaru' there was a chauffeur who had a room beside the garage under the billiard room. Annie's granddaughter Jennifer Jeffries remembers the chauffeur, Bentriss: 'His first name was a mystery; nobody ever called him anything but Bentriss. He came out from England more or less wedded to the Rolls-Royce and he had "RR" on his cap. "Oamaru" had a tennis court, which Annie converted into a beautiful rose garden. She had what was called at the time 'a lady's companion'. Katie Parker looked after Annie, doing odd jobs and taking her shopping. Annie was very put out when Katie left to be married.'

Jeffries recalled: 'My grandmother was very good to me. Each year my brother and I used to give her our own special Christmas present. We went to Coles in Chapel Street, which in those days had the slogan: 'Nothing over two shillings and sixpence.' We bought the most awful things. I remember giving her a black cat and looking back now it was awful, but when I went to her house she had it in her china cabinet. I was so pleased.'[1]

In 1930 Annie bought 'Seaview' at Mount Martha, on the Mornington Peninsula, some 80 kilometres south of Melbourne. 'Seaview' occupied more than 10 acres of prime land. In her will Annie directed that it be sold and the proceeds divided between her grandchildren with the plan to subdivide it into 38 allotments. This was disputed by the Mornington Shire, for 10 years, and eventually the grandchildren received $10,000 each.

In her last years Annie suffered from dementia. She died in her Toorak apartment 'Myoora'. Tom Ramsay did not make it to his mother's funeral. He was in London, where he was spending a great deal of time with his family. In 1955 Fergus was at Emsworth House, Penn, Buckinghamshire, where he scored a first in arithmetic. The headmaster wrote that he had settled down well. Anne was at school in Beaconsfield. Robin was at the Royal Academy of Dramatic Art. 'The Principal says he is not without talent but has a lot to learn.'[2]

Meanwhile, Tom was showing his devotion to famous cricketers. He was playing squash regularly with R. W. V. Robins. Captain of England in three Test series, Robins was particularly famous for dropping an easy catch off Bradman in the Third Test of the 1936–37 series. Bradman went on to make 270. His other famous cricketing friends included Gubby Allan, Denis Compton and Bill Edrich.

Compton and Edrich always stayed at 'Hascombe'. According to Tom's daughter Anne: 'They used to get up to all sorts of shenanigans. Bill Edrich was in Dad's dressing room, which had a bed in it. On the floor there was a tiger skin with teeth and a mouth wide open. The night before, they had way too much to drink. Bill got up in the night to go to the loo, fell over the rug, got his foot caught in the tiger's mouth and did a nasty injury to his ankle.'

These were different times. Cricketers regularly partied through the night before Test matches. Ex-aviators Bill Edrich and Keith Miller were famous for it. One night during the 1953 series, Miller and Edrich dallied until the early hours on the town. The Middlesex bowler Alan Moss commented: 'There is no one today with the character or ability to enjoy a party as Bill and Keith did, and then go out the next day and play cricket just as heartily.'[3]

Apart from enjoying the company of cricketers, in 1955 Tom Ramsay had his hands full. Relations with PPZ (Les Specialites PPZ) had deteriorated even further. The French company issued a writ against SRC (Société Rouennaise de Cirages) alleging breach of contract and asking for 250 million francs compensation. Following a long and arduous legal battle, which Kiwi eventually won, the agreement with PPZ was terminated and SRC won 45 million francs compensation. SRC now needed a new company to help with selling and distribution, so they signed a five-year agreement with Fly-Tox, an insecticide company. A Swiss company made a takeover bid for Fly-Tox, and Kiwi decided they needed their own factory and their own sales staff, with a change of name from SRC to Kiwi France. The company built a new modern factory at Sottesville-lès-Rouen, an industrial area near Rouen. It occupied an area of 45,000 square feet and was in full production by August 1969.[4]

Twenty-five years of service, 1953: Ted Harris, Albert Dobbs, Jessie Ley, Tim Cole and Bill Thompson

But Kiwi had been a powerful force long before then. By the 1950s the Kiwi name was internationally renowned. The polish was being distributed to over 150 countries. The Kiwi name was everywhere. In Melbourne the bird was even on the tram ticket. Turn over a penny ticket to read: 'If you want the best boot polish get Kiwi.'

In London, Dean & Son were producing little books for children. They carried cartoons for Walt Disney's Mickey Mouse, Minnie and Goofy. What a coup! Here were the world's most famous cartoon characters introducing young people to Kiwi:

> Mickey read a Magic book
> And thought he'd have some fun
> So he borrowed Goofy's old black shoes
> To show what could be done
> He held a cloth in front of them
> So Goofy couldn't see
> Minnie under the table
> Doing magic with KIWI!
> When Goofy saw his shoes again
> He shouted with delight
> I've never known my old black shoes
> To look so shiny bright

In 1949 there were advertising comic strips in American newspapers. In the first frame of one strip there is a furious female talking to her husband: 'Don't speak to me! You disgraced me at the party.' In the next frame up pops a little Kiwi: 'Your shoes didn't help you chum! They sure could stand a shine!' The husband looks at the Kiwi: 'Well, if it isn't KIWI – pal of my GI days!' So off he rushes to buy his can of Kiwi and his wife sighs: 'KIWI is our bluebird of happiness.'

In another strip a worried character is leaving the president's office: 'No raise! And the boss hardly listened to me. I wonder what's wrong.' Up pops little Kiwi again: 'Those shabby looking shoes ruined you. The boss is a stickler for neatness!' 'Why hello KIWI! You were the GI's No. 1 shoe polish in England and Australia!' So off he rushes to buy his Kiwi and the bird has triumphed again.[5]

In Hong Kong the *Star* ferry runs between Victoria Harbour and Kowloon. The *National Geographic Magazine* once listed this ferry ride as one of the 50 things everyone should do in their lifetime. Clearly on every step right down to the ferry side there was the message both in English and Chinese announcing Kiwi Shoe Polish.[6]

During World War I New Zealand troops were stationed at Bulford Camp, 12 miles north of Salisbury in England. They cut an enormous Kiwi into the hillside, bigger than the Hollywood sign in Los Angeles. It could be seen for miles. The Kiwi Polish Company thought this a great idea and maintained it in good shape for 25 years. Tom Ramsay visited it in 1936. By this time people were not thinking of Kiwi Diggers, but of boot polish.[7]

From the *Kiwi International Review*, 1970:
'Millions of people have seen the Kiwi logo repeated twelve times in English and Chinese on the front of these stairs leading from the Star Ferry Terminal in Hong Kong. Virtually a local landmark, the advertisement could not be more appropriately placed.'

Jacko, an Australian imitator of Kiwi

OPPOSITE

A collection of Kiwi imitators from across the globe — imitation is the sincerest form of flattery.

Then there were ads that caused trouble. In the 1960s Melbourne motorists who drove north along Punt Road towards Collingwood would note a large Kiwi sign. It read: 'Have you cleaned your shoes this morning?'

The sign was on the right just before the railway bridge. Cars unwittingly went through red lights and there were so many accidents the police ordered Kiwi to remove the sign. After their accidents motorists told the police: 'Sorry I was looking down to see if I had actually cleaned my shoes.'[8]

Imitation was the greatest form of flattery. Up until 1974 there had been at least 27 attempts to market imitations of Kiwi. These took place in countries as far as apart as Finland and Vietnam. Many of them were exact copies of the Kiwi tin and when opened the polish was just crude tallow. Some were just backyard operations and were not worth the cost of legal proceedings, but others were more serious and it was necessary to make a forensic examination of the polish to prove that they were fakes.

GENUINE (ENGLAND)

If imitation is the sincerest form of flattery, it is a great tribute to the fame of Kiwi Shoe Polish that so many illicit attempts have been made all over the world to pirate the brand image. Most of the firms concerned in this "rogues' gallery" were obliged to withdraw their products following court actions. In some cases public apologies were extracted.

GENUINE (NEW ZEALAND)

N. W. STEVENS & CO. LTD.
HOUSEHOLD DIVISION

AUCKLAND, NEW ZEALAND

World famous Kiwi Shoe Polish is manufactured in
AUSTRALIA, UNITED KINGDOM, UNITED STATES OF AMERICA,
CANADA, SINGAPORE, EIRE, FRANCE, MALAYA,
PAKISTAN, ITALY, JAPAN, PERU, NEW ZEALAND.

JAPAN

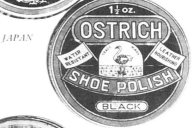

JAPAN

FINLAND

ISRAEL

JAPAN

WIKI

INDIA

KOREA

KOREA

MALAYA

SINGAPORE

CAMEL

KOREA

VIETNAM

RED BIRD
BOOT POLISH
BROWN

COMMUNIST CHINA

EGYPT

COMMUNIST CHINA
(Sold in Syria)

FORMOSA

OPPOSITE

The Kiwi design has remained consistent for more than a century. Variations in wording, language and opening mechanisms can be seen here. Not many products have lasted this long in the same form. From left to right, top row, second and bottom row:

BROWN
c. 1930s to 1940s, coin opening,
made in UK or Australia;
Thoroughly Waterproof

TAN
c.1930s to 1940s, coin opening,
made in UK for the Canadian market;

TRANSPARENT DRESSING
c. 1940s, coin opening,
made in UK for the Canadian market

TAN
c. late 1940s to 1950s, coin opening
made in UK for the Canadian market

BLACK
1950s, wing lever
probably made in Canada

JAUNE CIRE
1960s, wing lever
made in France

NOIR
1990s, wing lever
made in France

BLACK
1990s to 2000s, wing lever
made in Malaysia or Indonesia

BLACK
c. 1980s to1990s, wing lever
made in the USA

TOP AND BOTTOM
Kiwi Shoe Polish Handipack,
including mini brush and cloth,
made in the UK, 1960s

TOP RIGHT
Flat Kiwi polish printed tin
before pressing, produced in
France 1990s

The range of imitations was amazing. The Vietnamese polish was called 'Seadog' and it had a tiny picture of a walrus instead of a Kiwi. The Indian version was called 'Ostrich', boasting an ostrich instead of a Kiwi. Another was called 'Wiki', another 'Kimi' that featured an emaciated heron. 'Fuji' in Japan had a porcupine, 'Cock' in China had a rooster. There was 'Mammoth', which depicted that creature but, like Kiwi we were told it was 'water resistant'. 'Jacko', which had to be Australian, showed a very nice kookaburra and 'Venus', gave us a splendid armless naked Venus. They all had one thing in common: tins exactly the same shape size and weight as the honest Kiwi brand.[9]

Just occasionally there were good results. In 1953 two Japanese businessmen apologised for their misdeeds, announcing in the Tokyo newspaper *Yomiuri* that they had manufactured and marketed a shoe polish under the name of Kiwi for the past two years just because there was a popular demand for that brand. They said there was no excuse for what they did. They wanted to apologise and they promised not to do it again. Tom Ramsay commented that he had been protesting to the Japanese regularly since 1951.[10]

Kiwi kept on expanding. In 1952 it went to Canada and bought a factory in Hamilton, Ontario. In 1955 Kiwi bought the business of Irish Radium Products in Waterford, where there they produced a wide range of shoe and floor cleaning products. The big one was Singapore in 1953. The Japanese wanted this port back in 1941 so that they could dominate South-East Asia. For Kiwi it was also beneficial, as from here they could deliver their polish anywhere from Indonesia to Japan.

The first manager in Singapore was Bert Bulling, with a fascinating story. Bulling spent most of his life in Tientsin, China, where in the early days he was a subaltern in the Royal Regiment before going into the import–export business. The Red Army of Mao Tse Tung was pursuing the almost defeated Chiang Kai-shek, when he wrote a letter to Tom Ramsay 31 March 1949.

> About 12 noon on 15 January the situation was becoming too warm to be pleasant, so my wife, my daughter Barbara now aged 22 and myself decided to move into the basement, where lived the Chinese household staff who had added to their numbers by relatives. About 1 p.m. the house received a direct hit from a mortar shell, which reduced it to a shambles. On the dust clearing I saw one young Chinese woman on the floor, dead, and when I went into the passage to see how the other Chinese were, a hand grenade was thrown in and I received a couple of pieces in the leg. The 'Liberators' then entered and ordered us upstairs, where we remained until permitted to move ... My wife received a cut across the knee from the glass, but Barbara was unhurt. They were both fine examples to the Chinese of cool headedness, turning not a hair through a most unpleasant experience. Having got over this one I received a rude shock two months ago when the relatives of the dead girl took action against me, holding me responsible for her death. She was not employed by me. I refuse to accept responsibility but they want money out of me.

The shine that keeps leather *alive*

It's hard to "shake" a Kiwi shine. More than a surface sheen, Kiwi gives your shoes a rich glow that comes from deep within. And when a Kiwi shine begins to wane, a quick brush-up brings it back. All colors. Also, new KIWI RED and new KIWI WHITE SHOE CLEANER.

(Kee-Wee)

KIWI *shoe polish*

• Brown • • Black • • Ox Blood • • • Mahogany • • • Dark Tan • • Mid-Tan • • • Tan • • Cordovan • • • Blue • • Red • • Neutral •

Anthropomorphism in the form of Sherlock Holmes provides a new angle for the flightless kiwi bird in one of the many advertisements featured in US magazines. From *Life* magazine, 1953.

NEWS

A-45

from J. ROBERT MENDTE, Inc.
PUBLIC RELATIONS
317 SOUTH 16TH STREET
PHILADELPHIA 2, PA.

RECEIVED
NOV 2 1956

Concerning KIWI POLISH CO.
For Release At Will

Released to:
10 Wire Services
N Y & Phila Sports Editors

GOOD LUCK AT THE OLYMPICS

Jimmy Mills (right), soccer coach at Haverford College and coach of the Olympic Soccer team which has left for Australia to participate in the Olympic Games, rubs the team's temporary "mascot", a stuffed wingless Kiwi bird, for good luck. The stuffed Kiwi, valued at $600 because it is a disappearing species, was presented to Mills before leaving the East Coast by Lawrence Emley (left), president of the Kiwi Polish Co., of Pottstown, Pa., which has international headquarters in Australia. The Kiwi will travel with Mills and his team. The Kiwi bird comes from New Zealand. Emley collects the stuffed birds as a hobby.

30

Bill Ramsay presents Kiwi kits to members of the US Olympic team, 1956.

Lawrence Emley, president of the Kiwi Polish Company of Pottstown, Philadelphia, presents a stuffed kiwi to Olympic soccer coach Jimmy Mills, 1956.

Bulling fully expected looting, fires and destruction, but the 'liberators' were well disciplined, law and order was established, and by the end of February mail and telegraphic communication was restored with Shanghai. However, trade was almost impossible. Barter was permitted, but only the government could handle imports and exports. Bulling said he could see no hope for foreigners in China. Now he was asking whether Tom could find him a position somewhere. He knew his age was against him; he was 55, but perfectly fit. What's more, he had great experience in the import–export business and he was an expert accountant.

Tom Ramsay took four months to answer his letter. He wrote: 'I feel terrifically disappointed that after all your trials and tribulations I cannot do something more to help you. Quite frankly Bert, the position is that our organisation is, in pretty well most countries, set up on an idea of giving our own young executives a chance to plough forward.'[11]

Two years later, in 1951, Tom Ramsay changed his mind. He sent Bert Bulling to Singapore in preparation for the new factory. He decided Bert might be ideal because he was fluent in Mandarin. Fortunately for Bulling, Tom Ramsay did not realise almost nobody in Singapore spoke Mandarin. Hokkien and Teochew were the main dialects. Mike Fraser, another Singapore manager, said it was amazing. Two Chinese people could be sitting in a restaurant and if they spoke different dialects they would not understand each other, not a word.

FOLLOWING PAGES

Kiwi poster for school students displaying the history and production of Kiwi polish.

New Zealand's national bird, the Kiwi ,has no tail and practically no wings, and therefore cannot fly. It sleeps most of the day in a burrow, and forages for its food at night. The Kiwi lives on worms, insects, berries and beetles.

THE STORY of

The red and black tin with the Kiwi bird trade mark in the centre is famo
The raw materials are gathered from countries thousands of miles apart, th
each one can be detached for pasting into school project books.

1 The mid-Victorians treated their boots by cleaning them with diluted white of egg, and then by applying beeswax well boned in.

2 The first English blended polishes were made with a liquid base of beer or vinegar containing molasses, which was carbonized with an acid to form a black pigment. This was usually paper wrapped and known as Blacking. A moist rag was used to apply the Blacking to boots or shoes. It had no waterproofing effect and was inclined to smear off on clothing.

3 Next came the paste polishes we know today. These consist of three main ingredients (a) Blended waxes to give the shine, (b) Solvents which convey the polish over the shoe and (c) Dyes and scents which give the colour and characteristic odour. The advantages of these paste polishes are that they are quick and easy to apply, they give a bright shine and recolour the leather.

7 Another important mineral wax is Montan. This is extracted from brown coal, and is produced in large quantities in Germany. From this is made a synthetic wax which is gaining in importance, because it contains so many of the desirable properties of Carnauba and other expensive waxes.

8 An animal wax which has been used universally for years is Beeswax, which, as its name implies, is produced by bees. It is found in their hives in a cone-like form, and the bees use it as a store for their honey.

9 The best solvent known to the shoe polish industry is Pure Gum Spirits of Turpentine. It is produced in many countries, but the best comes from Savannah in U.S.A. and Indonesia. The turpentine pine tree is cut and gum exudes. The gum is collected and treated by distillation to obtain the Spirit.

13 The finished mixture is transferred into a pouring machine which is fitted with a hot water jacket, to keep the polish liquid. The new tins are passed under this machine and the correct amount of polish is automatically poured into each.

14 When the tins are full they are moved by conveyor belt through a refrigerated cooling tunnel in which the polish sets firm.

15 The belt carries the tins to the processing line where paper circles and lids are fitted. They are boxed and stored for a set period, so that the polish will mature and be perfect when presented for sale.

SHOE POLISH

...ld over, but do you know how the polish which goes in the tins is made?
...ed and processed to make your polish. Here is the story with pictures and

The female Kiwi weighs about 4 lbs. and lays an egg a quarter of her own weight. The male bird builds the nest and sits on the egg for 75 days of incubation, during which time he loses two pounds, or half his weight. The chicks when one month weigh about ⅔ of a lb. and eat half a pound of worms daily.

④ The waxes can be grouped into three types, 1. Vegetable, 2. Mineral and 3. Animal. The most important vegetable wax is Carnauba, because of its shining properties. This comes from Brazil, where it collects in the form of a dust on the leaves of the carnauba palm tree. The fully grown trees are 20 to 35 feet high, and natives cut off the fronds with special long handled knives.

⑤ The fronds are then collected and after being allowed to dry out they are beaten on the floor of a completely enclosed room, thus shaking off the wax, which after melting and resetting is bagged for shipment. Also an important vegetable wax is Candelilla, which is obtained from weeds growing in Mexico. Another wax, Esparto is found in certain North African grasses.

⑥ The chief mineral wax used in polishes is Paraffin, a by-product of petroleum oil. The colour and grade vary according to the country the oil is produced in. Paraffins play a large part in polish manufacturing as they have good preservative effects on leather

⑩ The majority of dyes used in shoe polishes are artificial colourings derived from coal tar. The dyes are usually dissolved in oil before being added to wax blends, as this process makes the colouring even.

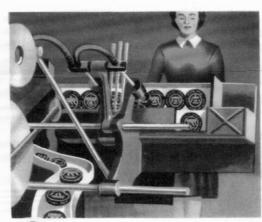

⑪ Containers made of tinplate are most suitable, as they are economical, strong and light. The tinplate is first printed when in the flat, and then the tins are stamped out by dies in very finely adjusted presses.

⑫ Having assembled all the raw materials and a container, the manufacturing can commence. The first step is to melt a selected blend of waxes so they can be thoroughly mixed. After melting the waxes the dye, solvent and scent are added. The mixture is then stirred at a constant temperature until ready for pouring into the tins.

⑯ Every Kiwi factory has an up-to-date laboratory where exhaustive tests are done on all raw materials and samples of finished polish, to ensure that a uniform high quality of product is maintained.

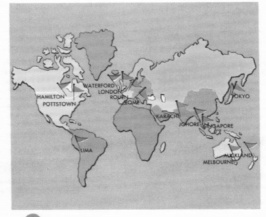

⑰ Kiwi was first manufactured in Australia, but now, owing to the foresight and pioneering spirit of the founders of the Company, it is also produced in England, Canada, New Zealand, Singapore, U.S.A., France, Malaya, Pakistan, Japan, Eire, Peru and Italy. In addition, Kiwi is sold in 150 countries and known everywhere.

⑱ And that is the story of shoe polish, and particularly Kiwi, a polish designed to enter the pores of leather to nourish and preserve, and to give a high shine with a minimum of effort.

POLISHING THE WORLD

iwi held its first international conference in the week starting 19 March 1963. Melbourne had not seen anything like it. Kiwi people came from all over. Bill Ramsay and Will McDougall came from London, Larry Emley from Philadelphia, Randy Mann from Rouen in France, Lloyd Zampatti from Singapore, a representative from N.W. Stevens Ltd from Auckland, Jack Lucas (General Manager Australia), and others came from all around Australia.

Kiwi chairman John Ramsay believed the overseas executives should get a better idea of what Australia was doing. He met top men at Sydney's airport, and immediately they were off touring to Port Kembla, where they spent two days at the BHP steel works looking at the manufacture of iron, steel and tin plate. John Ramsay thought this was part of their education; tinplate was used in a great number of Kiwi products. Then they drove to Cooma and spent two days in the Snowy Mountains, learning a little about the great Australian hydro-electric scheme.

The conference took place in the Grand Ballroom of the Southern Cross Hotel, which had opened only a few months earlier. For Melbourne this new style of American hotel was so modern and different from the grand 19th century Melbourne hotels like Menzies, the Windsor, Scotts and the Federal. Conservationists hated the idea of this new fancy place because it was going up on the site of the old Eastern Market, which dated back to 1847. Once a famous market for Melbourne, by the 1960s it had grown rather tired and was a sprawling home for flower sellers, tattoo artists, phrenologists, bookshops, ancient wine cellars, and even test-your-strength-machines. The legendary E. W. Cole of Coles Book Arcade in Bourke Street had his first stall there in 1873.

The conference opened with a battery of speakers, including the Victorian Premier Sir Henry Bolte, the American Consul General Mr F. S. Hopkins, the Lord Mayor of Melbourne Sir Maurice Nathan, and the Regional Director of the Department of Trade Mr R. B. Hines. Mr Hines was particularly complimentary, claiming Kiwi was one of the few Australian enterprises that knew how to export. Usually when he tried to encourage would-be exporters he would receive so many depressing replies: 'We can't compete. Our costs are too high. We are too far away from our overseas markets. The highly industrialised and established exporters would push us out of it.' Hines said the great thing about Kiwi was that it was so international people didn't realise it was Australian. He had British friends who thought it was British, American friends who thought it was

KIWI SHINES SHOES IN 110 COUNTRIES...

France in Vanguard of Retail Merchandising Advance, Improvement in England and Sales Excellent in Canada

THOMAS M. RAMSAY

FRANCE has made greater strides in retail business than any other country of Europe during the past twelve months, in the opinion of Thomas M. Ramsay, Joint Managing Director of Kiwi Polish Company Pty., Ltd., Melbourne, Australia.

Mr. Ramsay was in Toronto during the last week of August on his way back to Australia after his annual tour of the Company's factories in Rouen, France; London, England; and Philadelphia, Penn. Interviewed by RETAIL GROCER

there were many evidences that the production of consumer goods had increased substantially during the past year.

Government restrictions in England respecting sizes and other specified limitations of containers, were still having an adverse affect on retail trade but Mr. Ramsay stated he also found encouraging evidence of pick up. Distribution of goods was much improved over conditions a year ago.

Started in 1901

In addition to their factory in Australia the Company operates a plant at Oakland, New Zealand and prior to the last war also had one in Poland. Kiwi shoe polish is now sold in 110 countries. This great world-wide organization had its obscure and modest beginning in 1901 when the late William Ramsay, father of the present joint managing directors, Thomas M. and John Ramsay, originated the formula for the polish now so favourably known around the world. The trade name "Kiwi" was adopted in 1906 and originates

from a small nocturnal bird peculiar to Australia and New Zealand. The species had almost become extinct but the Australian Government has recently taken steps to propagate it.

Male Hatches Eggs

At Hawkes Bay fifteen of these little brown feathered creatures, with their uncannily phosphorescent plumage, have been hatched and reared to date, Mr. Ramsay told us. This bird sanctuary, he explained, is known as an acclimatization farm. The male bird hatches the eggs, one at a time, the female presenting him with another fresh egg as each one is hatched and so on for a period of eight weeks or more.

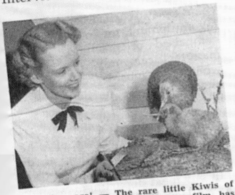

Here they are! — The rare little Kiwis of Australia. A short documentary film has recently been made of these birds and at your Editor's suggestion Mr. Ramsay will send a print to Langley-Harris and Company for showings to community groups in Canada. This illustration is reproduced from the December 1948 issue of Retail Grocer and Provisioner. Remember it?

AND PROVISIONER at the office of the firms Canadian distributors, Langley-Harris and Company, Ltd., he was quite enthusiastic about business conditions here. Sales of their famous Kiwi Shoe Polish in Canada were very gratifying, showing greatly increased volume, he stated.

France Modernizes

When in France a year ago, Mr. Ramsay said he found conditions in the retail outlets very poor. The untidy appearance of chain store units and of retail establishments generally had been pronounced. However, this year he had noted a great transformation. Premises had been modernized

Here, at Kiwi's Headquarters, Melbourne, Bill [?] Manager (grandson of the [?]

American, and it wouldn't be long before people in Pakistan thought it was Pakistani.

Tom Ramsay gave a very long speech in which he detailed the history of Kiwi, claiming that it would have been dangerous for Kiwi just to stick to shoe polish. It had to develop other products. One of the first, back in the 1920s, was White Cleaner. It had many uses. Tom could have let out one secret on Kiwi White Cleaner. Up at his Mount Macedon retreat, 'Hascombe', he used it in his marking machine and it made excellent white lines on the grass tennis court.

In 1941 there was a cleaner for webbing equipment, very useful for Allied troops in the field. In 1950 there was Kiwi Glint for glass and chromium. In 1952 there was Kiwi Sport, which was launched with a big promotion. It went down to the Antarctic with the Australian National Research Expedition. It kept boots waterproof for two days when tramping in snow and ice. It was splendid, too, for footballs. No longer need they be heavy and waterlogged. Even at the end of the match, footballs would stay light and easy to kick after an application of Kiwi Sport.[1]

In 1956 Kiwi bought the firm that made Shinoleum. Linoleum in the 1950s covered half the floors of kitchens and bathrooms in Australia. Shinoleum was there to give it a shine.

AT HOME
WITH THE
PURTELLS

Melbourne's leading jockey needs no introduction to racegoers. But at home with his wife he is much like any other suburban householder.

See also Page 4

Kiwi was always on the lookout or ways to promote its products. This front cover features Jack Purtell, famous jockey of three Melbourne Cup winners.

The same year Kiwi acquired Steprac, a carpet cleaner. The discerning buyer would note that Steprac was 'carpets' spelled backwards. If this wasn't enough, there was Kiwi steel wool under the trade name of Topsy. The following year the company bought a half interest in Parco Chemicals, which made aerosol cans, and after that came the old established firm of Bon Ami. Bon Ami had been a good friend to housewives as a powder household cleaner since the 1890s. Kiwi then acquired Kitten Products, manufacturers of car care products that sold directly to garages. There would be few motorcar enthusiasts who had not at some time used a little Kitten to polish their beloved chrome and steel machines.

There was expansion everywhere: Preston, Moorabbin, and Traralgon in Victoria where Kiwi was making cans for Melbourne manufactured Kiwi polish. There were factories in Caringbah, Milperra and Leichhardt in New South Wales, and the Susquehanna Metal Box Company producing exclusively for Kiwi US.[2]

Tom Ramsay mentioned some interesting home truths. When they opened for business in Philadelphia there had been a murder on their doorstep. They didn't find the body for a fortnight. Then whenever they went out for a sandwich they had to step over the Sterno drinkers. Sterno was a semi-liquid fuel. Put your Sterno in a rag, squeeze out the liquid then swallow it. 'Whallop,' according to Tom. However, he did not mention the terrible snowstorm at the Pottstown factory in 1958, when there was no electricity, no water,

OPPOSITE TOP

Feature article announcing Kiwi shining shoes in 110 countries

OPPOSITE BOTTOM

Bill Ramsay explaining the kiwi's peculiarities

no light and, of course, no heating. The workers were suffering. Tom Ramsay, who was on the spot, came to the rescue with an old Australian trick. He pulled out kerosene tins, perforated the sides, filled them with old newspapers, then lit them to provide instant warmth.[3] Fergus Ramsay recalled his father used this method to barbecue chops at 'Hascombe'. The chops almost inevitably were incinerated, but his mother Mimi always quietly cooked rival chops on the stove in the kitchen and swapped them for those that had been cremated.

Perhaps the most fascinating information to come out of the conference was that, although Kiwi was selling in 158 countries, almost none of it was coming from Australia, except for small quantities shipped to New Guinea and Fiji. Most of the exports to the Middle East and Africa went out from the UK. France supplied Europe, and then there were the shipments from Singapore all over South-East Asia. Canada and the USA supplied the Americas and West Indies.

The conference closed on Friday 22 March 1963 with a dinner at the Athenaeum Club. The guest speaker was John McEwen, the Minister for Trade. They consumed Saumon Fumé, Consommé Royale, Filet Boeuf Rossini, Soufflé au Fromage and finished with Very Old Macquarie Port and Courvoisier Napoleon Brandy.

What was it like to work for Kiwi in the 1960s? Alf Anderson was a sales representative in Rochdale, Lancashire. He left school at 15, worked in a grocer's shop then joined Kiwi in 1964, aged 18 at the time. He says there were 72 senior representatives and the UK was split into two regions, North and South. Both regions had a regional manager and then there were area managers.

Anderson was the youngest of eight children, and on his first day Kiwi presented him with a car, a brand new Ford Anglia. This was simply amazing for him as he was the first member of his family ever to own a car. His area manager Keith Lloyd drove it up from London and the family was overwhelmed when Lloyd said he didn't mind if Alf took his mother for a drive that afternoon.

The following day he had to drive to a local town and meet the area salesmen. Before the advent of big supermarkets, salesmen had to visit every little shop and make Kiwi known virtually in every street. They also had to visit all the shoe shops and the shoe repairers, which, like corner stores today, would eventually disappear.

A sales conference was held every year, which meant travelling down to London by train and staying at the Piccadilly Hotel. For a young sales rep to be staying at a four-star hotel was a very big deal, and Alf thought he had really arrived. The chief sales manager was Leslie Fraser Mitchell, tall, sleek with grey hair. One year, Leslie Fraser Mitchell organised the launch of a scouring pad called Qwik-Brite at the Piccadilly Hotel. As part of the business presentation they featured a stripper: the full bit, with stripper music and the young lady finishing bare except for Qwik-Brite scouring pads placed in three precise spots not suitable for general exhibition.

KIWI
SHOE CREAM

A new product, Kiwi Guard, was a liquid polish in a cone shaped container. On the top was a sponge in the shape of a Grenadier Guardsman's busby. Squeeze the tube and rub on the polish with the busby. Anderson thought this was supposed to revolutionise shoe cleaning. Kiwi Guard was only moderately successful, so it didn't make Buckingham Palace.

Kiwi looked after its staff. After a year Anderson received a promotion and his own Kiwi territory. Promotion meant that he switched from a Ford Anglia to a bright yellow Ford Cortina. Proudly he went out in his new car. After only two days he bent it in an accident and thought that could be the end of his time with Kiwi, but no. His district manager Keith Lloyd said, 'Don't worry about it.' His promotion was still on and his salary went from £400 a year to £700. On the strength of this he got married. He and his bride were both 19. Anderson remained with Kiwi for six years.[4]

Cam Smith worked in London for eight years. After studying accountancy in Melbourne he thought he could handle a balance sheet and a profit and loss account. His English-born father was a surgeon, and he urged Cam to visit Europe and to see something of the world before settling down. But he made one stipulation: 'You are going to have the time of your life. Put a date on it when you will finish.' So, aged 22, he sailed for London and indeed had the time of his life, so much so he didn't want to go home. When he called Bill Ramsay at Kiwi's London office to ask him for a job, Ramsay took him to lunch, and before it was over young Cam had a job as a management trainee.

Smith arrived at a time when Britain was just discovering supermarkets. Before this, Kiwi was sold almost entirely through small retail shoe shops, shoe repairers and hardware stores. The man in charge of sales was Fred Hunt, but Fred was of the old school too wedded to the old ways of distribution. However, there was Leslie Fraser Mitchell, a flamboyant character, who also had dealings with Alf Anderson.

Smith said Mitchell was a driving force in getting Kiwi into supermarket chains like Tesco and Sainsbury's. Kiwi's biggest problem was that, except for some minor items like furniture polish, it was a one-product company. It had been too comfortable over the years with armed forces contracts in the UK, USA, Australia and indeed even in Germany.

Fortunately for Smith, he had not been long with Kiwi when the Bristol sales manager suffered a knee injury and was forced to resign. Smith was promoted into a new job as temporary Bristol sales manager, with 14 representatives working for him. He had his

Kiwi poster featuring troopers of the Royal Canadian Mounted Police, 1957

OUI !

... OUI

OUI,
le nouveau
BLANC LIQUIDE KIWI
est digne
des plus belles chaussures
et des plus beaux jours.
Il ne laisse pas
de traces,
il tient et ne tache pas.

BLANC
liquide
KIWI

Son applicateur souple est très pratique. Sa bague-éponge, démontable et lavable, permet d'étaler sur les chaussures un blanc **vraiment** blanc. Son flacon, léger et incassable, ne se bouche jamais.

C'est **KIWI** et c'est tout dire !

ALJANVIC 285   Photo Derly

"E L L E" I9 Mai I96I

own company car, a Morris Traveller. Cam said: 'It looked like a mini Tudor house with wooden slats as part of the structure.'

Smith's temporary position became permanent and he rose rapidly on the ladder to become southern sales manager. He recalled: 'We had a sales force of 140 people, which was absurd. That's the way it was in those days. All manufacturers had huge sales forces. I was one of those who said we were spending far too much running a sales force when our distribution was proceeding well into the supermarkets.' As now, the distributors had to fight to get shelf space for Kiwi. The supermarkets would bring stock in from their warehouses, but then they would expect Kiwi employees to do the hack work by taking the product from the small local warehouse, not the regional warehouse, and putting it on the shelves.

In 1973 Smith returned to Australia where, after working as Kiwi's major accounts manager in Melbourne, he was posted to Queensland to run the Brisbane office.[5]

.   .   .

On 21 October 1966 the chairman of the Kiwi Polish Company John Ramsay was driving home in his Mercedes Benz. He crossed the Yarra over the MacRobertson Bridge, turned left into St Georges Road, Toorak, turned into Orrong Road, and as he approached Clendon Road he had a massive heart attack and crashed into a brick fence. He died instantly. He was 62 years old.

His daughter Jennifer Jeffries remembers the shock. A policeman came to report the terrible news to her mother Edith Ramsay. Jessie Ley, John Ramsay's secretary, a remarkable woman, and a brilliant do-everything assistant, immediately went to the Ramsay home to cook dinner for the family. The funeral was at the Toorak Presbyterian Church.

John Ramsay had suffered from heart troubles for a long time. In April 1952 he was diagnosed with an enlarged heart, and he was making regular visits to his doctor Clive Fitts, seeking relief from angina, which he had lived and worked with for 14 years. John Ramsay was born in 1904 and had three children: Jennifer, Bill and Simon. Both Bill and Simon had joined their father in the business.

The Ramsay brothers Tom and John were very different. Tom liked to be the front man, the talker, the one to spread the message of Kiwi. It was interesting that when there was a grand occasion like the international conference at the Southern Cross Hotel in 1963 it was Tom who made the keynote speech, not John, the chairman. *Who's Who in Australia 1966* is also revealing. There was a fine entry for Thomas Ramsay, saying that he had been Managing Director of Kiwi Polish Company since 1956 and that his recreations were Australian historical research, gardening and golf. The elusive John Ramsay, the elder brother and chairman of the Kiwi Polish Company since 1933, made no appearance in *Who's Who*.

They were both short men with moustaches but, according to John's son Simon, Tom was slightly more rotund. Simon worked for Kiwi from 1954 to 1956 doing all the menial jobs from mixing polish to driving a truck for £8 10s a week. He didn't get on with his Uncle Tom. He said, 'Eventually I told him where to stick his job,' so Simon left to work in the motoring industry.

It had been a good life for John Ramsay. He had his grand house, 'Devon' on 2 acres at 1 Whernside Avenue, Toorak, which he sold to Dr Ainslie Meares, the well-known psychiatrist, in 1951. He then bought a house at 60 Clendon Road, Toorak, next door to 'Cranlana', the former residence of the famous philanthropist and founder of the Myer Emporium, Sir Sidney Myer.[6]

Like his brother Tom, John Ramsay also had a country house. In the late 1930s he bought 'Koorootang', a historic mansion on the beach road between Mornington and Mount Martha. Set on 14 acres, Koorootang Court is now a retirement village in Mount Martha.[7]

John Ramsay's death in 1966 deprived him of the opportunity to guide Kiwi through another decision that would have a huge effect on its future. In May 1967 Kiwi went public, and its shares were listed on the Stock Exchange. The *Financial Review* had begun spreading rumours as early as 1962. The share issue, said the *Review*, would rank among the largest ever share issues in Australia, with placements in London, New York and possibly Paris.[8] Kiwi was already a well-known international brand with global expansion possibilities.

The *Sun Herald* in Sydney bewailed the disappearance of the great Australian family companies: Grace Brothers, Penfolds Wines, T. A. Field and R. W. Miller were all gone.[9]

In January 1967 Kiwi approached Sir Ian Potter, Australia's leading international financier to talk about going public. Potter was definitely the man. Peter Yule in his biography of Ian Potter tells a story that in the early 1960s Sir Ian was leaving a cocktail party to catch a flight to Bangkok. He had been talking to an American banker who said, 'I can give you a list of contacts you might be interested in.'

Sir Ian replied, 'I would appreciate that. I only know one person in Siam.' The American asked, 'And who's that?' Sir Ian answered, 'The king.'

It was the Potter international connections that sealed the move. Tom Ramsay and Mimi dined with Sir Ian along with leading people from Morgan Guaranty and thus the Kiwi float was underwritten by Potter and Company.[10]

The company was now Kiwi International Company Pty Ltd, with T. M. Ramsay as chairman and managing director. There were 10 million shares at $1 each. Eight million were issued fully paid to vendors and two million were offered for subscription. Another 10 million were held in reserve. The prospectus pointed out that for the year ending 31 August 1966 the consolidated profit of the Kiwi Polish Company was $1,262,144. Tom Ramsay anticipated that the company would pay dividends at the rate of 7 per cent per annum.[11]

There was a rush for the shares. The first day was 30 June 1967 and 99,600 shares sold by lunchtime. They opened at $1.50, 31 cents above the issue price, and reached $2.60 by the end of the day.[117]

•   •   •

In the same year as the float, Kiwi went into manufacturing in Africa, which provides a fascinating story on its own.

In 1967 Tom Ramsay hired a young man with potential, Michael Burnett. With a degree in economics from Sydney University, he had spent eight years with Unilever before he came to Kiwi as group marketing officer. Tom Ramsay called in Burnett and Dr Michael Searby, the group technical officer, and requested them to go to South Africa to look at the market. Until then the company had been using a CNA (Central News Agents) subsidiary as its distributor of imported Kiwi. It was an unusual partnership because CNA was akin to the UK's W. H. Smith chain, whose main business was selling stationery, books, newspapers and magazines.

Soon after his return from South Africa, Burnett reported that Kiwi had less than 5 per cent of what was already a sizeable market, and one that had significant growth potential.

Africa was an important market for Kiwi.

He suggested the company should seriously consider going there and building a Kiwi factory. Burnett said: 'Some months after, Tom called me in and said, "You think it's a good idea, why don't you go and do it."

Burnett reflected, 'At that stage I was only thirty and relatively naive, especially when it came to undeveloped markets, particularly one as diverse as Apartheid South Africa.'

The South African population was split into four groups: whites, blacks (Bantu), Indians, and Coloureds (most of whom lived in the Cape and were descendants of east Asians who were earlier imported to work on sugar cane plantations). The largest group by far were the Bantu. It was this group that constituted the greatest market potential for Kiwi.

Burnett discovered that only about 10 per cent of shoe polish sales in the late '60s were through supermarkets. The bulk of sales were made in small shops in the Bantu and Coloured townships, often via Indian wholesalers. He spent much time in the townships (with a Bantu rep) to learn about the market, and in so doing discovered that few white people ever ventured into the townships.

The black population at the time had three prized possessions: their hat, their transistor radio and their shoes. Shoes were particularly important. It was a matter of pride, particularly for men, to have shiny, quality shoes. And they took great care of them.

The market potential being clear, the question was how to establish Kiwi in this market. It was decided to set up a 50/50 joint venture with CNA and to build a new factory in South Africa to manufacture shoe polish and take on the dominant market leader, Reckitt & Colman, and their 'Nugget' brand.

The senior CNA executives were known to Tom Ramsay, and were keen on the venture, and were most helpful and welcoming to the new Kiwi general manager. Burnett recalls, 'CNA Chairman Alan McIntosh invited me to a number of black tie dinners at his home, guests being served by servants in white jacket and red sash. Always the ladies retired early while the port was passed around and the men had a pee on the front lawn!'

CNA were adamant that the factory be built in Heilbron, which was a Coloured homeland, an area specifically designated for Coloureds about 100 kilometres south of Johannesburg. Such a decision would certainly find favour with the Africaans government in Pretoria, which was clearly one of CNA's goals. And the land was to be free. Despite young Burnett's misgivings about not building in Johannesburg where the big market was, the combined pressure of CNA and Tom Ramsay won the day, and the factory was built in Heilbron.

Before it was completed Burnett was pulled out of South Africa in 1973 and returned home to become general manager of Kiwi's Australian operations in Melbourne.

While the original factory location was soon found to be wanting, and was subsequently relocated in 1974, Kiwi is today a dominant market leader in South Africa and more tins of Kiwi Shoe Polish are made in the South Africa factory than any other in the world

. . .

Peter Hunt, who had been managing operations in Nairobi, took over from Michael Burnett. The factory was fine enough, but Heilbron was bleak. If the township existed at all it was easy to pass without noticing. The land was a 'kindly' gift from the government, and it was not difficult understand why. Nobody else wanted it, and there was little encouragement to live there. Hunt managed the South African operations from Johannesburg. The factory manager, Dida Schmidt, lived in Heilbron. He was Afrikaans–German, and both Burnett and Hunt described him as a splendid man.

Hunt drove the 100 kilometres from Johannesburg to Heilbron once a week. 'I had an Alfa Romeo and I screamed down at a pretty fast rate and I always got booked for speeding in Sasolburg,' said Peter.

Sasolburg was half way between Johannesburg and Heilbron. When Apartheid attracted international opposition in the 1960s and South Africa suffered crippling economic sanctions, the German company Sasol was the first to start making petrol out of coal, an inventive and enterprising move. Hunt said six years supply of petrol was stored underground, just in case there was a war or civil disturbance.[118]

In those first years of production Kiwi had to compete against Nugget, which was all-powerful in South Africa. Kiwi had less than 7 per cent of the market. At Heilbron Kiwi had a sideline: Christmas crackers and decorations. Hunt took them to a Jewish wholesaler, Reuben, in Cape Town and he sold them to all the shops, where they were a popular line. How ironic: Kiwi crackers were selling better than Kiwi Boot Polish. CNA

Kiwi was important for shoe maintenance in Africa.

were big customers and Kiwi crackers were sold through all their outlets.

But there was one special customer: Harry Oppenheimer, the Gold and Diamond King, one of the richest men in the world. Every year a special parcel containing Rolex watches would arrive at the factory. Harry would order 20 or 30 dozen of the special handmade crackers. It was normal for the crackers to contain a joke, a party hat and a little trinket like a ring, a puzzle, or a plastic top. Harry's trinket was better than that: a Rolex watch.

. . .

Ivan McLaws from head office in Melbourne went to Heilbron in January 1973 and prepared a report. He said the quality of local labour in the factory was poor. They didn't respond to incentives or show desire to take leadership. Delays in transport were an unbelievable problem. It took two weeks for consignments to reach Johannesburg by train. As for Cape Town, that was six weeks. Send it all by truck? No! South African Railways successfully opposed an application for a road licence. Kiwi couldn't even get a licence for the critical Christmas period when it was essential to distribute the crackers.

So Heilbron was not the place to be, and not long after the McLaws Report, Kiwi closed the factory. It went into partnership with the Royal Beech-Nut company, a big South African company that specialised in confectionery and foodstuffs. It agreed to manufacture Kiwi products under licence at Chloorkop, just north-west of Johannesburg. Royal Beechnut had Kiwi until December 1983, and they improved sales to the point where Kiwi had 17 per cent of the market.

The big battle came after the Nicholas–Kiwi merger in 1982. The partnership with Beechnut came to an end. All the equipment went to Nicholas Kiwi's factory at Pinetown 15 kilometres out of Durban. From now on it was Kiwi that began to triumph all over Southern Africa.

·   ·   ·

Denis Shelley went to South Africa in 1970 on a teaching scholarship and taught for a short period. He then worked for eight years for a pharmaceutical company and subsequently in 1983 joined Reckitt & Colman, where he spent 10 years; four years in the Household and Care Division as their group marketing director. Reckitt & Colman were the producers of Kiwi's great rival Nugget, and unquestionably it was King of the Castle, with 75–80 per cent of the market. It was a market not to be ignored because South Africans loved their shoe polish and shiny shoes. The time was the early 1980s, and Reckitt & Colman made a disastrous mistake.

The Reckitt & Colman factory was just out of Johannesburg and the company chairman, Graham Higgo, called in experts to make an 'internal analysis'. How could they cut costs? Denis Shelley said they looked at every aspect; how Nugget was produced, how it was made, how it was packaged, and how it was distributed. Their dramatic move was similar to what they had done in Australia. They changed the formulation of the actual polish from a spirit-based formula to a water base. Next they wondered how they could make the tins easier to open. The classic method was a winged key on the side of the tin. They believed this could be improved by placing a small indent on the tin, like a thumbprint. Press down with your thumb and the tin would flip open.

Shelley said the trouble was that these changes didn't work. The new Nugget tin was not airtight. South Africa has a hot climate. The water base in the tin evaporated and the polish inside shrank, became hard and cracked. If you shook the tin you could hear the polish rattling inside. Would-be customers derisively called it 'the rattler'. Unlike in Australia, shoe polish was not just sold in supermarkets. In Africa it went out to the little villages, to shops with roofs of corrugated iron, and the Nugget tin had to be very robust to take the heat. Then there was the other aspect: some Africans believed Nugget no longer buffed as well as Kiwi. Where was the shine?

Shelley claimed it took less than eight years for a complete reversal of market share. When Nugget had sunk to just 40 per cent of the market, Reckitt & Colman started all over again: back to a spirit-based formula and back to the wing-nut can. But it was too late. Kiwi had become the 'gold standard', with its reputation for being the superior product of choice for the armed services and police force, greatly enhancing its reputation. It was a good example for future scholars how not to meddle with a successful brand. Kiwi rose to become completely dominant in Africa.

In 1992 Denis Shelley left Reckitt & Colman and joined Kiwi Brands as CEO of their office and the factory in Pinetown, just out of Durban, owned by Sara Lee. There was a nice piece of sleight of hand because the name Sara Lee was never mentioned. Shelley said if you asked for a list of Sara Lee companies quickly you would find out everything the conglomerate did all over the world, but not in South Africa. This was the land of Apartheid, and the United States had to be seen as politically correct and taking part in a boycott. So the Kiwi Brands business was tucked away in a Swiss holding company. When Apartheid came to an end in 1994 and Nelson Mandela became the new president, the scene changed and Kiwi Brands could call itself Sara Lee.

Business thrived. Shelley said: The Africans have a love affair with their shoes. They will pay an exorbitant amount for them. Their shoes are a status symbol, and they spend much more on shoes as a percentage of income than other groups. It's a ritual. You see them on a Sunday with other members of the family, friends and neighbours around the back step polishing their shoes. We did some promotion with schools. The whites didn't give a hoot what their shoes looked like. The schools, which gave us all the traction, were the black schools. We were selling 42 million cans a year and the population of South Africa was 40 million. That's a very high per capita use of polish.'[119]

When Shelley took over at Pinetown in 1992, Kiwi was mainly a single-product company, which he believed was dangerous should the market for polish ever turn sour. It was necessary to branch out and acquire more products. The timing was perfect because Sara Lee had just bought out some of Beecham's products. The Beecham business in South Africa was independent of Sara Lee in Europe. Yet Shelley was able to do his own mirror buy-out in South Africa and was able to acquire a whole range of deodorants, including Status and Body Mist. Status became the number-one deodorant in South Africa. No longer was the company just reliant on Kiwi.

In 2010 when S. C. Johnson & Son, Inc acquired Kiwi Brands, the Sara Lee factory at Pinetown at that time was the biggest manufacturer of shoe polish in the world. So this was the end of an era. Pinetown closed and all production moved to the S. C. Johnson facility at Roslyn, 100 kilometres north of Johannesburg.

RAMSAY
HOUSE

188

THE KIWI POLISH COMPANY
PROPRIETARY LIMITED

CHANGING TIMES

By 1968 Kiwi had been making shoe polish in Melbourne for 62 years. In that time it had blossomed into a company that was a household word akin to Coca-Cola, Kellogg's, Cadbury or Mercedes Benz. So it was a surprise to find that the headquarters of an international company was housed in a two-storey building in grubby Burnley Street, Richmond.

In the Kiwi building the international staff was upstairs, the Australian administration downstairs, and the factory was on three levels, including a mezzanine. The factory floorboards had matured like vintage wine; the timber had absorbed decades of wax and solvents. The thought often occurred that it could make a blaze to light up all Richmond, Burnley and even illuminate fashionable Toorak across the Yarra. The Kiwi factory went right through to Neptune Street, a typical piece of Richmond, a narrow street, designed for workers cottages and horse-drawn carts, never for cumbersome Kiwi delivery trucks.

From the window at Kiwi it was possible to see trams rattling down Bridge Road. Across the road, on the corner of Neptune Street, there was an establishment perhaps even more famous in the district than Kiwi, the Dover Castle Hotel. Friday nights were the big nights. The factory workers swarmed there at 4.15 p.m. Next the Australian Kiwi office staff would hurry over, immediately after finishing work at 5 p.m. The gentlemen from head office went elsewhere.

The Burnley Street factory was like an old shoe: one didn't want to throw it away, but the sole was thin and it had to go. Many employees remembered it with nostalgia. Kath O'Connor first went there in 1958 on trial for one day to work the switchboard. When first she saw it, she was terrified. She was used to a board with plugs; you plugged in to the chairman, you plugged in to the sales manager, you plugged in to marketing. No plugs on this one, just a dazzling display of lights. A fellow employee offered to give up her afternoon off to help her. Kath stayed for 15 years.

It was an old-fashioned company, and in the summer the building would heat like a furnace. Kath said the cooling system consisted of a block of ice on a kerosene tin with a fan behind. Will McDougall, a director, was kind. He would send out and buy ice blocks for everybody and sometimes even ice-creams. One day when the temperature hit 104 degrees Fahrenheit everybody was sent home.

Bev Thompson started as a typist–stenographer in 1950. She was there for a year,

Kiwi world headquarters,
188 Burnley Street, Richmond

and then came back six years later and remained until the company sold to Consolidated Foods Corporation in 1984. Bev said there were no Christian names. Everybody was Mr, Mrs or Miss, except for Tom Ramsay. When he received his knighthood in 1972, there was a careful decision. They would not call him Sir Thomas (jokingly sometimes pronounced Thomarse), but Sir Tom.

Slacks for female staff were forbidden, so the ladies had to wear skirts and stockings. The office supervisor and private secretary to Tom Ramsay was Miss Jessie Ley. It was definitely L.E.Y. So don't get the spelling wrong. 'I am not Chinese,' Miss Ley would say. Jessie Ley began as an accounting machine operator in 1930 and never married. Bev said, 'She was very strict. If we ever left the room to go to the ladies room she would time you. She had a funny manner, very gruff, but she was very kind to anyone who needed it.'

The pay was not good, but there was a genuine family feeling about the place and an understanding that you were safe if you worked for Kiwi. Kath O'Connor said that when her husband died Jessie Ley gave her three weeks off. Tom Ramsay came to the funeral and the Ramsays sent flowers. There was a staff issue of shares and Kath had to find

£200. She wrote a letter to Tom Ramsay saying she was sorry, she had a child to support and £200 was beyond her. Kath still received her shares and Tom Ramsay paid the money.

Back in the 1950s and 1960s members of the Melbourne Cricket Club received two ladies tickets. Tom used to hunt down staff members and ask them if they wanted to go to the football. Bev remembered she and Kath went to the MCG one day, when she dropped Tom's precious ticket and it slipped a foot down into a grate. There was much panic, for it seemed irretrievable, until an official came and pulled up the grate. Yes, Tom was often kind, but they all agreed if you wanted something out of him or you wanted to do serious business, it was important to see him in the morning, never in the afternoon. Tom frequented the Athenaeum Club, where he always had a good lunch.

If at times the Burnley Street factory seemed to belong to another age, it did have a touch of real class. Over the doorway there was the Royal Warrant, the Coat of Arms of His Majesty King George VI, granted to Kiwi not long before the king died in 1952. The warrant next passed to His Royal Highness the Duke of Edinburgh. That story even made news in New York. The *Wall Street Journal* reported that Prince Phillip drove an Aston Martin, ordered his theatre tickets from Ashton & Mitchell Ltd, and used Kiwi to shine his shoes. However, it was difficult to imagine Prince Phillip downstairs at the palace, applying Kiwi to his royal brogues.[1]

The Royal Warrant was strict indeed. In 1973, when the 'By Appointment' began to appear on some of Kiwi's other products, there was a threatening letter from the Royal Warrant Association, Buckingham Gate, London, saying: 'We have been informed by the Lord Chamberlain that the Warrants Committee has had occasion to consider a bad breach of rules . . . therefore felt obliged to issue the strongest possible warning . . .' because they had used the warrant for White Cleaner.

His Lordship's warning was heeded immediately as the warrant applied to Kiwi Shoe Polish did not apply to products other than this.[2]

Like a family with too many children, Kiwi had to find a bigger house. It all began with a firm called Simpsons, custom packers. Simpsons were down by the Yarra River at the south end of Burnley Street on the corner of Barkly Avenue, Richmond, exactly where the Board of Works planned to build the South Eastern Freeway, later to be called the Monash Freeway. So in 1968 Simpsons had to move, and they bought 40 acres of market garden land at Heatherton Road, South Clayton. The 1960s was a time when big frogs liked to swallow little frogs or even frogs their own size. It did not matter if they were indigestible, or not on their diet.

The company secretary Russell Martin who had been with Simpsons for 11 years remembers the time well. Simpsons started in 1888, making cardboard boxes and cylinders. Their products included bleaches White King, Magic King and Drip Dry King, and their range continued to expand. They formed a holding company called Simalex and took over or merged with a number of companies. They found themselves in the hair business with hair dyes, hair dryers and everything associated with hair. Next there was a

Opening of Clayton factory, 1972. John Wicking and Tom Ramsay with Sir Rohan Delacombe.

firm called Vactric, which specialised in the door-to-door selling of electrical appliances, sewing machines, floor polishers and paint sprayers. Few people behind the doors were interested. Vactric was bleeding with bad debts. The share price of Simalex, which was well over a dollar, came down to 29 cents.

In 1969 Kiwi acquired Simpsons, who had already moved to the 40 acres at South Clayton, and the fit could not have been sweeter. As Russell Martin put it, 'Kiwi bought Simpsons and they bought me too.' Martin finished as finance director for Nicholas Kiwi.[3]

Kiwi spent two years building a modern factory on 4 acres at Clayton, and leased the rest to the Board of Works. This was no ordinary move. Kiwi had 12 factories scattered around Australia, and the plan was to bring them all under one roof. The movement of equipment and complex machinery, to say nothing of staff and families, could only be imagined. Just eight years earlier Kiwi had closed its tin manufacturing factory at Traralgon in Gippsland. Back in 1955 decentralisation seemed a good idea but, just as Kiwi found at Heilbron South Africa, freight costs could be prohibitive. There was a cry of pain from Traralgon. The president of the Develop Traralgon Association Chris

Humphrey said it was just the old story: The lack of real understanding of problems industries face when they go to the country.[3]

The man who had the responsibility of bringing everything under one roof was Malcolm Daubney. Born in Lancashire, he was a mechanical engineer employed by shipbuilders Vickers Armstrong, Barrow-in-Furness for nine years in their engineering design office. He married an Australian girl, Beverley, in 1965, emigrated to Australia and joined Kiwi Australia at Burnley Street, Richmond, Victoria as works engineer.

White King bleach became a household name in Australia.

The big move could only be described as a nightmare. In the official Kiwi directory for 1968 there were 37 different products. There were items one wouldn't expect, like Kiwi Polishing Cloths, Super Lavender Disinfectant, White Eucalypt Disinfectant, Kiwi Bowl Polishes, Clever Mary Paste, Shinoleum Floor Polish, Lane's Emulsion, Miss Jacqueline Shampoo, Kitten Kleen-a-Screen Windscreen Cleaner, and Bon Ami Toilet Cleaner. The integration of the Australian manufacturing operations was further complicated by the fact that all these products had to be continually manufactured during the relocation of the plant to meet sales demands.

Daubney had to bring together factories in Perth, Adelaide, Brisbane, three in Sydney and three more in Melbourne. Two box-making companies, one Melbourne and one in Sydney, remained in their original locations because of their unique manufacturing requirements and proximity to their specialised markets. 'Truckloads of previously unknown and unidentified raw materials arrived at Clayton from interstate operations which they had stored for years,' said Malcolm. 'We had to progressively dispose of thirty-two truckloads. We didn't tell John Wicking, the zone director about that. Better he didn't know. He hated waste.' New plant and new packaging filling equipment came from the United States and England. It was all open and running by October 1970.

Kiwi may have consolidated 37 products at Clayton, but the special triumph from the Simpsons takeover was White King bleach. No longer was it fashionable to have shiny shoes. Sales of Kiwi Shoe Polish were on the decline, but every kitchen in the land needed a bottle of White King, and the day came when returns from White King bleach went way beyond those of Kiwi Shoe Polish.

Fergus Ramsay remembered that White King was not always regarded as the perfect product: 'We used to get letters from people, they just happened to be wearing their best cocktail dress when they opened a bottle of White King. It fizzed and the bleach left white spots all over their most expensive dress. Would Kiwi please send $500 so that she could replace the dress? Another woman complained that fizzing White King sprayed over the bathroom wall and spoiled the lovely wallpaper. We would send a rep around to check whether the complaint was genuine, but usually it was better to compensate rather than have a nasty court case about it.'

They discovered why White King was fizzing. At Clayton they were using water from the Board of Works. The board's pipes were old and rusty and flecks of rust were causing the bleach to fizz.[5]

On the other hand, there were letters from people who were delighted with the product. For example, John Thomas Campbell wrote that he was very pleased with White King. For the past eight years he had been using it to clean his false teeth. White King actually had a sales brochure announcing there were 36 ways of using White King from cleaning false teeth to preserving cut flowers.[6]

By 1 January 1972 everything was going well at Clayton. The Governor Sir Rohan Delacombe had been there to inspect the plant. But even better than that, the name Thomas Meek Ramsay appeared in the New Year's Honours List. He was now Sir Thomas Ramsay, with the order of Commander of St Michael and St George, 'for public service and services to commerce'. Apart from his success with Kiwi he had been president of the Royal Historical Society of Victoria, president of the Chamber of Manufactures and an outstanding benefactor to his old school, Scotch College. He received 170 letters of congratulation, which he put carefully in alphabetical order. They included two from Sir Robert Menzies and two from his former wife Betty Grounds.

THE AUSTRALIAN
Financial Review

7c

Printed by David Syme & Co. Limited, 250 Spencer Street, Melbourne,
for John Fairfax & Sons Limited, Broadway, Sydney.

Friday, July 14, 1972

KIWI FACES TAKEOVER MOVE

There was bad weather ahead for Sir Tom. The annual report for 1971–72 revealed a profit slump of 38 per cent. The group result fell from $1,384,335 to $858,330. The causes were difficult trading conditions in almost every country where Kiwi operated. Profits in Australia were not improved by all the travail involved in consolidating manufacture at Clayton.

With a sagging share price, the question was being asked by finance editors as to when and how much a predatory company would bid for Kiwi. Sir Tom admitted: 'For years many firms have been beating at our door either for a merger or a complete takeover.' Now the names were appearing in the news, and they included Procter & Gamble, American Home Products, S. C. Johnson, Beatrice Australia, Philip Morris and Gillette. Reckitt & Colman denied it was making a bid, but the *National Times* reported that didn't mean it wouldn't happen.[7]A few days later, at the end of July 1972, the Clorox Company of the United States offered $31 million cash for Kiwi International Company Ltd. It was the largest all-cash offer made up to that date in Australia. In effect Clorox was offering $3 a share, when during the year Kiwi shares had been as low as $1.40. Clorox was a former subsidiary of Procter & Gamble. Its chief product was a bleach of the same name. The Melbourne *Age* reported that Kiwi heirs, the Ramsays, the McDougalls and the Wickings, held well over half the capital, and they stood to collect $20 million.[8]

The Kiwi directors recommended that shareholders accept the bid, but what did Sir Tom think? The *Sun News Pictorial* reported that Sir Tom was a sad man. Rex Davis wrote: 'At first it was hard to believe this of a man whose family investment companies stand to make nearly $8 million, but it was soon clear from moistened eyes and pauses in his speech that he meant what he said. "I'm an Australian. I believe we should fight hard against any overseas takeover … Dad started this thing. He died at 42. I've been with the company since 1920. How do you think I feel? I walked round the factory today and was extremely sad." '[9]

Resulting from this interview there was some anonymous hate mail. One shareholder cut out the *Sun News Pictorial* report and scrawled across it: 'This is a sellout of the country. You stop the takeover or you will be shot dead. Shit Ramsay! Traitor of the country!'

Thomas Ramsay receiving his knighthood from Governor-General Sir Paul Hasluck, 1972.

The takeover bid met with a hostile reaction in Federal Parliament. The Opposition Leader Gough Whitlam said: 'Perhaps someone can tell me how selling another part of Australian industry into foreign hands is in Australia's interests, but I doubt if anyone can.'

The Clorox Company eventually withdrew its offer. It had planned to raise $15 million to finance its offer. The US Securities Exchange Commission rejected its share issue.[10]

None of this was good for Kiwi. Profits to 28 February 1975 dropped 69 per cent and Kiwi made history by not paying a dividend.[11] At the annual meeting in February 1975 Sir Tom spoke of the losses made in Europe. Two years earlier Kiwi France had bought a French subsidiary, Purador, which sold deodorants for lavatories. The price was $1 million and there was a $22,000 loss from Purador in the first year, with the result that Kiwi France was showing a deficit of $133,980. On 20 May 1975 Kiwi $1 shares sank to 28 cents. Shareholders could only look back wistfully to the Clorox offer of $3. Just one member of the family, Ian McDougall, jumped in at the first mention of the offer

Wedding of Jean Ramsay to Dugald McDougall, Singapore, 1925

and sold 83,000 shares at $2.60. This created some family tension, reported the *National Times*.[12]

Tom Ramsay did not forgive Ian McDougall for selling his shares. He considered Ian to be one of the family, and thought they should never break ranks. There were three McDougalls, all very different. Their mother was Jean Ramsay, daughter of William Ramsay, the founder of Kiwi. In 1925 she had married the dashing Captain Dugald McDougall, whom she had met when her boat stopped at Singapore; they became engaged three days later. There wasn't much time, as the boat was going on to Colombo. He proposed by writing on the menu at Raffles Hotel, 'Will you marry me?' They married a year later. The captain managed a rubber plantation in Malaya, and a few years later he and Jean moved to London. Tom Ramsay offered him a job in the London office. There they had sons Dugald Ramsay McDougall, born 19 May 1926, William Stewart McDougall, born 2 May 1928, and Ian Duncan McDougall, born 27 June 1931.

All three sons were sent to Australia to board at Geelong Grammar School. Ian was there from 1940 to 1944, just nine when he went to junior school. Dugald, the eldest, left school to join the Royal Air Force, but by the time he did any training the war was virtually over, and it was unlikely he saw action. He joined Kiwi in August 1944 and became responsible for UK technical development and manufacturing plants in West Indies, India and France.

Will McDougall worked for Kiwi almost immediately after he left school. He rose rapidly in the London office. In 1963 he was the UK general manager, and he came out to Australia for the 1963 international conference. He never married and loved parties and entertaining. He finally left England for Australia in 1968. His friend Lee Barr described him as a kindly thoughtful man, the first with a present or a bunch of flowers when anyone was sick. Although living in Melbourne, he was responsible for Europe and Africa. He spent six months of the year travelling through Europe, South America, Africa, even countries like Nigeria, where he said hotels were appalling, with frequent power failures.[13]

Will McDougal, UK general manager and director of Kiwi

Will was a director of Kiwi from 1967 through to the 1980s. In 1983 he retired as a senior executive but continued on the Nicholas Kiwi board until the Consolidated Foods takeover. Not long after this he began to get pains in the wrists. He had blood tests and his

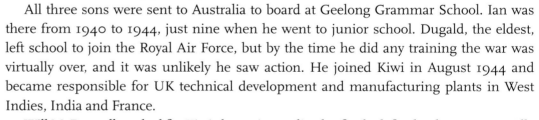

doctor gave the terrible verdict of chronic leukaemia, and he had five years to live. Lee Barr said on that very day he was due to lunch with friends. Unfazed, he carried on as before. For his 70th birthday he invited 13 of his friends for a grand celebration on Hayman Island near Queensland's Barrier Reef. Will footed the bill for all the food and accommodation. The food and wine were splendid, with plenty of crayfish and champagne. Will thought it unlucky that they were a group of 13, so he included a 14th member, a teddy bear dressed in a dinner jacket. Will died two years later on 6 October 1999.

Ian was the youngest of the McDougall brothers. After he left Geelong Grammar School he read Scottish Law and English at Cambridge and went into advertising. In 1955 Tom Ramsay found him a job in marketing for Kiwi. He worked in the Paris office, visiting the factory at Rouen one day a week. In Paris he met Moreli McLaren, whom he later married. It was an interesting liaison: Moreli's father was a director of Reckitt & Colman, Kiwi's arch rival in the shoe polish business. Reckitt & Colman made Cherry Blossom and Meltonian shoe polish in England and Nugget in other parts of the world, including Australia. 'Yes, I was a Nugget girl and I had a huge loyalty to Cherry Blossom', said Moreli.

After Paris the McDougalls went to Singapore, where Ian worked with Lloyd Zampatti. They had four boys: Dugald and Torquil were born in Singapore, and Hamish and Callum in London. Ian returned to London in 1961 to be marketing manager. In 1970 he became general manager and in April 1973, as Moreli put it, 'He was given the push.' Tom Ramsay wrote in his notes: 'Ian McDougall is leaving of his own accord. He is taking it well.'[14]

'Own accord' was hardly the way the McDougalls saw it. He was sacked. Moreli said, 'It was unbelievable the way it happened. Ian was very bitter. You would think he had done something absolutely awful when he hadn't done anything at all.' Ian had two years without a job, and then he found one with Devon County Council and later with Midlands County Council.

John Wicking with Anthony Eden, later British Prime Minister, Egypt, 1941

The dismissal, if one could call it that, caused a rift in the family. Moreli believes that Will was the one who had to break the news to Ian that his service with Kiwi was no longer required. Ian and Will did not speak to each other for 10 years. Yet Will was kind hearted and always remembered to get in touch with his nephews on their birthdays and at Christmas. Moreli said, 'The rift all ended when Tessa got married.' In 1986 Dugald's daughter Tessa married in Majorca, where her parents had chosen to retire. The brothers and their families gathered there for the occasion. Moreli said, 'It was really good. We decided this non-speaking was ridiculous. Life was too short and we were all great friends again.'[15] (Ian McDougall died on Good Friday 9 April 1993.)

Was Ian sacked because he sold shares during the Clorox bid? Perhaps not. More likely it was the serious state of Kiwi finances. There had been bad reports from both the UK office and from France. 1975 was the year in which Kiwi did not pay a dividend, so the board was looking for a new start. Ian was one of the casualties. Both Bill Ramsay and John Wicking went to London to see what could be done.

There were some radical changes. Michael Burnett returned from South Africa in 1972 to become general manager of the Australian operations. J. W. (Bill) Ramsay, managing director, was soon to be pushed aside to be joint managing director together with John Oswald Wicking.

Wicking was an imposing man 193 centimetres (6 feet 3 inches) tall. He had married Janet Tompson, the only daughter of Walter Tompson, the accountant, and Madge, the famous early pioneer automobile driver of 'Bayonet', and sister of the Kiwi founder William Ramsay.

The Wickings had a large property, 'Ponkeen', at Ruffey near Euroa, some 200 kilometres north of Melbourne. In 1965 Tom Ramsay drove up there and invited him to become a director of Kiwi. Wicking was educated at Scotch College, studied accountancy, and at the outbreak of war was the 60th volunteer from Victoria to join the AIF (Australian Imperial Force). He was a sergeant by the time he was 19, and he went to Egypt and Libya as a lieutenant with the 2/7th battalion of the 6th Division. His war included being torpedoed and bombed. He was fighting for the defence of Crete when parachuting

John Wicking and Janet Tompson,
Melbourne, 1946

Germans invaded. He told a story about how they took refuge in the mountains. The German bombers came over and he screamed to his men, 'Don't go down that well, get behind it.' Some of the men did go down the well and they were all killed. Wicking survived but was captured and taken to Germany. He attempted to escape three times, and on each occasion he was put into solitary confinement for long periods.

The war ended in Germany when General George Patton with his pearl-handled revolvers rode into the Stalag prison camp aboard a Sherman tank. Following him was a truck with a donut kitchen manned by girls who looked like Hollywood starlets. The half-starved prisoners of war looked on amazed. Wicking said Patton announced: 'Men you are free. You can do what you like.'

Wicking found his way back to England and returned to Melbourne. In the meantime his fiancée Janet Tompson had spent years at home not knowing whether he was alive or dead. As soon as Wicking got out of the army in 1946 they married. After all of his traumatic experiences, the thought of sitting behind a desk as an accountant was too dreadful to contemplate. He spent the next 19 years turning the 2,000 acres of 'Ponkeen' into a model farm.

From 1969 Wicking was the Australian zone director for Kiwi. He had a reputation for being tough but fair. Malcolm Daubney said: 'He never liked surprises or hearing bad news second hand. If there was anything going wrong you had to tell John. For five minutes he would call you all the names under the sun then he would say, "Okay, how are we going to fix it and he would never mention it again." ' Michael Burnett said one of his favourite phrases was: 'I don't want to find any black snakes under rocks, okay?'[16]

Wicking had a special technique when visiting factories. First he would arrive early before the office opened and would head for the waste bins. He always wanted to see what was being thrown away. He liked to wander round and talk to the workers, chat to the girls, and with his charming manner he would find out what was going on. By the time he spoke to the managers they were surprised at how much he knew.

In October 1974 Sir Tom Ramsay wrote to Bill Ramsay, who was managing director of Kiwi in London. The letter was marked 'Confidential'. He said: 'I am certain that you are aware of the seriousness of the present position of the company, and the important part that the United States and France has to play in the overall situation of the company. It appears to us that the position has become even more serious and alarming in the last two months.'

Sir Tom referred to the loss during the previous year of $20,646, and he said the outflow of funds was serious. He added the rider that the poor results didn't just apply to the UK and France, but to the whole organisation.[17]

Bill Ramsay replied that he was well aware that trading conditions were serious. He made two suggestions: either merging with another company in the UK or integrating the manufacturing operations of Britain and France.[18]

Sir Tom decided now was the time for some drastic action. He sent John Wicking and the company secretary, Russell Martin, to look at the operations in both England and

France. Wicking had only been in London for a few days when he sent back some caustic comments about conditions in Britain. He had a particular distaste for the then Labour prime minister, Harold Wilson.

> Under the present Government there appears no hope for industry. The lethargic attitude of the English and their lack of fight to prevent socialisation. Strikes and lack of production inevitably lead to a lower standard of living. I believe there is little hope for this country. I am sure the pound will be devalued over and over again. I feel that the Conservative party will not be able to restore the harm done by the Labour party even if they win the next election.[19]

In 1965 Jan-Willem Taminiau left Holland for England and found a job in the marketing department at Heinz. Two years later in London, when reading the *Daily Telegraph*, he noticed Kiwi was looking for an overseas sales manager. He remembers a meeting in London with the sales manager, Eric Willoughby, and the local managing director, Will McDougall, which lasted from 6 p.m. to 9 p.m. 'I finished with half a bottle of Campari in my stomach. To my surprise, a week later I got an invitation for a final interview and dinner with Will. No doubt he wanted to check whether I ate with a fork and knife. I got the job.'

In 1971 Kiwi sent Taminiau to Nairobi as general manager for East Africa, covering Ethiopia, Kenya, Tanzania and Uganda. There was little trade to be had in Tanzania, which was under the influence of the Chinese. The Chinese had copied Kiwi polish, and were exporting it to the Tanzanians. Uganda was suffering under the dictator Idi Amin, and it was difficult getting money out of there. Taminiau actually met Idi Amin at the Kampala Club. His impression? 'Large and fat.' However, Kiwi sold well in Kenya. 'Africans,' he said, 'like their shoes. They polish them in the morning and they polish them again at night and perhaps even again at lunchtime. In France they polish them once a year.'

Taminiau had been in Nairobi two and a half years when he received a telephone call from Bill Ramsay. There was a new job waiting for him. He was to fly immediately to Paris. The following week at the famous Paris Hotel de Carillon, he conferred with Will McDougall from London and John Wicking, now zone director for Europe. Taminiau was to become the general manager for France. His wife Ineke was listening in to the conversation on another telephone. She said, 'No! Don't accept it.' She thought they were too happy in Nairobi. The power of Kiwi prevailed.

The original tin sent to London in 1927. The tin is attached to a framed cartoon from the *Post*, May 1972, with the caption, 'Ah Kiwi 1927. That was a very good year!' Cartoon by Douglas Tainsch

Taminiau and Ineke had barely settled at Rouen when it became clear that John Wicking wanted to close down the factory and shift everything to Ealing in London. PA Management Consultants had made a study confirming this was the economic thing to do. It was understandable why Kiwi wanted Ealing to be the headquarters for European production. The Ramsay family had created history by starting their overseas production there in England 63 years ago.

Taminiau noted there had been a coal miners' strike in England. In Wales alone, 135 pits closed, plus 35 collieries and 85 private mines. The miners had demanded a 45 per cent pay increase. The effect was disastrous. The British Government had to introduce a three-day working week to save electricity. The strike lasted until the end of the month. The miners finished up the highest paid union workers in Britain and were now feeling their power. In late 1973 they voted to strike once more. Prime Minister Edward Heath refused to compromise. He declared a state of emergency, and once again Britain had a three-day working week. The strike was resolved after an election on 28 February when Harold Wilson's Labour Government took over.

Taminiau said the PA consultants had another look at the situation and decided now it was more profitable to close down the Ealing factory and move production to France.[20]

John Wicking had been influenced by what he saw as a dismal future for Britain, and there were other factors. French regulations on closing companies and retirement of staff were so stringent it made economic sense to concentrate manufacturing at Rouen in France.

Late in 1975 the Kiwi factory at Bramwill Road, Hangar Lane, Ealing, London W5 went up for sale. The brochure announced that the factory was 100,850 square feet on 3.4 acres, brick walls with asbestos roof sheeting, all valued at £575,000. Vacant possession available early 1976.

The UK did not have exclusive rights to strikes. On 5 January 1979 the workers in the Kiwi factory at Rouen started a strike that lasted eight weeks. The year started with savagely cold weather. On 3 January it was so cold it was impossible to heat the factory satisfactorily, so the management decided to send the workers home and still compensate them for the day lost. The next day, according to Taminiau, it was possible to get the temperature to between 14 and 16 degrees Celsius. It was still too cold to work, so once again the factory closed, this time on union orders. It was Friday, and everyone returned to work on Monday. Kiwi refused to pay for Friday's walkout, declaring the workers had been on strike. So the battle was on, everything came to a halt and union stewards also stopped the non-strikers from working.

As with all strikes, simple moves become more complicated. It wasn't about the cold weather anymore; the union wanted an immediate 10 per cent increase in salaries, an increase in the company's contribution to the Works Committee (1 per cent of total salaries), an increase in holiday pay, better working conditions, and payment for all days lost in the strike.

The strike became increasingly bitter. Crowds of up to 800 gathered outside the gates, fighting with the police. The Communist Party took up the union cause. On 20 February the unions and the Communist Party organised a demonstration in front of the local prefecture. There were 600 present, and the protest became so violent that the police had to use tear gas grenades. The next day the communists organised another demonstration, and the Electricity Union cut off all electricity for three hours. The union leader then telephoned Taminiau and threatened to cut off electricity for the whole area, bringing the docks to a standstill and stopping the trains from Paris.

Taminiau was determined to reject all the union claims, but in the end they did make a small gesture. They would increase the year-end bonus from 1,500 francs to 1,900 francs, but on no condition would they increase salaries or pay for the days lost. The unions accepted the Kiwi proposal and returned to work. Taminiau claimed the company didn't actually lose anything by the strike. They kept the production lines working by using all their executives in the factory, all secretaries, non-union members, plus non-strikers.[21]

Back in Australia other problems arose. When Bob Shatterley president of Clorox, visited Melbourne in 1972 he made a takeover offer. Malcolm Daubney was at the office in Clayton when Shatterley expressed his concern about the future profitability of Kiwi, particularly Kiwi Australia. John Wicking offered to bet Shatterley $50,000 that Kiwi Australia would be in the black the following year. This was too much money; the bet never took place. Obviously Wicking knew what he was about because the turnaround was extraordinary. On 24 March 1976 the *Financial Review* reported that after four years of struggling Kiwi International was heading for its most profitable year ever. The group announced a net profit of £827,326 for the half year. That was 239 per cent higher than the previous profit, and a dramatic upturn in Kiwi's fortunes. The company had been paying no dividend at all, but now the dividend would be 4 cents a share.

Trevor Sykes of the *Financial Review* claimed the main reason for the improvement seemed to be that Kiwi had straightened out its problems in Europe. If only he had a found a taker, John Wicking would have won his bet.[22]

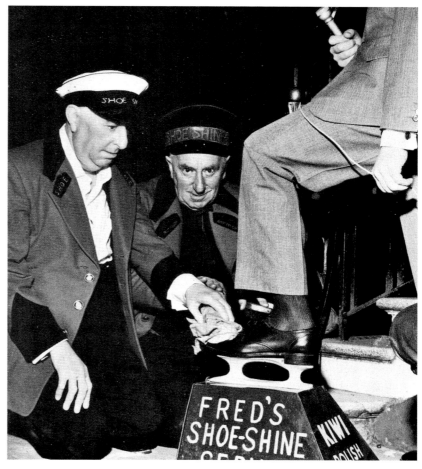

Shoeshine man Fred (centre) helps his wax companion shine a reporter's shoes, at Madamme Tussauds, *c.* 1972

13

TOM RAMSAY RETIRES – KIWI MERGES

**M**en who are powerful often hate the idea of retirement. They think no one else can do the job. Maybe the archbishops of the Anglican Church inspired Tom Ramsay. Unlike the popes in Rome, they retire at 72. This was Tom Ramsay's age when he announced his retirement at the Kiwi annual meeting in Clayton on 16 January 1979. When he gave his last company speech he told board members he would step down at the annual general meeting in January 1980.[1] The new chairman and managing director would be John Wicking. The newspapers on 12 January published pictures of Sir Tom in an unlikely pose busy cleaning his shoes. In one picture, there he was in his office down on one knee, coat off, wearing an immaculate striped shirt with gold cuff links, polishing his shoes with a large brush. With Kiwi polish, of course.[2]

According to his daughter Anne, he was a disciplinarian. When heading for school one's shoes had to be perfect. In their house at Struan Street, Toorak there was carpet down the stairs from the first floor. That carpet was lovely for Anne: she could use it to polish her shoes all the way up.[3]

A farewell dinner was held for Tom at Maxim's restaurant in South Yarra. Maxim's was one of Melbourne's top restaurants, and the 40 guests included most of the family. Kiwi director Malcolm Daubney said, 'We racked our brains over what we could give him. What do you give a rich man who has everything.' Finally they settled on the Coat of Arms, the Royal Warrant to Kiwi from King George VI. They had it freshly painted and beautifully mounted on fine timber. Tom was not impressed. He made his feelings clear to John Wicking. Perhaps he expected something grander. A full-sized billiard table perhaps? Or maybe a painting by the highly prized Australian Impressionists Tom Roberts or Arthur Streeton?[4]

•   •   •

Tom Ramsay was never lavish with salaries, but he did look after his staff. Senior executives travelled first class, and they lived well when they were posted to far-off destinations like Africa, the Middle East or North America. But it did not pay to question his authority. Larry Emley was an example. Larry was the man Tom met on a plane in 1948 while he was flying across the United States. He hired him to start Kiwi's operations in Philadelphia.

Seeing that he was in the US, he had the appropriate title, 'President'. He tended to live like one, and he was a success. Sales of Kiwi products in the US far outshone those in Europe and anywhere else in the world. Because of this, Larry was under pressure from his executives for salary increases and better pensions. He telephoned Ramsay in Melbourne making demands to him and the Kiwi board. We do not know what Emley actually said, but Tom Ramsay was furious.

On 29 May 1969 Ramsay sent this cable to Emley: 'Your telephone conversation this morning deeply resented. Explanation or tender your resignation.' In another cable he said: 'Cannot accept such managerial insolence to the Board.'[5]

Emley cabled back: 'Accept my immediate resignation.'

The reply to this on the same day, 29 May, sounded like the coup de grace: 'Under circumstances power of attorney held by you on behalf of the company hereby revoked.'

Then there was another cable from Emley. This time direct to Tom's house at Airlie Street, South Yarra. 'I am shocked and amazed at your reaction. Insolence never intended. The whole matter has got to be a misunderstanding or breakdown in communication.'

The next day Larry Emley was most contrite: 'In the name of my father and mother I apologise totally for my words. Would like to stay on to see the job through.' Larry did actually stay in the job, but relations with Tom Ramsay were never quite the same. There was an event that undoubtedly sped Larry's retirement. Michael Burnett, who became president of Kiwi USA in 1977, said Larry occupied Kiwi's house, which was really a 30-acre farm complete with stables near Pottstown. Larry belonged to a group known as the Pickering Hunt, and he used to ride with them most Thursdays in the summer. It was an old-fashioned hunt: horses, jumping fences, red jackets, the full bit. Whenever Tom visited Pottstown, Larry would organise a cocktail party. On this particular night one of the guests said to Larry in Tom's presence, 'Larry we missed you today at the hunt. Where were you?' It was common knowledge that Thursday was Larry's day for the hunt, and Jay Smith, his vice-president sales often took Friday off in the summer to play golf.[6]

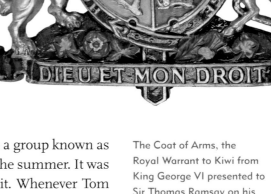

The Coat of Arms, the Royal Warrant to Kiwi from King George VI presented to Sir Thomas Ramsay on his retirement, 1980

•   •   •

It is very likely that Tom knew about this ahead of time. Larry was eased out or 'retired' at the end of June 1974. There was a testimonial dinner for him on 8 June and D. F. Wood his successor presented him with a boomerang. Tom sent a letter of apology regretting his inability to be present at the retirement party.[7]

Lady Mimi Ramsay

Tom spent nearly all 1979 touring Kiwi outposts around the world. He went to South Africa, Kenya, Pakistan, Thailand, Malaysia, Singapore, Indonesia, Fiji, USA, UK and France. Everywhere there were farewell dinners. In Fiji the staff presented him with a curious clock shaped like the shell of a turtle. In Singapore he and his wife Mimi received a watercolour painting of the House of Parliament in Singapore.

Kiwi produced a special farewell booklet with a smiling Sir Tom on the front cover, and inside were the words: 'Over the 50 years that Sir Tom Ramsay has been with Kiwi our financial picture has become rosier every year.'

'When I started with the company,' recalled Sir Tom, 'Our financial statements were measured in hundreds. Today we are looking at millions. Back in 1938 I spent three solid hours getting a first order out of the New York shoe people. Hard talking, hard selling. But I got the order and I was immensely pleased with myself. The order was for three and half gross of shoe polish.'

According to Malcolm Daubney there was no doubt he was the driving force in the company and his ego was huge. Industrial chemist Ivan McLaws remembers back to the 1950s: 'In the mornings at Burnley Road he would arrive in the car park out the back and he would make a point of walking right through the factory. In the English style, he called everyone by his or her surname. No Christian names. The then factory manager was Laurie Charters, a big man, a lovely man, but when Tom Ramsay saw something that upset him, he would say: "Charters, you fool," and dress him down in front of everybody, that was Tom. But when you got to know Tom over the years he proved to be a very nice man.'[8]

His daughter Anne confirms that he was very generous: 'Dad was pretty strict with us. He was also stern when it came to dinner time, and I was pretty much the only one at home because the boys were at boarding school. At dinner time unless you talked about things Dad wanted to talk about he wouldn't listen. He had to hold the floor all the time. If you didn't agree with him there was hell to pay.'

He also had a sense of fun, and he would stagger his children by doing strange and funny things. Anne recounted: 'We had been to Fiji quite a few times and he had an interesting collection like a kava bowl and a grass skirt and woven place mats. One day he got into the Irish whiskey and he dressed in a grass skirt. Then he put a place mat around his head like a headdress and we had this kava ceremony. I don't know what he put into the kava but it was very alcoholic and looked like mud. We had a fireplace, and behind that was the kitchen and it was open to the sitting room. Dad went round and round shouting 'Wallah! Wallah!' He used to enjoy his alcohol, sometimes a bit too much. In the early days at Mount Macedon there used to be get-togethers with the locals. There were times when Dad and Mum dressed in maids and butlers outfits. He liked dressing up.'[9]

Tom's son Dougal agreed that his father had a great sense of fun: 'He had a naughty sense of humour and he loved telling jokes. His repertoire was huge, and that supply of jokes seemed endless. Yet sometimes he had a fearsome temper. If Tom came home from the office he would retire to his library and have a few martinis, his favourite drink ... He used to start the day with a Fernet Branca, which was a deadly sort of aperitif.

Sir Thomas Ramsay by William Dargie, 1979

He had a slug of that before he went to the office.' One expert on the drink wrote: 'The easiest way to describe the taste of Ferna Branca, it's kind of like a hit in the nose. Your brain hurts, your eyes sting and water. You cough a bit. Then as soon as it begins a warm wave of relief washes over and you are left baptised and golf ball eyed awake.'

In his retirement Tom sat up night after night cataloguing his papers. He had a genuine interest in Australian history and he was the darling of the antiquarian bookshops. Whenever anything valuable arrived, the bookshop would immediately contact him. He left a pile of bound receipts and appeared to buy a book almost every day. One wonders how he ever managed to read them, but he did have a remarkable collection. In 1967 he gave an address to the Friends of the Baillieu Library at Melbourne University. He told the 'Friends' that his collection even then had grown so large he had to divide it into sections and then sub-sections, covering biography, anthropology, natural history, photography, art, pictorial, manuscripts, education, politics, magazines, reference, and voyages by explorers.[10]

Under 'Voyages' he had *The Principal Navigations, Voyages and Discoveries of the English Nation Made by Sea and Land, Richard Hakluyt, 1589*, written in Latin and Old English. He also owned Sir Richard Hawkins' vellum bound copy of *Voyage into the South Seas*, published in 1622. William Bligh fascinated him. His daughter Anne said he went off to Norfolk Island on his researches one time, and Mimi wondered when he was going to come back. His library contained 24 books on Captain Bligh and Norfolk Island, including one written by Bligh himself in 1790. He pronounced to the Friends of the Baillieu Library: 'I defend Bligh as one of our more colourful characters, carefully and thoroughly trained by notable captains such as James Cook. I was much amused in reading a review of a book entitled *Who Caused the Mutiny on the Bounty?* by H. E. Maude. The reviewer advanced the theory that the mutineer Christian, torn away from a successful love affair and thrust into the celibacy of naval life, developed a homosexual attraction towards Captain Bligh.' Tom Ramsay added that it would have been interesting to hear William Bligh's language when he was told about that one.

Ramsay sold one of his books, Samwell's *Narrative of the Death of Captain Cook*, for $22,500. The book dealer, Derek McDonnell of Woollahra, Sydney was shocked by the price. He said it was really only a pamphlet and this represented $592 a page.[11] Ramsay left most of his huge collection to his old school, Scotch College in Melbourne.

Much of his correspondence in his retirement was taken up with requests for money. He was very generous. He nearly always said 'Yes', and his gifts were mostly amounts of $5,000 or $10,000. In 1986, for example, he gave away well over $100,000. There was $10,000 for State Relief, $10,000 for the Royal Historical Society, $10,000 for the Flying Doctor Service, $5,000 for the Baker Institute, $10,000 for Anti Cancer and $10,000 for the Victorian State Library. In 1985 he gave $200,000 to the Museum of Victoria. Every year since, the museum (now Museum Victoria) has granted a fellowship entitled the Thomas Ramsay Science and Humanities Fellowship. It was a rare gift. Not many philanthropists think of the humanities when they are handing out money.

Tom Ramsay retires with his Kiwi polish kit and the famous Kiwi Black polish. Photo from the *Sun*, 1980.

John and Janet
Wicking, c. 1982

· · ·

John Wicking was the first non-Ramsay to run Kiwi. Described as a tough man in business, he was tall and physically imposing, with an undeniable presence. Like Tom Ramsay, he had to command, and he was probably the only man who could stand up to Tom. He liked the peace of his cattle property 'Ponkeen' near Euroa in Victoria. His wife Janet, the only child of Walter and Madge Tompson, niece of the founder William Ramsay, was a significant shareholder in Kiwi at the time. There was little need for John Wicking to leave the comfort of 'Ponkeen', but Tom Ramsay at once saw that John Wicking was a leader and a man with talent. Starting in 1964, Wicking came to Kiwi two days a week, three days a week, then ultimately full-time, rising to director, zone director and then managing director.

· · ·

When John and Janet bought 'Ponkeen' the property was in a poor state. They employed six Italians who had recently migrated to Australia. They could speak little English and were illiterate. They worked hard clearing land, building fences and they slept in the shearing quarters. Liz Cooper, daughter of Frank Newman, John Wicking's best friend, said at night they would sing wonderful songs. Legend has it that John Wicking noticed that one of the Italians always turned up late and disappeared early. Was he 'swinging the lead?' 'No,' said the Italian, 'I Cookie.' ('I am the cook.'). The name Cookie stuck, but his real name was Giuseppe Saglietti. He came to Australia in 1948 from Alba in the Piedmont region of Italy, one of 13 brothers and sisters.

Wicking taught Cookie English and they became good friends – so much so, there was a complete trust between the two men. Wicking made Cookie the manager of 'Ponkeen', making it possible for him to work full-time for Kiwi. In 1997 after Janet's death, Wicking decided to sell the farm to Cookie for $1. There had to be a witness, and Liz Cooper was in the kitchen at 'Ponkeen' when Cookie handed over his $1 payment for a property of 2,000 acres that was worth millions. The Wickings had no children and John said he could never repay Cookie for everything he had done.[12]

Cookie's son Peter Saglietti said John Wicking continued to love 'Ponkeen'. He could pick almost to a minute when John and Janet would arrive every Friday afternoon then leave again on Sunday.

.   .   .

For more than a decade before he became managing director there had been rumours that Kiwi and Nicholas Aspro would one day merge. The companies were so similar. George Nicholas was a chemist, and until 1914 all aspirin came from Germany made by the giant Bayer Company. Bayer was careful with its patents all over the world. When war broke out Germany could no longer export to enemy countries. So George Nicholas in Melbourne, using kitchen utensils borrowed from his wife, paraffin tins and primitive apparatus, set about making his own aspirin. He had some success, but the result was smelly and impure. Then another chemist, Henry Woolf Shmith, walked into his shop, and after many experiments they produced aspirin of extraordinary purity. On 12 June 1915 they applied for the right to use the trade name Aspirin, and by 17 September they had the blessing of the Federal Attorney General, W. M. Hughes. Henry Woolf Shmith, seeing the mounting costs of marketing the product, sold out to the brothers George and Alfred Nicholas, which is possibly one of the most unfortunate financial decisions one person ever made in Australia.

The Federal Government went back on its decision to allow the Nicholas Brothers to use the word 'aspirin', so in 1917 they invented a brand of their own: Aspro. George Nicholas explained that 'As' were the last two letters of Nicholas and 'pro' was for product. To reduce a remarkable history into a few words, Nicholas Aspro, like Kiwi, spread around the world, making splendid fortunes for members of the Nicholas family.[13]

Forceful men with strong egos ran the two companies. Maurice Nicholas was the chairman of Nicholas Aspro. He was the son of Alfred Nicholas, brother of George, the founder. Sir Tom Ramsay, son of the founder William Ramsay, ran Kiwi. Tom had his beloved weekend retreat 'Hascombe', across the road from another historic Nicholas house 'Alton' in Mount Macedon. Maurice had his property 'Strathalbyn' at Sassafras, next door to 'Burnham Beeches', which George Nicholas built at the end of the 1920s and early 1930s. It had a theatrette with 'talkies', an electric pipe organ, orchid houses, gardens with artificial waterfalls, and a dairy with prize dairy cows, all set in 50 acres. It was art deco in design, with images of koalas and possums on the outside. Some said it

Maurice Nicholas, Chairman of Nicholas Aspro

looked like an ocean liner. Maurice's house was a smaller version next door, designed by the same architect, Harry Norris.

Maurice and Tom were great friends. Both had been divorced and went on to successful second marriages. Maurice married Phyllis Mein in 1938, daughter of a well-known grazier. They were divorced in 1953. On a visit to Sweden he met the beautiful Margareta Ahlin, and they were married in Stockholm soon after Maurice's divorce. Tom, after his divorce from Betty in 1941, married his beloved Mimi. Mimi was born in Rangoon, where her father J. W. Richardson had been a timber merchant.

So these men had much in common. They were often at each other's houses and they travelled overseas together. Tom's daughter Anne remembers the time when Maurice and Tom stayed at the same hotel in Bray, England. They had no adjoining door between their two rooms, so they made a hole in the wall. They were not popular with the management. Since they were such friends, many wondered why it took so long for these two great Australian companies to join forces.

Tony Nicholas, Maurice's elder son, claimed that their personalities were too strong. They couldn't decide who would be chairman. 'The story goes,' said Tony, 'they met and one said, "I'll be chairman." "No," said the other, "I'll be chairman." And that was the end of that.'[14]

Nothing could happen until these two men were no longer in power. Maurice died in 1976 and Tom stepped down in January 1980. Now there was an interesting situation. Lindsay Cuming was chairman and chief executive officer of Nicholas and John Wicking was chairman and chief executive officer of Kiwi. This was the first time in the history of both companies that a member of the family had not been in charge. Cuming had spent two years with the law firm Hedderwick Fookes & Alston, but he realised the legal world was not for him so he joined Nicholas. He had an illustrious career with Nicholas in Europe and North America, and rose to be president of Nicholas International in 1972. He took over from Maurice as chairman in 1976.

In late 1981 Cuming had raised the idea with the Nicholas Board of getting together with Kiwi with the aim of creating a larger and stronger company, being able to defend itself against any potential takeover. The Nicholas Board gave Cuming approval to contact John Wicking.

Cuming rang Wicking in March 1982 suggesting that they have lunch together, and at Wicking's suggestion they met at Le Gaulois Restaurant in Syndal, an outer Melbourne suburb, where they were unlikely to be seen together.

The outcome of the luncheon was that Lindsay and John agreed that if any business union eventuated it had to be a genuine merger, and that they would discuss the matter with their respective boards on this basis for approval to proceed further. The rest is history.

A meeting between Wicking and Cuming took place in June 1982. Recommendations were then put to the boards of Nicholas and Kiwi, and were largely accepted. The big news of the merger was in all the newspapers on 16 September. 1982 Chanticleer in the

Financial Review stated it made such blinding sense he couldn't understand why it had taken so long.

Both Nicholas and Kiwi agreed to appoint David Haynes of Tricontinental Bank to facilitate the merger process.

John Wicking was pleased with his results. The Nicholas Kiwi Group for the first full year ending 30 June 1983 showed an operating profit of $21,653,000 (up 39 per cent on the previous year) on sales of $311,518,000 (up 16 per cent).[15] Most mergers are in fact takeovers. But in this case, a merger took place legally, with neither company buying out the other. It was designed and put together as a genuine merger.

The *Financial Australian* claimed Danny Hill, a Perth mining entrepreneur, had spurred it all on. Hill had been busy buying Nicholas shares, and now had an 8 per cent interest in the company. This wasn't true, because all the machinery for the merger was in place before Danny Hill made his report. Tony Nicholas, who made his own assessment for Nicholas shareholders, said it was very likely that the merger of the two companies made it more attractive to overseas companies.[16]

Maurice Nicholas, Mimi Ramsay, Phil Nicholas, Tom Ramsay, Marge and Sam Pearce – ready to go to the races

The deal was that Kiwi shareholders would receive five shares in Nicholas Kiwi Ltd plus 60 cents for every four Kiwi shares held. Kiwi shares on 16 September closed at $1.75 and Nicholas at $1.60. Chanticleer claimed that the Ramsay family controlled close to 50 per cent of the shares in Kiwi and the Nicholas family had about the same in their company. In their report Tricontinental listed the owners of the 8,121,501 Nicholas shares. It was difficult to pick out all the Nicholas family shareholders because many of them were listed under the names of private companies. However, two were interesting: Mr Krov N. Menuhin (France) 50,000 shares and Mrs Zamira Benthall (UK) 30,000 shares. Marston M. Nicholas appeared on the list with just 500 shares

In March 1938, after a concert at the Royal Albert Hall, the Australian conductor Bernard Heinze had introduced brother and sister Yehudi and Hephzibah Menuhin to brother and sister Lindsay and Nola Nicholas, children of the Aspro founder George Nicholas. Yehudi, the internationally acclaimed violinist, aged 21, married Nola, and Hephzibah, a brilliant pianist with an international reputation, aged 17, married Lindsay Nicholas. Neither marriage lasted. Hephzibah lived with Nicholas on his grazing property in the Western District of Victoria for 13 years. They had two sons, Kronrad and Marston, before they divorced. Yehudi had two children with Nola, Krov and Zamira, the exotic names on the share list.

The merged company had 47 factories around the world and was selling in 170 countries. According to Lindsay Cuming Nicholas Kiwi had become a significant Australian company now being number 17 on the Melbourne Stock Exchange. Nicholas was strong in Australia, UK, France, across Europe and Indonesia. Kiwi was strong in Australia, UK, North America, Africa and Asia.[17]

The squabbling between Tom Ramsay and Maurice Nicholas as to who should become chairman was resolved with the appointment of Lindsay Cuming as managing director of Nicholas Kiwi Ltd and John Wicking as chairman. But within a year the first annual report of Nicholas Kiwi already gave John Wicking the title 'Chairman and Chief Executive'. Lindsay Cuming said: 'John and I didn't really hit it off when we sat down together. As chairman he was also executive chairman. While everybody said the merger should have happened a long time ago, I was never sure our culture as companies was all that compatible. We had our pharmaceutical products and consumer divisions as well. We operated on much larger margins ... We had different ideas on how the company should develop.'[18]

Lindsay Cuming stayed on for another year as a director, but he was keen to retire, to live with less stress, and many companies in the city of Melbourne were eager to have him on their boards. The directors listed in the 1983 Nicholas–Kiwi annual report were: J. O. Wicking AM, Chairman and Chief Executive; H. J. Nicholas OBE, Deputy Chairman; A. M. Nicholas, M. J. Armstrong, C. M. Beddow, A. D. Lapthorne and S. D. M. Wallis, all formerly Nicholas; and W. S. McDougall, R. S. Martin, and W. V. Reid OBE, all from Kiwi. Three former directors of Kiwi had gone to important posts overseas. Malcolm Daubney was now vice-president Asia, Michael Burnett was vice-president Americas, and Jan-Willem Taminiau was vice-president Europe.[19]

The difference in the culture of the two organisations, Nicholas and Kiwi, was fascinating. Nicholas always paid executives and employees extremely well. Nicholas had good superannuation, and the Nicholas family enjoyed great benefits. Kiwi on the other hand was tight-fisted, working on narrow margins, and most wary of any pennies that went astray. In 1972–73, when Kiwi Australia was operating at almost a loss, John Wicking, zone director and acting general manager, refused to use a company car. He always drove his privately owned car, which at the time was a Mercedes Benz. Then, as a cost cutting measure, he sold his Mercedes and bought a humble Toyota Corolla, and senior executives had to downsize their cars accordingly. The joke around Kiwi was: 'Soon we will have to ride motorbikes.'

Following the merger with Nicholas Aspro the contrast became almost absurd. Hilton Nicholas had a chauffeur-driven Rolls-Royce, which was owned by the company. According to John Wicking, now chairman and chief executive, this wouldn't do. He suggested that Hilton buy the Rolls and take on the chauffeur at his own expense. This he did not do.

The Ash Wednesday bushfires on 16 February 1983 were traumatic for the Ramsays. On this day 47 people lost their lives in Victoria and 28 in South Australia. There were

3,700 buildings destroyed, and 3,700 sheep and 18,000 cattle burned. Most of Mount Macedon was razed. Six people died in the area and 234 houses went up in flames. The fire approached Macedon through the Wombat State Forest, defoliating 80 per cent of the bush in its path. The fire travelled 45 kilometres from the Calder Highway to the summit of Mount Macedon in 15 minutes.

By extraordinary good luck, two mansions escaped destruction: Tom Ramsay's 'Hascombe', and 'Alton', the property of the Nicholas family, just across the road from each other. Built by Sir George Vernon in 1875, 'Alton' was bought by George Nicholas for his family in 1928. The original single-storey house, described as Gothic Revival became double storey, and it had 28 acres of garden.

On Ash Wednesday Tom and Mimi Ramsay were in Melbourne. Their son Dougal was at his house in Kyneton. At first light the next morning, he decided to check on 'Hascombe'. Trees were down along the way, but he knew the back roads. Incredibly 'Alton' and 'Hascombe' were still standing. A fireball had gone right across the top of them. Dougal said that when he arrived a hedge beside the house was burning. He put that out along with other spot fires.

Hilton Nicholas, son of George, had been a pilot with the RAAF during World War II. He flew a light aircraft over 'Alton' the same morning. He said he could see the manager on the roof putting out fires. Dougal waved to Hilton up above.

Dougal said 'Hascombe' lost many trees and valuable shrubs in the fire, but Tom and Mimi were particularly distressed at the horrific death in the fires of Jane Fraser, whose husband Doug was a master at Geelong Grammar School and a particular friend of Tom's. Their son Mike worked for Kiwi in Singapore in the 1970s.

The fire destroyed two churches, the Church of the Good Shepherd at Upper Macedon and Holy Trinity at Lower Macedon. They were both Anglican churches and their congregations decided to combine in building one church midway between the remains of the former buildings. They called the new church the Church of the Resurrection. Tom Ramsay started the building fund with a gift of $10,000, then served for two years on the fundraising committee.

Mimi Ramsay made a donation for brochures and handouts. She decorated a brochure with a Constance Spry rose, the artwork of Lady Law-Smith. The new church opened in November 1986 and the centrepiece was a dazzling stained glass window by Leonard French, who had created the glass ceiling at Melbourne's National Gallery. Shirley Nicholas, widow of George Nicholas, inventor of Aspro, donated the window.[20]

BUILDING THE KIWI EMPIRE

A quality control laboratory was an essential part of every Kiwi manufacturing factory for ensuring that the quality of Kiwi products never varied. Raw materials, containers and final product were tested, and the size of the laboratory varied from one to about eight persons, depending on the size of the factory.

nfortunately it is not possible to tell the stories of all of the many remarkable people who have worked for Kiwi. Most of them are now out of touch, and even if we could find them this story would run to six volumes. The Kiwi policy was established very early. Don't export: it's better to manufacture on the spot, whether it be Britain, France, USA or Africa. That is the only way to avoid punitive tariffs and to establish friendly relations with often hostile governments. So many of those who worked for Kiwi had their passports stamped with almost every country on earth.

During his Kiwi career Ivan McLaws and his wife Pat lived in 23 houses. McLaws was born and educated in Geelong. In April 1949 he noticed that Kiwi was advertising for a female laboratory assistant. Jobs for industrial chemists were hard to find, but Sheila Sullivan, the head chemist at Kiwi, must have liked him regardless of gender, because he got the job.

Selecting ingredients for the famous polish was a restricted task entrusted only to the person in charge of quality control. One of McLaws' jobs was to select dyestuffs from the large, coded drums that contained them. The dyestuffs would come in large drums, unmarked except for code numbers. There could be some 30 drums, and McLaws would tell the storeman he wanted the lid off that one, then that one. He was climbing over the drums one day and he didn't realise the lid on the drum on which he was standing was loose. He was the perfectly correct chemist, wearing a suit, shirt and tie. In he went. It was good dye. All his clothes were ruined, and despite frequent showers and baths it was a week before his skin returned to its normal colour.

McLaws' first overseas posting was to Singapore in 1960 as assistant manager to Lloyd Zampatti, a science graduate from Perth posted by Kiwi to Singapore in the same year. It was a difficult time for both McLaws and Zampatti. Malaysia and Indonesia were in a state of armed and political opposition, which had the name 'Konfrontasi'. Indonesia, under President Sukarno, objected to the creation of Malaysia. McLaws said: 'Sticks of gelignite would be stuffed up drain pipes. Niggling things, you would never know when the next one was going off. A bag of explosives was left at the Australian Trade Commission in Singapore. It exploded in the entrance. Kiwi, through Chinese wholesalers, had quite a big business with Indonesia until Konfrontasi, but then it ceased. The only way anyone could do trade with Indonesia was by barter, using illegal gunboats. They would go over to Indonesia with things like sewing machines and radios, and come back with loads of

John Murphy, senior chemist, joined the Kiwi head office laboratory in 1962 and worked for Kiwi until 1999. He worked on product development and quality control, provided technical service to African and Asian factories, and was plant engineer at Clayton.

rubber and tin. Just occasionally they thought shoe polish was a very negotiable item and we would send that.'

Indonesians loved Kiwi, not only because it was good for polishing shoes, but it was also very effective for staining timber. Wood carvers in Bali, Djakarta and all the tourist centres used Kiwi for colouring their statues, beautiful heads and smiling Buddhas. Another senior Kiwi chemist, John Murphy, who spent time in Indonesia, said many a tourist who thought he was buying an Indonesian antique was sadly mistaken. That antique was probably carved the previous day and its apparent antiquity was all due to Kiwi.

After President Suharto replaced Sukarno, Indonesia finally accepted the existence of Malaysia in August 1966, the year McLaws and his family went to Nairobi in Kenya. Kiwi bought a company called Kenya Chemical Industries. McLaws hired an architect, built a new factory and started making shoe polish. They also inherited an insecticide from Kenya Chemical Industries. Nairobi is almost on the equator, so it was a marvellous place for mosquitoes and almost everything that crawled, including white ants, ready to devour any timber that was available.

McLaws said they were successful selling shoe polish in Kenya. 'We had a big team of shoeshine boys, not only in Nairobi, but in every provincial town throughout East Africa. We made sure they had a little jacket and a cap, and we supplied them with Kiwi at a very discounted price. They had a shoeshine box and they would sit up one end and the customer would put his foot on the other. Shoeshine boxes were everywhere – airports, in the streets – if you went to a country town inevitably you would find a shoeshine boy.'

McLaws' job involved much travelling, but it was not a bit like Australia. The unmade gravel roads were disastrous on tyres, so they always travelled with two spare wheels. Nairobi was on a plateau 5,500 feet above sea level. For holidays they would go 300 miles down to the coast, setting out at night so that they could get to their destination while it was still cool. 'Of course we had trouble with animals that were likely to burst out in front of you. We equipped the car with spotlights. Elephants were the biggest worry. They were unpredictable. Then there were giraffes, rhinos, impala. Even small animals could cause damage if you hit them. One time we had a leopard in our garden. You would know it was a leopard. It had a distinctive cough.'

The McLaws stayed in Nairobi for four years before they had to leave because their two daughters needed a proper education. Then there was the Kikuyu tribe. 'They were making armed attacks on houses near us, which could be quite brutal. Usually a team of eight or 10 hit the servants quarters which were remote from the house, threaten the boys who gave them entry to the kitchen, through the house. Usually you were sitting at the dinner table, everything so peaceful, then boom! They wanted everything you had. Fortunately it didn't happen to the house we were in, but I had a button under my foot in the dining room. It was a connected to a five mile siren, which our neighbours would hear, and that was the signal for them to call the police.'

The McLaws family returned to Australia, and at the end of 1969 McLaws was setting up a factory in Djakarta, Indonesia. In 1971 he took over from the manager Joop Van

Kiwi polish is used to colour carvings and statues to create an 'antique' effect.

Kiwi found its way into many countries and the advertising of the brand found a myriad of ways to reach the market.

Dijk, who was suffering from hepatitis. A manager in Djakarta had to learn about life quickly. If one wanted to start manufacturing, then one needed at least a dozen different permits with an official stamp on a dozen different pieces of paper. There had to be a permit to employ labour and also a permit for fire protection. The obvious thing would be to import high-quality fire extinguishers from Australia, but no, you had to take the fire extinguishers supplied by the local fire brigade.

Despite the red tape, Kiwi did well in Indonesia. They took over a Chinese company that had a well-known disinfectant, Densol, which flooded the market. When he first visited the factory there was a team of 10 squatting on the floor; no conveyors, no tables. They filled litre tins with Densol through a hole in the top. A fellow with a hot iron soldered a disc of metal over the hole. They taped a 3-inch nail to the side of the can. When the customer wanted to use the disinfectant he punched two holes in the top with a hammer. When Kiwi took over their manufacturing methods were updated.

•   •   •

Geoff Rout, like Ivan McLaws, rarely stopped moving. He was a chemical engineer who joined Kiwi in 1962 after a stint with the Gas & Fuel Corporation. Rout had three years in London in Kiwi's Ealing research laboratory, and as project engineer in the 1980s he went to Malaysia, Singapore, Indonesia, Taiwan, Philippines and China, doing his round of 14 factories two or three times a year. An intriguing factory was in Taoyan, a town south of Taipei in Taiwan. Malcolm Daubney in 1988 had bought for Kiwi the Diamond Shoe Polish Company, and the Chinese produced excellent shoe polish. Rout explained that their way of manufacturing belonged to the 19th century. There were two rooms, one a hot room where the shoe polish would be made in steam-heated vats and girls hand-filled

Densol disinfectant, available in bottles and tins of various sizes.

As well as the successful Densol and the traditional shoe polish (rebranded as 999), Kiwi produced a range of other commercial and domestic products in Indonesia.

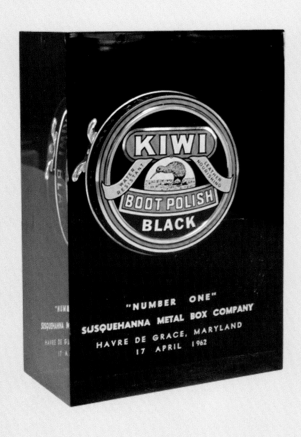

"NUMBER ONE"
SUSQUEHANNA METAL BOX COMPANY
HAVRE DE GRACE, MARYLAND
17 APRIL 1962

'NUMBER ONE'
KIWI (THAILAND) LIMITED.
BANGKOK, THAILAND.
27 NOVEMBER 1985

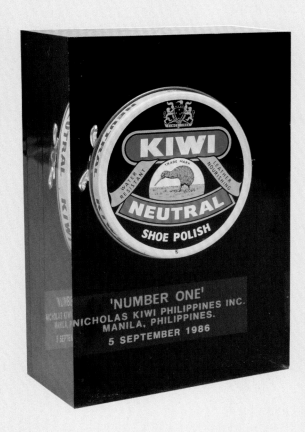

'NUMBER ONE'
NICHOLAS KIWI PHILIPPINES INC.
MANILA, PHILIPPINES.
5 SEPTEMBER 1986

"NUMBER ONE"
KIWI UNITED TAIWAN CO. LTD.
TAIPEI, TAIWAN
24 FEBRUARY, 1989

little dippers. They would pass these through a window into the cold room, and there another team of girls would hand-fill individual cans.

The smell of turpentine in the room was so overpowering that the girls had to wear masks to cope with the fumes and heavy protective clothing to keep out the cold. Rout said within a year they had put in a cooling tunnel and an automatic filling machine.

Rout had another story about the Taoyun factory. When he first arrived the factory manager was a Chinese man, Elton Shu. Rout was startled to see, right there in the factory, the head of a Buddha with two burning candles, and recalled: 'He told Elton Shu, "We are going to have to remove your God from the manufacturing area. We can't have that in a flameproof area," and he said, "Why not?"

' "Because in the flameproof area we are going to put in flameproof electrical Shu equipment and we can't have any sparks. And we can't have candles being lit."

'Shu said, "But he is our God of Safety." I went away and thought about it that night. Next day I said to Elton. "What's the most important thing to someone from China?" And I knew what he would say. He was a big bloke and he liked his food. He said, "Food is the most important thing."

'I said, "Elton, what we ought to do is take your God down to the canteen and he can look after the food." He thought that was a marvellous idea. We took the Buddha down into an underground bunker we had converted into a canteen. Honour was preserved all round.'

Geoff Rout also spent time in China. The China story began with Malcolm Daubney, who was the vice-president Asia. It was never easy dealing with the Chinese. Negotiations went on for years. He said, "First we went to Shanghai and dealt with a company called Golden Cock, their shoe polish can was almost the same as the Kiwi shoe polish can except for the brand name. I suggested that they should change their brand name to Golden Cockerel, which they did."

It was Rout's job to go to Tianjin every two weeks to check on the factory. After six months he found he had to be there full-time: he was to stay for two years with his wife Janice in the Hyatt Hotel. He recalled: 'The first week I was there we had a disaster. The Chinese company was called the Golden Rooster. We had 80 per cent and the Chinese Government 20 per cent. It consisted of three factories each with its own Chinese supervising manager. One of the managers left his keys locked inside his office. So a girl on the factory staff said, "I will get it for you."

Because his window was open she climbed out through the window, to go round to his office. 'As she was clambering over the roof, she went through the asbestos cement and fell to her death. So in that first week there was a large investigation into why our company didn't take a stronger control of the factories it owned.'

Then there was another problem. Before Kiwi went to China it was legal for anyone to make Golden Rooster shoe polish, and they did it with government blessing. The Chinese Army was insolvent, and the soldiers were poorly paid. So the army set up its own manufacturing kettles for shoe polish with the government's blessing. Because of the language barrier, Kiwi knew nothing about this. While doing due diligence, Geoff Rout

OPPOSITE

Four 'Number One' tins sealed in solid blocks of resin for eternity. All have the Royal Warrant printed on the top of the lid — the Royal stamp of approval boosted the brand and translated into sales.

was surprised to see a second-hand plant being installed at the factory, but he couldn't find out why. After a year they then discovered that Golden Cockerel was manufacturing at night, using Kiwi packaging, Kiwi cans and material to sell to the army. To make matters worse, they were using cans and cartons that Kiwi had rejected or weren't up to specification.

There was a real kerfuffle leading to a confrontation between legal people and the army. A Chinese colonel begged Kiwi not to tell the newspapers that the Chinese Government was allowing their own people to fake a national product. Was it ever stopped? Rout says maybe it was brought under control, but China is a big place, and months later they heard the polish was being made illegally in Szechuan.

.   .   .

Lew Bell joined Kiwi in 1965. He had been a solicitor at the Melbourne law firm of Arthur Robinson. He recalled: 'I was grossly underpaid and I thought I was confined to Melbourne for the rest of my life. So I went around the world for six months. Then I came back and wrote to a number of companies. I wrote to Bill Ramsay and asked him for a job. He looked me over. I don't think too many people wrote to him for a job, maybe he was flattered. He gave me a job in the Burnley Street head office. There weren't too many in the head office. There was Tom, John and Bill Ramsay. There was Michael Searby, who was in charge of the technical side, Jervis Leary and Les Jeffres, the secretary, who I had a great bond with. Jerv Leary, a director, worked in a corner office, which had a huge map of the world all over one wall. He liked to stick in pins to identify Kiwi activities in all the various foreign parts.

'Then there was Lloyd Zampatti. He was an extremely good executive and very ambitious. The system was that if anyone was wanted to take a phone call, his name would be called out on the loud speaker. The story was that Zampatti had his name called regularly, and Tom would think, 'That guy's important, he's wanted everywhere.' The annual meeting would be a big occasion. All the Ramsay women would come, Edith, Mimi, Joan Best, John Wicking's wife Janet, and they would be told what their dividend was. I was just the young bloke standing round trying to be polite.

'I was a sort of projects officer and I did things like protecting trademarks. Tom had tremendous vision about that. He wanted the Kiwi trademark protected all around the world. Everyone wanted to copy it, and he pursued everyone who did. Another key reason for my being there was listing the company on the ASX.'

In 1967 Tom Ramsay posted Lew Bell to Singapore, where he worked first with Lloyd Zampatti and then Michael Taylor. 'The big thing was to get a licence to manufacture in Indonesia. I would go up and down and the only hotel to stay at in Djakarta was the Hotel Indonesia. Sick of it I can tell you. This was just after President Suharto threw out his predecessor Sukarno, who had put a complete freeze on investment. The only Australian company that had survived through this was Nicholas Aspro. Now it was easy to get a licence, and we were the first to go through, along with the Australian Dairy Board.

'In Singapore I had an apartment paid for by the company, a servant and a car. A pretty good life for me that was. I used to work very hard for them. We had a factory at Hillview Avenue, just near the nine and a quarter mile post on the Bukit Timah Road. I have been out there since. Now it is all housing developments. You can't even recognise the street. Our principal products were shoe polish, white sandshoe cleaner and some household cleaning products. I was always blasting head office in an undiplomatic way on improving the product range. The white shoe cleaner would come in a little glass jar. You put it on white sandshoes. The Singapore schoolchildren always looked immaculate … clean clothes and brilliant white sandshoes.'

Bell left Kiwi in 1971, aged 30, to do an MBA at the Wharton School of Pennsylvania. As an early scholarly task he wrote a thesis on Kiwi. He wrote that it was a company that could never last. It was doomed to failure. 'I couldn't have been more wrong,' he said.

Kiwi polish coming off the production line in Singapore. In 1967, the Singapore Armed Forces contracted Kiwi to provide boot polish for every soldier.

•   •   •

Michael Taylor was another one of Kiwi's extraordinary characters. A major in the British Army during World War II, he saw service in Borneo, where he met his Dutch wife Helma. She was a tall commanding woman with a forceful personality who worked in the nursing industry. Michael was large, somewhat rotund and wore thick glasses. He was hugely gregarious and his colleagues claimed he had the enviable gift of making instant friends with people he met for the first time, whether at a cocktail party or elsewhere.

He worked for Kiwi throughout Asia and Africa. Ivan McLaws first met him in Singapore in 1962 when Taylor was being transferred to Karachi. Lloyd Zampatti had initiated manufacturing in Pakistan in partnership with the Pervez Industrial Corporation, and Taylor was to become president. McLaws and his wife rushed about to find things the Taylors would need to set up house in Karachi: crockery, bed linen and even a car. McLaws had to find a car that could be serviced in Pakistan. He bought a German Opel.

Malcolm Daubney revealed that Michael Taylor had another gift: a musical ear. He could mimic almost any voice. 'Talk to Mike Taylor and he would mimic you and you would think it was you. You could be in a lift and he would do Tom Ramsay and you could swear Tom Ramsay was standing behind you.' He was also a great linguist. He could go to a country and in a remarkably short time pick up the language. McLaws said Taylor

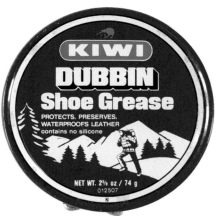

A selection of products that were originally formulated in the USA and later manufactured by factories in Singapore and Australia

went to India, and after being there for a couple of months he could speak Urdu. He had no trouble with French; after being in Singapore he spoke Malay; and in South Africa, according to McLaws, he had a perfect Afrikaans accent.

During the 1960s Taylor was in East Africa, where he was constantly on the move. McLaws claimed that he travelled more miles for Kiwi than anyone else he could remember. As area manager for South-East Asia, including Indonesia, he covered the region before travelling all over Africa: to Nigeria, Ethiopia, Somalia, Congo, Ruanda, Burundi, Uganda and Tanzania. He was also involved in distribution in South Africa before Kiwi started producing polish at Heilbron. Africa was not easy. Many of the countries were rife with tribal warfare, and normal means of communication did not exist. Kiwi had to be either bartered or smuggled across borders. McLaws said: 'In the office when we were doing some planning, suddenly from the other side of the desk he would say, "I am just going to close my eyes for a minute, then immediately he would be off to sleep. Ten minutes later he would resume the conversation as if there had never been a break."'

Michael Taylor spent his last five years in Singapore from where his markets included Thailand and Japan. With a chauffeur-driven car, he lived in a vast house in the most fashionable part of Singapore. In 1974, when Kiwi profits were on a steep downturn, it was time to economise, and the Taylors had to move into a leased apartment. There were still stories a-plenty about Taylor. On a visit to Singapore, Malcolm Daubney discovered that Michael and his wife Helma liked to play the cello in the nude in their apartment.

After Michael Taylor retired in 1975, Allan Herman, marketing manager for Kiwi in Australia took over in Singapore. One of his first jobs was to sell the huge house the Taylors had formerly occupied. It took six months before it finally sold for $450,000. The new owner did it up and two years later it sold for over $2 million.

Shoeshine people were hard at work in Africa at airports, in the streets, and in most small towns.

THE CHALLENGING FUTURE

OPPOSITE

In 1980 Kiwi was already a global force to be
reckoned with. John Wicking, chairman and managing
director, wrote: 'I am confident we are heading into a
decade of growth and prosperity unprecedented in the
75-year history of our company.' Kiwi around the
world employed 1,475 people.

I n 1980 Kiwi was showing confidence in the future, with every good reason for optimism. In 1979 sales had been $78 million. In 1980 they jumped to $92 million. John Wicking, chairman and managing director, wrote: 'I am confident we are heading into a decade of growth and prosperity unprecedented in the 75-year history of our company.'[1]

Kiwi's key to success during its long history was almost entirely due to their entrepreneurial marketing, particularly in the early days, long before radio and television when they developed unique and creative advertising material, a 1916 silent cinema advertising film and clever, colourful and eye-catching advertising posters. Equally important, they successfully and consistently transferred manufacturing technology from Australia throughout the world.

Around the world Kiwi employed 1,475 people: USA 289, followed by Australia 225. France had 217. Fiji was a big surprise with 146. There were 85 staff in Singapore, 58 in Indonesia and 30 in Canada. The UK, now that production had crossed the Channel to Rouen in France, was down to 67. In England, the home of Guy Fawkes and the gunpowder plot, Kiwi had taken over K & M Candles, and then acquired Hovells, which produced Christmas crackers and cake decorations. Hovells had been in business since 1854. They took Christmas very seriously indeed, and they sold their products to all the big stores like Harrods and Fortnum & Mason. They advertised an exclusive range of Christmas crackers from £20 to £140 for a box of six. However, the matrons who didn't patronise these stores could go to Selfridges for a cheaper range including cameo candles. The factory was at Yalding, a village near Maidstone in Kent that dated back to the days of the Doomsday Book. Its top attraction was a medieval stone bridge 450 feet long, built in the 1400s. What a change this was. The biggest money earner for Kiwi in the UK was a Christmas cracker company.[2]

The United States accounted for about a third of worldwide sales and an even higher percentage of profit. It was unparalleled for an Australian company to perform in the toughest retail market in the world. This success had its origins in Tom Ramsay's foresight when Kiwi began manufacturing in Philadelphia in 1947, an arrangement that lasted until 1954 when Kiwi moved its operation to Pottstown, about 60 kilometres north-west of Philadelphia. The site had drawbacks. Close to a river that had a habit of flooding almost every five years, it sometimes left the shoe polish factory awash. Legend has it that Tom Ramsay on one of his regular visits had to be carried to the entrance. In 1980 Kiwi moved further along Highway 421, in the direction of Reading, to Douglassville. It cost $4.24 million to build a superb new factory and offices, 127,000 square feet, big enough for the entire US staff. The cost of moving from Pottstown was another $400,000.[3]

In January 1977 Michael Burnett went to Douglassville as president of the Kiwi Polish Company (USA Division) and zone director for North America and South America (later Kiwi Brands Inc. to reflect aspirations and actions to diversify the product base). Previously general manager of the Kiwi Australian operations, this was a promotion. His predecessors were Larry Emley and then for a short period another Kiwi director, Donald Frederick Wood. Burnett moved into the country estate originally bought for Kiwi by Larry Emley. It was an 1840 two-storey farmhouse on 30 acres with woods, stables and a riding circuit.

When Burnett arrived in America, the shoe polish scene had changed. Paste polish was selling well, and black was the favourite (about 75 per cent), but growth was no longer there. Women didn't care for their shoes: They would sooner buy a new pair than clean them. As for the young, sneakers were all the rage. Burnett said: 'In mid-winter on one of my field trips to Chicago there was snow everywhere. I saw all these women walking down the street wearing lovely dresses, but ... in sandshoes or sneakers ... I asked why. I was told they all wear sneakers to work then change into proper shoes when they get there, so they won't get dirty. When going home they put on their sneakers again.'

Sneakers were in, so the obvious solution was to bring out a sneaker cleaner. However, the market

Kiwi produced new cleaning products for sneakers, which became popular in the 1960s and 1970s

was very small and this did not solve the problem. Kiwi paste polish was still the top seller, but sales did not expand. Burnett took a risk and bought a sophisticated high-speed filling machine for liquid shoe polishes, which cost over $200,000, an enormous price at the time. It put life into the sales of liquid shoe polish, which did great business, not quite as great as the paste polish, but big nevertheless. In the old days the military was the top customer. At every camp there was a PX, the equivalent of a normal supermarket. The military loved Kiwi, but compulsory military service came to an end. It was vital to keep producing new products, so every year there was something new: suede cleaner, Kiwi shoelaces, Kiwi waterproofing, shoe creams in 20 colours. When the price of footwear soared in 1977, Kiwi acquired the technology for those who wanted to repair their boots and shoes at home with 'Shoe Patch' and 'Boot Patch'.

A wonder product was Bloo toilet cleaner. Pop a tablet in the cistern and it turned the toilet water into a fetching Mediterranean blue. Allan Herman, general manager of Kiwi Australia, flew to England and gained the rights from Jeyes Ltd for Australia. Burnett initially had his doubts about it for the US market, but later launched Bloo in the USA with considerable initial success. It was such a different concept and American supermarkets hadn't seen anything like it. However, the product came with a brilliant animated television commercial. The voice-over was done by Kenneth Williams, the British actor–comedian, famous for his roles in the Carry On films and appearing with Tony Hancock.

Burnett said that for two to four years they did great business. It was a real breakthrough for Kiwi in the household products market. However, American Home Products, a company with vastly superior muscle, paid Kiwi the maximum compliment. They came out with their own version of Bloo, spending many millions in advertising. Life in the Bloo market was never as good again.

There were a number of reasons for the success of the American operation. First there was Larry Emley. There was also a wonderful vice-president manufacturing, Bill Jamison. Burnett particularly remembers Jay Smith: 'Jay was a very aggressive guy, chunky, an American, he may have been an ex-marine. Jay was vice-president sales until 1976. He was a bloody good salesman and tough as nails ... Jay was tough with the customers both verbally and mentally. He would almost order the customers to stock Kiwi. Eventually he got fired because he was too aggressive with his boss, the president Don Wood ...'

The Nicholas–Kiwi merger took place in 1982. While the Nicholas business was substantial in Europe and Africa, the business in North America amounted to only $5 million per year, and was not profitable. Their major product was Ambi, a skin cream lightener sought after by black women. It originated in Zimbabwe and was sold by Nicholas in a number of African countries.

It was decided to merge the small US Nicholas business into Kiwi Brands, USA. The Wisconsin factory and the New Jersey admin/marketing offices were closed, and the business concentrated in Douglassville. It was profitable the following year.

But there was a problem. About this time Nicholas was planning to launch a new product, Ipso, in the US. This was a sweet like the popular Tic Tac mints. Ipso, made in Ireland, was a very clever idea. It came in little boxes, which could link with one another like Lego. The theory was that once Americans became fascinated by building little houses or castles out of Ipso packets, they would become addicts for the sweets. However, it was not that easy. No matter how good the product, it would be hard to break into the massive US confectionery market without very substantial advertising support. To facilitate the launch Nicholas had $800,000 worth of Ipso inventory stored in a warehouse at the time of the merger.

It soon became apparent that a US confectionery launch was an impossible dream. So, what to do with the Ipso inventory without incurring a disastrous write-off? This was the problem. Burnett had retained three Nicholas employees, two from the laboratory and a bright 23-year-old brand manager, Steve Stanbrook. Burnett handed the problem

to Stanbrook, who went on a big sales hunt. He called on many confectionery makers with little success. One day he came into Burnett's office and said: 'I have found this firm Keebler, I think they might be interested. I told them they could have Ipso at cost price.'

Keebler was the second-biggest biscuit company in America, the makers of Sunshine and Keebler biscuits. They took over Sunshine in 1996. The Sunshine pioneers were Jacob and John Wiles. In 1902 the Wiles brothers agreed they would like to build a factory that was full of sunshine. And so Sunshine biscuits was born. In 1912 they built a factory on Long Island, New York, that had 1,000 windows. The Keebler biscuit brand was a much bigger brand than Sunshine in 1982.

In the 1980s, as there was little growth in shoe care products, Kiwi US continued to look for new products. One of these was Jonny Mop, a toilet bowl cleaner. It had a short plastic handle and came with disposable paper pads, and the theory was that it cleaned the toilet and left a fresh, pleasant fragrance. Publicity for toilet cleaners was not easily organised, but Burnett managed to get a five-minute interview with the famous Joan Fontaine on her television show. It was hardly prime time, but it did go to TV stations all over America. A still photograph showed a determined Burnett holding up a Jonny Mop, with the Academy Award actress Joan Fontaine to one side.

In Australia Kiwi Dark Tan or Kiwi Black were hardly the jewels in the Kiwi crown any more. Finding a tin of Kiwi in a large supermarket could sometimes be difficult. In

ABOVE LEFT

Bloo toilet cleaner is remembered for its advertising with Kenneth Williams performing the voice over on the animated TV version.

ABOVE RIGHT

Jonny Mop, a toilet bowl cleaner, had a short plastic handle and came with disposable paper pads.

1981 Kiwi was selling 53 different products in Australia alone, and the leader in all these products, the real crown jewel was a bleach called White King, which had come to Kiwi with the takeover of Simpsons in 1968. In 1980 Kiwi built a Cloromat factory for $750,000 at Clayton. John Murphy, the industrial chemist and manager in the 1990s, said at its peak they used 50 tonnes of chlorine a month and 30 tonnes of sea salt a week. Demand was so high at times they had to run two shifts a day. Sodium hydrochloride was the main ingredient for White King, and this was put into bottles at a 4 per cent concentration.[4]

In 1980 Allan Herman, general manager of Kiwi Australia, launched Jeyes Bloo Toilet Cleaner and Martha Gardener's Wool Mix. In her day Martha was a well-known figure in Melbourne, who offered a solution to every household problem. Anything you wanted to know about stains cooking, smells, washing, or how to grow your geraniums from cuttings, Martha was your girl. If your dog did something frightful on the white living room carpet, there was only one hope: go to Martha. She ran a radio program for 30 years, was on television and had a column in Melbourne's *Herald*. She even had her own publishing company producing a best seller titled *Martha Gardener's Book: Everyone's Household Help*. It was full of marvellous stuff: how to clean greasy overalls, how to stop sausages from oozing out either end, how to get rid of silverfish with Epsom Salts, and when you have a plague of fleas, easy, put mint under the mattress.

The marketing people at Kiwi did a deal with Martha and produced her Wool Mix. On the label the bottle had a picture of Martha looking like everyone's all-knowing

Vanessa Williams, Miss
America, signed up by Kiwi for
supermarket promotions.

Martha Gardener's Wool Mix was one of many well-known products added to the Kiwi range.

grandmother. Martha was quick to point out that Wool Mix was a marvel. You could use it to clean anything: silk, rugs, dressing gowns, velvet, furniture, grass stains on sleeping bags; and there was one particularly crafty line saying it could clean ice-cream stains off car seats.[5]

Was there anything Kiwi did not touch? In 1980 Kiwi produced a publication called *The Future Report*. The Public Relations Department had worked hard. Maybe the little New Zealand kiwi bird could not fly, but Kiwi the company that stole its name was now 75 years old and it had spread its wings to almost every place on earth. In Nairobi 1,000 shoeshine boys were using Kiwi. In Bali Kiwi was essential for polishing and colouring woodcarvings. In Norway Olympic ski teams were using Kiwi on their boots and, for an even greater test, Kiwi was there when Norwegian climbers were on the way to the top in the Himalayas.[6]

The Hamilton factory in Canada was a modest affair: 5,000 square feet and employed only 25 people compared with Kiwi's great factory in Douglassville, Pennsylvania, 127,000 square feet and a staff of 289. Kiwi Canada had produced a frypan cleaner that had the name Rapide, ideal in an area where they spoke English and French. 'Rapide' was simply fast in both languages. Then they had a product Mink Oil, which contained a small proportion of oil from processing of mink skins for fur. Its ingredients were silicone and lanolin, designed to waterproof boots in harsh Canadian winters.[7]

One of the most intriguing of Kiwi's operations was in Suva, Fiji. It was intriguing because here Kiwi made no shoe polish at all. That was interesting in itself, because there were nigh on 150 employees. This was in a country where there was racial tension. It was the Fijians who owned the land, but it was the clever Indians who were the businessmen and ran the economy. But the Kiwi factory employed a mix of both races. In 1980 on the staff list there were names like Mohammad Shah, Stetareki Ralulu, Annais Wong, Alumita Kabulevu, and Abdul Ishrat Wahit, Madhawan Sami, Atunasia Vakaloma. They worked well together. The biggest nightmare must have been organising the pay list.

The story began with Claude Israel, born in Melbourne in 1881. As a young man he went to Fiji and set up an import business, C. Sullivans (Pacific Islands) Limited. Why it was called Sullivans is not known. Maybe he thought Israel Pacific was too confusing. Among his imports was Kiwi Shoe Polish. When he retired, his son Mark took over, and in 1963 Kiwi acquired 50 per cent of the company. Two years later UEB, United Empire Box Company of New Zealand, came into the business and brought its expertise in manufacturing board containers, toilet tissue, paper bags and even bags used in supermarkets. There was another move in 1973: Bowater-Scott of Australia, the big paper company formed a joint company with Kiwi and acquired all the previous Fijian interests.

In 1978 Mark Israel retired at 60 and his son Simon, the third generation to be involved, took over the business. Simon was just 28. He concentrated all the spread-out operations into one large factory in Suva. One of the best money earners was a safety match, similar to Bryant & May Redheads. Simon said Fijians used a lot of matches. Not so much for lighting cigarettes. This was an island nation, and getting electricity to outer areas was difficult and expensive. So the matches were used for the lamps – kerosene lamps, and the famous Coleman lamps – that one had to pump to provide a splendid glow.

They exported all over the Pacific as far as Papua New Guinea and Tahiti. Apart from Kiwi Shoe Polish they imported famous brands like Wrigley's chewing gum and Gillette razor blades. And was Kiwi a big seller? Not exactly. Fijians did like bare feet, and the favourite footwear was the leather sandal, which they did polish with Kiwi.

In 1980 Caxton Industries in New Zealand made a takeover bid. Simon Israel said the Kiwi board decided it was a compelling offer and that was the year he left Fiji. John Wicking, Kiwi's chairman and managing director, commented to Israel: 'I knew your father and grandfather. You have a nose for business. Why don't you go to work in Asia for Kiwi?' So Israel ended up in Asia. He went to Thailand, he went to the Philippines, he went to Indonesia and he went to Singapore. There were few places in the world where a young man could not work for Kiwi.[8]

International Kiwi conference, Melbourne, 1980.
This was the last that Sir Tom Ramsay would attend.

STANDING

Ian McLaren, Director; Bob Kenny, Canada; Peter Hendry, Indonesia; Russell Martin, Director; Jan Lagerburg, Kenya; Grahme Dixon, Director; Graham Henderson, Company Secretary; Michael Burnett, Americas; Will McDougall, Director; John Wicking, Managing Director.

SEATED

Mark Israel, Fiji; Brian Ashford, United Kingdom; Sir Tom Ramsay, Chairman; Jan Taminiau, France, Malcolm Daubney, East Asia; Allan Herman, Australia.

THE
AUCTION

OPPOSITE

John Wicking, Chairman
of Kiwi International and
Nicholas Kiwi

In 1982 John Wicking was 64 years old. He had been a prisoner of war during World War II, captured by the Germans in Crete. He had seen through the merger of two great companies, Nicholas Aspro and Kiwi International.

He would stay on as chairman, but he was looking to retire as chief executive. Putting head-hunters Egon Zehnder into action, they found Brian Healey, a man with excellent credentials.

Healey had worked with the British firm Gillette, and then Associated Electrical Industries, moving in 1961 to Australia as marketing manager. He later worked for Nabisco in Australia and the Asia-Pacific area, eventually becoming senior vice-president of Nabisco in London.

John Wicking met Brian Healey in London in Easter 1983 when he asked Healey if he would be interested in replacing him as chief executive of Nicholas Kiwi. It would have been a hard decision. It meant a significant drop in salary, but the idea of returning to Melbourne was enticing, since he had three children still living in Australia. He eventually managed to join Nicholas Kiwi in January 1984. He was in for a shock when first he arrived at the Melbourne office: 'I had come from my position with a large international company. I had an office in Berkeley Square, a chauffeur and a car. I had an office in Reading, New York. I had the right to use a private jet. Then when I came to Kiwi I went out to this place in Heatherton Road, Clayton. The local tip was across the road, where the seagulls used to come at 4 p.m. every day and crap on the cars that were parked there. But the next five years were probably the happiest I ever had in my career. I never got carried away by the benefits of a senior executive.'[1]

Brian Healey made a quick assessment of the merged business. If Nicholas had been an English company and Kiwi a Melbourne company, he had doubts that they would ever have got together. However, they did so because the families knew each other well, plus the fact that both companies in Australia owned natural health products – Nicholas with Nature's Way and Kiwi with Golden Life. Kiwi also had a substantial interest in the Australian publicly listed Faulding pharmaceutical company. The contrast in the company policies could not have been more extreme. Nicholas was not particularly interested in keeping costs down, whereas Kiwi was frugal, almost in the extreme. Nicholas was extremely generous, Kiwi the opposite. Yet there was a geographic balance.

Australia was the only place where they were both reasonably strong. Nicholas was strong in Europe, Kiwi relatively weak. In America Kiwi was very strong, whereas Nicholas was virtually non-existent. In Asia Kiwi was strong, but Nicholas virtually non-existent except for Indonesia. In Africa Kiwi had a presence in Kenya, Zimbabwe and South Africa, but in relative terms Nicholas was far stronger.

Nicholas was a high-margin business. The cost of producing Aspro was minimal. The difference between cost of production and selling price was about 80 per cent. For Kiwi it was less than half that. Brian Healey stated: 'The great contribution John Wicking made in the first two years after the merger shook the money out of the pockets of the Nicholas side of the business.'

Healey had been in the job barely two months when things became interesting. Lloyd Zampatti, stationed in Singapore from 1967 to 1971, had been Kiwi's chief executive for Asia. As a side interest he had become president of the Singapore Chamber of Commerce. He had met trade delegations from Perth and he was offered the job of chief executive of Swan Brewing. He was there for 11 years, and then became managing director and group chief executive of Castlemaine Tooheys at their brewing headquarters in Brisbane. In 1984 Australian drinkers were going through a cultural change. Beer had always been the top drink. Sales had always gone up and anyone who invested in beer was sure to find gold. But in the 1970s and 1980s, Australians discovered another type of gold. They were developing a thirst for wine. In 1984 The *Australian Financial Review* officially described the Australian beer market as 'stagnant'.[2]

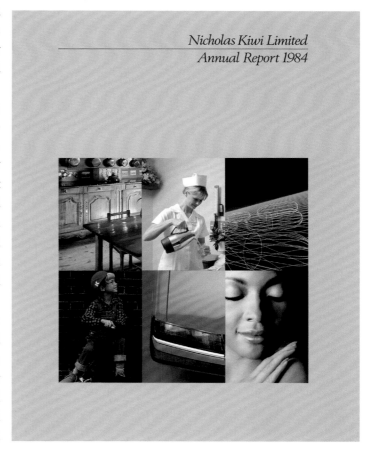

Nicholas Kiwi Limited
Annual Report 1984

Zampatti undoubtedly saw the falling beer market a big worry, but perhaps he wanted to return as the Prodigal Son to lead an all-powerful company in which years ago he had just been a servant. On 5 July 1984 Castlemaine Tooheys made a $307 million bid for Nicholas Kiwi. *Australian Business* reported that Zampatti just went in cold. Castlemaine Tooheys held no shares in Nicholas Kiwi and they had never spoken to Kiwi management.[3] The offer was $4 a share, or $3.75 plus one of its own shares, for two Nicholas Kiwi shares. If nothing else, the offer lit up the Stock Exchange. A million shares changed hands in one day. Nicholas Kiwi shares which had been selling at $2.70, finished the day at $4.05.

The directors of Nicholas Kiwi immediately rejected the offer. They declared it was totally unrealistic, and strongly recommended that shareholders retain their shares. Considerable control was possible because the Nicholas family together with the Ramsay family held 45 per cent of the shares. The *Age* in Melbourne quoted one market analyst: 'It's vertical integration at its best. You could go out on the town and get stuck into the XXXX (a Queensland beer owned by Castlemaine Tooheys), move onto some Seaview (a Champagne maker controlled by Castlemaine) and then, when you wake up with a hangover, you reach for the Aspros.' The *Age* was too shy to mention what the broker suggested should be done with the shoe polish.[4]

Lloyd Zampatti, speaking at a Securities Institute lunch in Melbourne, said: 'We believe, together we will have a great Australian institution.' He described the bid as not a takeover, but a merger. He was linking Castlemaine Tooheys' 'cash turbine' to the Nicholas Kiwi 'profit engine'. He added: 'I only hope that Nicholas Kiwi will come to appreciate the opportunities that our financial strength will give them.'

Business Review Weekly reported that Castlemaine Tooheys had not followed normal procedure, which was to buy up shares in Nicholas Kiwi before they made their bid. They could have bought, say, 9.9 per cent at $2.75. *BRW* commented: 'The modest Melbourne headquarters of Nicholas Kiwi shows little sign of being at battle stations and Brian Healey does not look a worried man. Actually, he has played for much bigger stakes.'[5] Even so, the Nicholas Kiwi board took out full-page advertisements in the major newspapers advising shareholders not to sell their shares. At the same time, Zampatti wrote to Nicholas Kiwi shareholders asking them to support the bid in light of significant financial benefits.

To emphasise their rejection of the Castlemaine Tooheys bid, on 9 August 1984 Nicholas Kiwi announced a one-for-six bonus issue and higher dividend payouts. As a result of the bonus issue shareholders received a 34 per cent increase in dividends for the current year. Nicholas Kiwi announced an expected profit of $26 million for the year to 30 June – up from $21.6 million for the previous year. Just to drive the point home, managing director Healey forecast a 15 per cent rise in profit for the coming year.

Indeed, something better was in the works. As *Australian Business* put it, all eyes were on the share market, but in Chicago in Consolidated Foods Corporation's head office overlooking Lake Michigan Chairman and Chief Executive Officer John H. Bryan was attracted to the thought that the global brand of Kiwi's shoe care products would be a natural fit with their household and personal care division, which Cornelis Boonstra, president Consolidated Foods Corporation and Douwe Egberts International in the Netherlands, was actively developing. In 1982 Boonstra had met John Wicking, chairman Kiwi Polish Company in Melbourne tentatively exploring the possibility of Consolidated Foods acquiring the Kiwi shoe care brands. Wicking at that time was heavily involved in the merger of Nicholas and Kiwi, so there was a polite thank you, but no thank you.

Boonstra joined Consolidated Foods when President of Intradal, which they acquired in the 1970s. Intradal had a range of household and personal care products that included the Tana and Erdal shoe care product range. The Kiwi shoe polish brands would complement Tana and Erdal, which had a strong presence in Europe, Canada and Australia. Consolidated Foods were not primarily interested in the Nicholas ethical pharmaceutical products, and in 1992 sold them to Roche for a handsome profit. However, they were interested in the Nicholas personal care products, which included the Radox brand.

Consolidated Foods of Chicago had a $17 billion turnover in 1984 and 150,000 staff worldwide. They not only had Sara Lee frozen foods and bakery items, but they were big in meat, coffee and apparel.

John Bryan decided to call Nicholas Kiwi's Chief Executive Officer Brian Healey to express his interest in the acquiring of the Australian shoe care and pharmaceutical company. Morgan Stanley International's Simon Orme in New York assisted by Bruce Bockmann in their Sydney office were engaged by Bryan to advise them on the acquisition. At the same time Graeme Samuel of Hill Samuel, merchant bankers in Melbourne, was advising Nicholas Kiwi, as he had done a few months earlier when Castlemaine Tooheys made an unsuccessful bid for Nicholas Kiwi.

Negotiations started to become serious, with Jim Carlson, Consolidated Food's Vice President Acquisitions assisted by Simon Orme, Morris Kramer a senior partner with Skadden Arps and Brian Healey and Graeme Samuel along with chairman John Wicking and John Walter from Clayton Utz leading the Nicholas Kiwi negotiating team.

Meanwhile, the market was beset with as much intrigue and rumour as an Agatha Christie mystery. Reckitt & Colman, the huge UK group was planning a new share issue to raise $160 million. Why? Reckitt & Colman specialised in household products, which included Kiwi's great rival Nugget. Everyone knew the slogan: 'Did you Nugget your shoes this morning?' Now did they want to Nugget Kiwi? Barrie Dunstan in the *Australian Financial Review* wrote: 'I believe Reckitt & Colman is the favourite to emerge as a second bidder for Nicholas Kiwi.'[6]

On 28 September 1984 Reckitt & Colman came out of hiding and bid $4.60 cash for the shares in Nicholas Kiwi or $3.95 after the capital had been expanded on a one-for-six bonus they planned to make on 12 October. Nicholas Kiwi shares bounced up again, this time to $4.45.

As Nicholas Kiwi was on the market, Chairman John Wicking, Chief Executive Officer Brian Healey and Finance Director Russell Martin, flew to Hawaii primarily to explore all possible options to enhance Nicholas Kiwi shareholder value and to discuss with Nabisco the possibility of merging their Australian interests with Nicholas Kiwi, but this proved not to be viable. Wicking and Healey returned to Melbourne and Martin flew to New York. In Chicago it was a different story because in October 1984 Consolidated Foods was beginning to believe that Nicholas Kiwi was a more tasty morsel. John Bryan, Chairman and Chief Executive of Consolidated Foods flew in a private jet to Melbourne with his corporate executives.

Consolidated Foods was smarter than Castlemaine Tooheys. Quietly they began buying up Nicholas Kiwi shares, and by 2 October they had 5.48 per cent of outstanding Kiwi shares. The same day, Consolidated Foods came out in the open. The company announced an offer of $4.80 for Nicholas Kiwi shares. The offer was unique and complex, and craftily designed by Graeme Samuel with the assistance of John Walter of Clayton

KIWI
PRODUCTS
ACROSS
THE
GLOBE

PROTECTS YOUR SHINE MILES LONGER.

JIKA SEPATU ANDA SEPUDAR KERTAS INI ANDA PERLUKAN KIWI 'EXTRA SHINE'

KIWI MET LA MODE A VOS PIEDS.

La Palette Mode Kiwi
LE CUIR QUI VIT EN COULEURS

Utz in Melbourne. They would pay $453 million for all Nicholas Kiwi operations overseas, but the Australian business would remain Australian owned and run by Australians as a separate entity. The Foreign Investment Review Board could not quarrel with that. All those factories across Africa, Europe, Asia and America were beyond the Foreign Investment Review Board's control.[7]

Maureen Murrill in the *Herald* wrote that for Nicholas Kiwi shareholders this was like winning a quinella at Flemington. They received cash in hand plus an interest in an ongoing Nicholas Kiwi operation. Brian Healey was delighted. He said: 'This particular operation enables us to give major benefits to shareholders and keep the company together.' It was also attractive to Nicholas Kiwi shareholders because Consolidated Foods Corporation contracted Nicholas Kiwi Australasia to manage all the international operations for an agreed management fee.[8]

It was becoming a football match, with each company trying to score goals. On 17 October Reckitt & Colman spent $47 million buying Nicholas Kiwi shares until they had 14.9 per cent of the company. They also upped their offer to $4.20 a share ex-bonus. This was effectively 20 cents better than what Consolidated Foods was offering. Meanwhile the board of Nicholas Kiwi decided on the urging of John Wicking that the whole issue would be resolved on 31 October with an extraordinary meeting of shareholders.[9]

In the next weeks there were rumours and counter rumours. Bryan Frith in the *Australian* wrote that shareholders were not being given enough time. 'The Nicholas Kiwi affair has now reached the extraordinary situation where the directors are determined to press on with a meeting to seek shareholder approval to the sale of the company's major assets, despite the fact that some shareholders may be effectively disenfranchised from voting. In fact it is entirely possible that some shareholders may have their shares voted contrary to their present intentions.'[10]

Finance editors were describing the coming auction as the biggest in Australia's history. On the Tuesday 30 October 1984, auction eve, Reckitt & Colman, upped their bid to $5 a share, and went to the Supreme Court in an attempt to delay the meeting. Reckitt & Colman were continuing their share buying even at prices over $5. Now they held 20 per cent of Nicholas Kiwi. Their last-minute bid before the court failed

The auction took place at the Kiwi factory's canteen in Heatherton Road, Clayton. One might have expected the grand ballroom at Melbourne's leading hotel, but no, the scene was a humble, typical staff canteen where the only decoration was a very well-known picture of Her Majesty, Queen Elizabeth II. There was room for 200 shareholders or voters, some of whom arrived by expensive limousines. John Wicking, still chairman of Nicholas Kiwi chaired the meeting, and he promised to be impartial.

It began at 10 a.m. Brian Healey told the packed canteen that the Nicholas Kiwi board was unable to come up with a recommendation to shareholders. It was up to the shareholders to decide. The media described it as an auction, and an auction it was. Melbourne had never seen anything like it; two huge companies fighting it out for supremacy. Each company raised its bid twice and there were long delays as each one was

THURSDAY

Herald

KIWI'S CRUCIAL TRIAL

Printed and published by H. A. Gordon, 54 Canterbury Rd., Toorak, 3142, for The Herald & Weekly Times Ltd., regd. office 44-74 Flinders St., Melb.

assessed. Ultimately they were dead level. Once analysed, the bids were worth $5.25 each.

The Reckitt & Colman bid was attractive to those who wanted instant money: $5.25 in cash for every share or $2.40 cash plus one share in Reckitt & Colman Australia, worth $3. The money would arrive within days. Reckitt's chief executive was John West. The *Financial Review* thought he had a remarkable resemblance to the famous England Test cricketer Alec Bedser. West said he would stick by his promise, and his company would stand by the share market and deliver $5.25 for everyone who wanted their money immediately. Reckitt & Colman made a submission to the government that they would merge their business with their Australian section and make Australia their headquarters

"What's a good-looking bird like you doing in a place like this?"

Herald cartoon, 1984

for the Asian Pacific region. This surely would soothe the Foreign Investment Review Board. Graeme Samuel believed that Reckitt & Colman would have difficulties in getting the Foreign Investment Review Board's review for their proposed offer.[11]

On the other hand, Consolidated Foods adopted Graeme Samuel's creative plan. They would establish a new company called Nicholas Kiwi Australasia, which would own Australian and New Zealand assets only. They would get all of Nicholas Kiwi's overseas operations plus a 15 per cent shareholding in Nicholas Kiwi Australasia. Shareholders would receive $4.42 in cash and a share in a scaled down Australian company worth 83 cents. There was a sentimental edge to this. The Nicholas and Ramsay families would be feeling they were not completely selling their heritage; their Aspro and their Kiwi would still have a stake in Australia. An important consideration for the board was that Nicholas Kiwi Australasia would be given a contract to manage all the Nicholas Kiwi's overseas operations, which meant all the existing staff would be maintained.

Bruce Bockmann, a New Yorker of Morgan Stanley, said they had no experience of company acquisitions in Australia, so they called on Keith Halkerston of Baring Bros Halkerston, a local merchant banker. It was Halkerston who made the Consolidated Foods bid at the auction. Bockmann thought it wise to have the bid coming from someone who had an Australian accent. Halkerston used a number of phrases that none of the Americans understood. 'It was good Aussie lingo,' said Bockmann.

At one stage Bockmann went outside for a breather. He met one of the Kiwi workers, who said he was the factory cleaner. 'What's going on there?' said the cleaner. Bockmann replied: 'We are having a debate as to who might buy the company.'

'I don't understand what you mean.'

'Well, think of this as a horse race. Two guys are running but neither of them understands where the finish line is.'

'Oh, I got it.'

'He didn't of course,' said Bockmann. 'No one had any idea where the finish line was.' Indeed it was touch and go as to which company would get the prize. An independent shareholder who they didn't know got up to speak. Yes, everybody knew what happened to a company in a small country when it is taken over by a large company from a country outside. 'The first thing that happens,' he said, 'is they get rid of a lot of people. They change the organisation. They get the culture all mixed up with their own. As far as I am concerned, Reckitt & Colman is just going to take this company, which we have built up over the years, tear it apart, and integrate it into their own organisation. I don't think we should let that happen. I think we should vote for the company which will give us a chance to maintain control of the international operation and still have our own company here in Australia.'

David Pike, a representative of the Prudential Insurance Company, which had 985,000 shares, asked for an adjournment so that his company could assess the tax implications of both offers. The chairman of the meeting John Wicking rejected the idea, saying, 'What did you come here for, for God's sake?'

Mr Pike: 'I came here to make a decision, but not to be railroaded. I'd like to go back to Sydney.'

Mr Wicking: 'You can't go back to Sydney. The matter has to be decided by five o'clock, because that's a condition of Consolidated's offer.'

The matter was indeed decided by five o'clock, almost to the tick.[12]

At 3.30 p.m. John Wicking applied the gag and the shareholders started to cast their votes for either the Reckitt & Colman or the Consolidated Foods offer. Twenty-four hours before the meeting Nicholas Kiwi had received 37.5 million open proxies of the 76 million eligible to vote. Right on 5 p.m. Wicking was handed a piece of paper on which there was a single word: 'Carried'. Consolidated Foods was the winner.

Brian Healey, chief executive of Nicholas Kiwi, commented later: 'I have only ever lost sleep twice in business. The second night after this deal was done I didn't sleep. I wasn't sure I had done the right thing. My fears were misplaced. The relationship we had with Consolidated Foods Corporation was fantastic. They treated our management and me generously. They treated us no differently to people where they owned businesses 100 per cent and it turned out a very good working relationship.'[13]

John Bryan said that while in Melbourne he was impressed with John Wicking and that he was 'a good guy, honest and ethical at all times'.

The *Age* reported that the Nicholas family would receive $110–120 million, the Ramsay family $85–95 million, and Reckitt & Colman, who had bought so many shares, $90–95 million. So there was a fine consolation prize for the loser.[14]

Nicholas Kiwi Australasia had a short life. Consolidated Foods did not stick with its unbecoming title. It adopted the name of its products, famous in supermarkets, Sara Lee. There was hardly a person in the United States who was not aware of Sara Lee apple pie. The government in Canberra relaxed the Federal Investment Review Board rules. In 1984

Consolidated Foods was allowed to hold only 15 per cent of Nicholas Kiwi Australasia. So the company stopped buying at 14.9 per cent.

Now all was changed. On 19 August 1986 Sara Lee offered $3.80 for each of the shares it did not own in Nicholas Kiwi Australasia, a cash total of nearly $250 million. The directors of Nicholas Kiwi recommended acceptance of the offer. So it was all over, and another Australian company was gone.

The *Age* said it was a good deal. The $3.80 compared with a stated net tangible asset of just 68 cents, so this was a staggering 22 times the 1985–86 earnings per share on the end-year capital. In terms of the original company shareholders ended up getting a total of $7.08 an old share, or $6.83 after allowing for the cost of the new Nicholas Kiwi rights issue.[15]

There were a number of red faces of 'couldabeen' rich champions. In 1984 when Castlemaine Tooheys offered $4 a share for Nicholas Kiwi and the board took out full-page advertisements advising shareholders not to sell, there were ultra conservatives who believed the Castlemaine offer was already too good to be true.

It was sad, even tragic, that Nicholas Kiwi was Australian no more, but the cash rewards for the shareholders could not be ignored. Once a successful family company goes public, its fate is inevitable; a hungry suitor is always waiting across the road or should one say across the water.

There was one little postscript. When Sara Lee completed its takeover in 1986, the big American company asked John Wicking for his resignation with a letter that he was required to sign. It was very official indeed. John Wicking, the departing chairman was not pleased. He signed that letter and wrote on the bottom, 'Get stuffed,' and he said, 'They think I can't write my own resignation letter.'

Malcolm Daubney commented: 'That happened all right. I saw the letter.'[16]

Shoe shiner, London, 1980s

SOMEWHERE SOMEONE *just* *went to work* in SNEAKERS.

(what a pity)

KIWI
SINCE 1906
SHOE POLISH
"Shines, Nourishes & Protects"
BLACK
NET WT. 2½ OZ. (70 g)

You don't see CEOs walking around in ratty tennis shoes. They wear wingtips with a fresh coat of KIWI shoe polish. And this particular polish has been making their black shoes blacker since 1906.

The reason we've been around so long is simple: your footwear is a reflection of who you are. So don't scuff it up. *Because a well polished shoe is a sign of a well polished man.*

- Kiwi

www.kiwicare.com

BRINGING A SHINE TO THE WORLD

OPPOSITE

Kiwi, now owned by S. C. Johnson & Son, Inc., is one of Australia's oldest and best known world brands.

ir Tom Ramsay died on 27 January 1995 aged 87. He had suffered from cancer for seven years, and Dame Elisabeth Murdoch wrote that it was terrible to see him becoming frailer and frailer.[1] Added to this his eyesight failed. Macular degeneration meant he could not drive a car and he could not read. For a man who loved history, loved books and possessed one of the finest private libraries in Australia, this was hard to bear. His daughter Anne said he used to catch the city tram into the Athenaeum Club for lunch nearly every day, and in the end he became rather grumpy.

There had been adjustments. On 23 March 1988 'Hascombe', Tom and Mimi's retreat at Mount Macedon was sold and in October 1994 Tom and Mimi moved out of 23 Airlie Street, South Yarra to a much smaller property across the road at number 22.

Secretary Pamela Radford visited him every week for three and a half years. She was helping him to write a history of Kiwi. Her last visit was to the Alfred Hospital on the Monday before he died. She said she always looked forward to her visits and she found him 'great fun'.[2]

After Tom's death Mimi answered hundreds of letters, which came from all parts of the globe. They were from captains of industry like Sir James Balderstone, chairman of BHP, politicians like Sir Charles Court, Premier of Western Australia, Ian Sinclair, leader of the National Party, plus letters from libraries, hospitals, museums, schools and all manner of relief organisations. Dame Elisabeth Murdoch sent a large bunch of roses.

. . .

John Wicking AM, chairman of Kiwi International and then chairman of Nicholas Kiwi died on 11 June 2002. His wife Janet, only child of Madge and Walter Tompson and granddaughter of the founder William Ramsay, had died six years before. Like Tom, John Wicking had a long bout with cancer. Early in January, Wicking's friend Snow Swift rang from Sydney to report that he and his wife Georgie were going on a final overseas trip.

'So am I,' said John.

'Where to?'

'In a box,' said John. 'In a box upstairs.'

Snow flew down from Sydney to have lunch with John and left on his trip the next day. John Wicking took his final trip five days later.[3] Malcolm Daubney played snooker with him most afternoons, and Frank Newman, his long-time friend, played once or twice a week. On the afternoon of John's death Frank was there. It was the first day Malcolm had not seen John wearing a suit and tie. He was sitting up in bed. Frank had a brandy and soda, John had his usual gin and tonic, and Malcolm a whisky and water. John was smoking even though he was on an oxygen tank. Frank and Malcolm left his house at 6.30 p.m. and Malcolm said he would be back the next day to tell him about Cookie's funeral, which was taking place at Euroa. John never heard about the funeral. He died at 10 p.m. that night.

The death of Cookie might have speeded his sudden collapse. Just a week before, his dear friend Cookie, the Italian worker to whom he gave his farm 'Ponkeen' for $1, had died in an accident. The date was 4 June. Cookie was driving a truck with grain and a tractor on the back when it went off the road and he was killed.

John Wicking's mother Jeannie went blind in her later years. This was something Wicking never forgot. He donated millions to the Association for the Blind, now known

as Vision Australia. He was on the board of the Association for the Blind for 18 years and president from 1972 to 1984. Since John and Janet had no children, on his death, after some initial distribution to family and friends, he left $45 million to the J.O. & J.R. Wicking Trust, which is professionally managed by Equity Trustees. In November 2015 the trust was valued at $103 million, and since its establishment in 2004 it has distributed or committed over $40 million. People when talking of the Wicking Trust tend to forget Janet, who in fact was the biggest shareholder of all the members of the Ramsay family.

The trust is remarkable in itself, and set to outshine many Australian trusts, including the famous Felton Bequest. The trust had certain priorities in its giving: the blind and vision impaired, the aged and those suffering from Alzheimer's disease. However, the most interesting part was that approximately 15 per cent of the trust's income was to go back every year for reinvestment.

John and Janet had inherited one of the best private collections of Hugh Ramsay paintings. Over the years they had been generous in donating Ramsay works to many schools, galleries and institutions, particularly in Victoria. In the 1990s, when Betty Churcher was the director, they had decided to leave their entire collection to the National Gallery of Australia (NGA) in Canberra. When Janet died in 1996, John presented their treasured portrait of her mother, *Madge*, to the Canberra Gallery, with the proviso that it be permanently on display. At the time of writing this is not so.

Betty Churcher retired the following year, leading to the appointment of the young Irishman, Brian Kennedy, as the new director. Wicking went out of his way to establish a rapport with Kennedy, inviting him to his house to see his paintings and entertaining him at his beloved Australian Club. Alas, Kennedy, facing his own crisis at the NGA, failed to measure up to John's high expectations. Wicking lost patience and changed his will, and the paintings were left to Liz Cooper, Frank Newman's daughter, and Patricia Fullerton, Hugh Ramsay's biographer, to decide their fate.

It is impossible to estimate their worth, since Ramsay's pictures were rarely sold at auction and, like the Wickings, other family members who inherited his works, generally tended to donate them to institutions, where his talent could be appreciated by the public. Of the 17 works in the Wicking collection, four were presented to the National Gallery of Victoria, one to the National Portrait Gallery and others to regional galleries in Geelong, Ballarat, Castlemaine, Mornington, Launceston and the Ian Potter Museum of Art at Melbourne University. The National Gallery of Australia received none.[4]

OPPOSITE

Kiwi advertising was aimed at many markets

·　　·　　·

In August 1986 Sara Lee had complete control of Nicholas Kiwi at a total price of A$703 million having previously in 1984 paid A$453 million for all the Nicholas Kiwi International business and 15 per cent for Nicholas Kiwi Australasia and A$250 million for the remaining 85 per cent of Nicholas Kiwi Australasia in 1986. It was a benevolent

takeover. There were no wholesale sackings and executives held their positions. The old tale of big fishes swallowing smaller fishes went on and on, even though smaller fishes at times were so big they became indigestible. In 1987 Sara Lee acquired the consumer products division of Akzo, the giant chemical company.[5] In 1987 Brian Healey realised quickly that everything was becoming too big, but Melbourne was small time. Sara Lee was selling 90 per cent of its household products outside Australia and 60 per cent in Europe. They would have to shift headquarters either to London or the Netherlands. He told Michael Burnett: 'There's no way I am going back to that stinking weather.' But he had stronger reasons: Melbourne was now home, not only for him, but also his wife and his children. Michael Burnett was the one who should go.

In 1988 Burnett became chief operating officer of Sara Lee Household and Personal Care Division in Utrecht. This division included 50 companies and in 35 countries with a turnover of 2.2 billion dollars. Then Sara Lee owned Douwe Egberts, dealers in coffee and tobacco products, an ancient company that dated back to 1753. So the combination of

Sara Lee and Douwe Egberts along with the previously acquired Intradal, Nicholas Kiwi and Akzo Consumer Products (ACP) was located in the Household and Personal Care Division. The division was initially located in Akzo's offices in The Hague.

So this was the new world of Sara Lee, and of the old Melbourne head office staff of Nicholas Kiwi, just six went to Utrecht from Australia. Russell Martin became the finance director, Rob Owers was his assistant, John Johnson handled accounts, Ian Jungwirth was the internal auditor, and Peter Thomas, formerly of Nicholas, controlled human resources.

Peter Thomas was general counsel and company secretary of Nicholas Kiwi. He followed Burnett, who had already been there six months, Thomas said: 'I had the job of persuading the others to go to Holland. Except for Michael none of them wanted to be there, but once there none of them wanted to come back. I stayed for three months with a Dutch couple who had a house in Wassenaar, a leafy outer suburb of The Hague.' There was one amazing thing about Wassenaar. It had several cricket grounds, and the Australian team always played there when it was on tour.

Sara Lee had a factory in Utrecht built originally for Douwe Egberts. In late 1988 the Household and Personal Care Division relocated from The Hague to the Douwe Egberts offices in Utrecht. A year later in December 1989 they moved again into the new premises built adjacent to the Douwe Egberts complex in Utrecht. Thomas said you could smell the coffee kilometres away. Coffee was on tap all day and he drank so much that by the end of the day his hand was trembling. Then there was the tobacco. Douwe Egberts didn't make cigarettes, but they specialised in cigarette and pipe tobacco. When Thomas went to a formal meeting the cigarette smoke was sometimes so thick you could cut it with a knife.

At this time there was a remarkable event, which could only be described as ironic. Just as Coca-Cola and Pepsi Cola were deadly enemies, Reckitt & Colman's Nugget was the deadly enemy of Kiwi in Australia. In the United Kingdom it was Cherry Blossom. John Bryan, chairman and CEO of Sara Lee had met John West, CEO of Reckitt & Colman, both in London and Chicago, to discuss the possibility of Sara Lee acquiring their shoe care business. Subsequently Reckitt & Colman suggested Burnett come to their factory at Hull to talk about it. He said, 'They wanted every i dotted, which caused considerable delays. However, we did eventually negotiate a deal that was a million dollars less than the asking price.'

Burnett said that obviously this was a good deal. He was thinking of Kiwi and Esquire, Reckitt & Colman's liquid shoe polish in the United States. So altogether they would have had 90 per cent of the market in the grocery and drug self-service stores. He had sent a memo to his president, Cornelis Boonstra, in the Netherlands telling him this was a good deal and it would give them stronger pricing for their liquid polishes in the US.

Sara Lee subsequently bought the Reckitt & Colman shoe care business in October 1991. A portion of the purchase was made by Kiwi Brands in the USA and part by the

Kiwi UK company. Less than $15 million of the Reckitt & Colman value of the business was ascribed to the USA portion of the purchase for USA antitrust compliance reasons. Under USA merger control regulations, mergers and acquisitions of a certain size must be pre-notified to the government. If the Federal Trade Commission thinks a merger or acquisition is anti-competitive, it will deny clearance. Sara Lee was concerned that its acquisition of the Kiwi shoe care brands in 1984 when combined with the Reckitt & Colman brands would lead to such a large market share that the Federal Trade Commission would move to block the transaction. By ascribing less than $15 million, the threshold for compliance based on the deal size test, Sara Lee thought they did not have to pre-notify.

The Federal Trade Commission thought otherwise and began a proceeding against Sara Lee that ended with them being fined $3.1 million. Burnett recalled attending the proceeding, and his memo to Boonstra regarding the potential market opportunities in acquiring the Esquire brand in the USA was used in evidence. Subsequently Sara Lee had to divest the Reckitt & Colman brands.

This was not the only time Kiwi had got into bed with the enemy. Reckitt & Colman had a dazzling array of products, and Nugget was just a tiny part of the range. Nugget sales in Australia had diminished over the years, probably because of high manufacturing costs and supermarket pricing pressures. In 1983 David Glanville, Nicholas Kiwi's Australian general manager and Roy Price, the factory manager, negotiated an agreement with Reckitt & Colman that they would make Nugget for them at the Clayton factory. Kiwi used the same tins, the same Formula M, and the same snap lid opener. So if a gentleman, who was passionately loyal to the brand encountered, 'Did you Nugget your shoes this morning?' he would not have realised an extraordinary detail: he was actually polishing his shoes with Kiwi.

The story goes back to 1972 when Nugget came up with a new idea: They reduced the quantity of white spirit in the polish and used 50 per cent water. Of course this made the polish cheaper to produce. Furthermore they introduced the snap-top can. The snap-top can had a pressure point, so when the user pushed down their thumb, God willing, the can popped open. The Nugget move caused concern through Kiwi Australia's head office. They would have to do something similar or Nugget could possibly capture their market.

Geoff Rout had been working in the Kiwi laboratories for over three years seeking to find a water-based formula. The big problem was evaporation: once water started to evaporate, the polish would crack and shrink. So the new mixture had the title 'Formula M'. It went into tins with the snap lid, which was more airtight. Formula M became better than the Nugget water-based recipe.

Kiwi produced Nugget in Australia for Reckitt & Colman right up to 1996, but ultimately sales were minuscule and manufacturing in Australia ceased. The reason for this was that possibly the production of Kiwi was on a larger scale and it was cheaper to produce; and Nugget had higher production costs, which were passed on to the retail

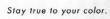

trade resulting in higher retail prices. Perhaps the real cause was that Reckitt & Colman was a great international company with a vast array of products, and therefore shoe care products perhaps had a lower profile.

Kiwi producing Nugget in its own tins was a delightful irony, but there was another. When Sara Lee took over Nicholas Kiwi the contract included a number of across-the-counter pharmaceuticals, including the famous Aspro tablets. For a company that dealt in cakes, apple pie, and household care products it wasn't a good fit. Malcolm Daubney said that many within Nicholas Kiwi thought that Consolidated Foods Corporation was in such a bustling takeover mood and preoccupied with the possibility of acquiring the global Kiwi brand that they hardly seemed to give any thought about the pharmaceuticals.

Early in 1991, the SaraLee/Douwe Egberts board decided to sell the Nicholas business, as they wished to focus more on their household and personal care brands. They were also aware that this OTC (over the counter) business could be worth more to a pharmaceutical company.

The sale memorandum was widely circulated to the leading pharmaceutical companies and around a dozen expressed strong interest. Of these, six were invited to Utrecht to visit the data room and question Tony Jamison, chairman of the Household and Personal Care Products Board, about the business. Jamison was the executive responsible for this divestment. All six submitted offers and two of these were invited to the SaraLee/Douwe Egberts lawyers' office in New York for the final showdown. Following contract negotiations, they were asked for their final offers.

With their more liberal attitude to the contract and an increased offer of US$821 million, Roche were declared the winners. At four times sales, this was a high price but it was recognised by all those interested that it was rare for a leading European OTC business to come onto the market. In addition, with its existing OTC sales of leading vitamin brands, it gave Roche the critical mass they needed to achieve their aim to form a separate OTC Division. For Sara Lee, it gave a good return on their Nicholas–Kiwi investment because they got slightly more for the Nicholas pharmaceuticals than what they paid originally for the total Nicholas Kiwi business.

The Roche and Sara Lee Corporation/Nicholas OTC operations were a good fit geographically and Roche's vitamin brands – Redoxon, Supradyn and Berocca –added a strong, growing product category to the Nicholas OTC business led by Aspro and Rennie. The combined business grew rapidly and by the late 90s had become one of the top three OTC businesses in Europe.

By the turn of the century, Roche decided to concentrate all its resources on its two principal divisions: Prescription Medicines and Diagnostics. Accordingly, they spun off Givaudan (global leader in flavours and fragrances) in 2000, sold their fine chemicals business in 2003 and, finally, divested the OTC business in 2004.

Not unexpectedly, the OTC business was purchased by Bayer, with whom a possible merger of OTC operations had been seriously considered in the past. Bayer paid US$2,900

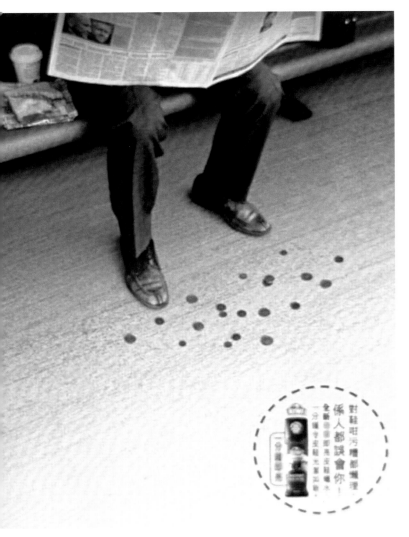

million for the business, 2.4 times Roche Consumer Health's sales of US$1,200 million, and overnight became one of the top three OTC companies in the world.

After 90 years, Aspro had gone full circle, from its roots in George Nicholas's small pharmacy in Melbourne, where George became the first in Australia to synthesise aspirin following the embargo on supplies to the Allied nations as a result of the outbreak of World War I, back to the German company that had introduced the original Aspirin brand to great acclaim in 1899.

So what was Sara Lee doing with Kiwi shoe care products internationally? In 1995 the company interviewed 3,500 people in eight countries to find out what people were doing with their shoes. The news was startling: There was little interest in putting a brilliant shine on one's shoes. That had been out of fashion since the 1960s. They asked 20 questions about what was important in a pair of shoes. Brilliant shine came in Number 17. People were not even interested in having shoes repaired; once they looked a little old they threw them out.[6]

Perhaps the dispiriting survey had some effect, but the truth of the matter was when Sara Lee acquired Nicholas Kiwi in 1984 a diverse portfolio of consumer products was viewed as a strength. However, in the 1990s a diversified portfolio was beginning to be viewed as a liability and was falling out of favour with Wall Street analysts. Following John Bryan's retirement in 2000 management began to look at its smaller businesses and the geographic markets where they were not growing or competing successfully. Subsequently the whole of the Household and Personal Care group, which included Kiwi, fell out of favour. These businesses were too small compared to their global competitors such as Procter & Gamble, Colgate, Unilever and S.C. Johnson. Sara Lee decided therefore to divest itself of several product groups and Kiwi was one of them.

•   •   •

On 31 December 2010 Sara Lee sold its Kiwi products to S. C. Johnson, an American company with 13,000 employees and an annual turnover of more than $9 billion. The global business manufactures domestic products such as furniture polishes, air fresheners, glass and surface cleaners, household insecticides, insect repellents, and of course now Kiwi products.

A press release read: 'S. C. Johnson is pleased to announce it has reached an agreement to acquire Sara Lee's global shoe care business including the beloved Kiwi brand that has been caring for families' shoes around the world for more than one hundred years.'

Founded in 1886 in Racine, Wisconsin, USA, S. C. Johnson has some historical similarities with the Ramsay family enterprise. S. C. Johnson is still a private family-owned business, now in the hands of a fifth generation of the Johnson family. Its brand, starting with parquetry and wax floor care products has, like Kiwi, been a favourite with consumers for more than a century. S. C. Johnson began selling products in Australia in 1917, and had entered the market in Great Britain in 1914. It is a global enterprise with manufacturing facilities around the world, and has many leading brands.

At its peak Kiwi was manufactured in 24 factories worldwide, selling more than 250 million cans of shoe polish annually which, placed end to end, would span the distance between Melbourne and London.

As for Australia, the Nicholas Kiwi factory closed in 1990, but production at Heatherton Road continued at Clayton until 1998. Through the 1990s there were 21 production lines producing a variety of products from toilet cleaners to disinfectants and car polish. Kiwi Shoe Polish was a small item. By far the biggest was White King bleach.

Australians who had believed that Kiwi and Aspro were as Australian as the Digger hat perhaps still thought they were Australian. Sadly, this was not so. Aspro was made in

Gaillard, Northern France. As for Kiwi, the marvellous shoe polish that had its beginnings back in 1906, pioneered by William Ramsay and Hamilton McKellan in Bouverie Street, Carlton, nothing was the same any more. Everyone was proud of Kiwi. It was as Aussie as Vegemite, MacRobertson's Cherry Ripe, Foster's Lager, Drizabone and Rosella Tomato Sauce. Kiwi, with the same marvellous formula, was still available on the shelves at one's nearest Australian supermarket. The tin looked much the same – well almost. The cover carried the line 'Shines, Nourishes and Protects . . . Since 1906.' The kiwi bird was still there, but it looked very different from the bird of old. William Ramsay may have disowned it, although given his entrepreneurial spirit he would have probably embraced the change. But here was the real blow: the polish wasn't made in Clayton in Australia; it wasn't even made in Richmond. There in tiny print that almost required the use of a magnifying glass, was the message: Made in Indonesia.

Sad, perhaps, but Kiwi was always very much a player in the competitive market culture. In its time Kiwi had eaten many smaller fish; in its turn, it was itself eaten by a much larger fish.

Everybody who worked with Kiwi – and all Australians, for that matter – should be proud that Kiwi was probably the most successful manufacturer in Australian corporate history: the brand, recognisable by the flightless little bird that started flying in Australia, has flown around the world for over 100 years and continues to do so.

NOTES

CHAPTER 1
A VOYAGE FROM HUMBLE BEGINNINGS

1 *Essendon Gazette*, 4 January 1901.

2 *City Men*, YMCA, Melbourne, 1 May 1904.

3 Family Bible.

4 Adams, D. S. (ed.), *A Layman's Religion: Essays on Religious Subjects*, Lothian, Melbourne, 1924.

5 *The Encyclopedia of Melbourne*.

6 Anthony Trollope, *Australia and New Zealand*, Chapman and Hall, London, 1876.

7 Fullerton, Patricia, *Hugh Ramsay: His Life and Work*, Hudson, Hawthorn, 1988, pp. 1, 138.

8 Ramsay, John, Journal of the Voyage from Glasgow to Melbourne, 5 March–8 June 1878.

9 ibid.

10 ibid.

11 ibid.

12 Fullerton, Patricia, op. cit.

13 *Argus*, 16 January 1879.

14 *Sydney Morning Herald*, 4 March 1879.

CHAPTER 2
MARVELLOUS MELBOURNE

1 Adam, D. S. (ed.) Ramsay, John, *A Layman's Religion: Essays on Religious Subjects*, Lothian, Melbourne, 1924.

2 Wicking, Janet (daughter of Madge Tompson, nee Ramsay), 'Memories of Clydebank', *c.* 1980.

3 Ramsay & Son advertisements, Ramsay archives.

4 Fullerton, Patricia, *Hugh Ramsay: His Life and Work*, Hudson, Hawthorn, 1988.

5 ibid.

6 Adam, D. S. (ed.), op. cit.

CHAPTER 3
KIWI ANNIE

1 *The Cyclopaedia of Victoria*, Vol. 1.

2 Dunstan, David (ed.), *Victorian Icon: The Royal Exhibition Building, Melbourne*, Australian Academic Publishing, Melbourne, 1995.

3 Rickard, John, 'The big picture', in Dunstan, David (ed.), *Victorian Icon: The Royal Exhibition Building*, The Exhibition Trustees in conjunction with Australian Scholarly Publishing, Melbourne, 1996.

4 Fullerton, Patricia, *Hugh Ramsay: His Life and Work*, Hudson, Hawthorn, 1988.

5 ibid.

6 ibid.

7 Letter to John Ramsay Snr, 24 September 1919.

8 Interview, Noelle Maberley Smith, 18 July 2011.

9 Hugh's father was Richard McClelland. He married Hamilton McKellan's daughter Irene.

10 Letter from Hugh McClelland, 20 October 2011.

CHAPTER 4
MUD, MANURE AND SHINY SHOES

1 Ramsay, T. M., Personal notes.

2 *Manufacturers Monthly*, 15 July 1979.

3 Letter to William Ramsay, 18 April 1912.

4 Letter to William Ramsay, 27 March 1912.

5 Letter to William Ramsay, 12 December 1912.

6 Letter to William Ramsay, 13 September 1912.

7 Letter to William Ramsay, 4 December 1912.

8 Letter to William Ramsay, 10 January 1913.

CHAPTER 5
KIWI AT WAR

1 Ramsay, T. M., Personal notes.

2 Hewat, Tim (ed.), *Advertising in Australia: The Force that Feeds the Market Place: A Working Paper on the Merits and Some of the Sins of Advertising*, Ure Smith, 1975.

3 National Film and Sound Archive.

4 Kiwi Board Minutes, 1916.

5 Barnett, Stephen and Wolfe, Richard, *New Zealand! New Zealand! In Praise of Kiwiana*, Hodder & Stoughton, Auckland, 1989.

6 *Smiths Weekly*, 15 October 1932.

7 Original program, Kiwi files.

8 Ramsay, T. M., Personal notes.

9 *Melbourne Directory*, Sands & McDougall; 1925 telephone book.

10 Interview with Nuki Monahan, granddaughter of James Ramsay (third son of John Ramsay Snr).

CHAPTER 6
LOOKING AFTER BUSINESS

1 Ramsay, John, *A Layman's Religion: Essays on Religious Subjects*, Lothian, Melbourne, 1924, p. xxi.

2 Kiwi Board Minutes; Ramsay, T. M., Personal notes.

3 Ramsay, T. M., Personal notes.

4 James Ramsay, Letter, 28 April 1927.

5 William Ramsay, Letter, 28 April 1927.

6 Ramsay, T. M., Personal notes.

7 Minutes, Kiwi Annual Meeting, 20 December 1933.

8 Dr Ramsay, Letter to John Ramsay, 15 January 1932.

9 John Ramsay, Letter to T. M. Ramsay, 5 October 1933.

10 Dr Ramsay, Letter to Tom Ramsay, 15 December 1931.

11 Ramsay, T. M., Personal notes.

12 McCalman, Janet, *Struggletown: Public and Private Life in Richmond*, Melbourne University Press, Melbourne, 1984.

13 Ramsay, T. M., Personal notes.

14 ibid.; Blake & Riggall to Dr Ramsay, 18 November 1933.

CHAPTER 7
THE FRENCH CONNECTION

1 *Australasian Grocer*, 20 October 1927.

2 Kiwi Board Minutes, 26 February 1935.

3 Clerehan, Neil., *Age*, Obituary, Betty Grounds (formerly Mrs Betty Ramsay), 25 February 2009.

4 *Herald*, *Age*, *Sun*, 5 April 1946.

CHAPTER 8
WORLD WAR TWO

1 Wikipedia, 2012.

2 Tom Ramsay to his brother John Ramsay, 30 September 1938.

3 *The Kiwi Story: The House of Ramsay 1905–1951*, Melbourne, 1951.

4 Tom Ramsay to his brother John Ramsay, undated.

5 Letter from Randy Mann to John Ramsay, 28 June 1940.

6 Letter from Madame Marinier to Randy Mann (translated from French), 20 March 1945.

7 Zecchini, Pierre, Memo (translated from French).

8 Report on Rouen factory, translated from French, by P. Letournelle, 19 September 1944.

9 *Argus*, 20 February 1941.

10 Ramsay, T. M., Personal notes.

11 McCalman, Janet, *Struggletown: Public and Private Life in Richmond*, Melbourne University Press, Melbourne, 1984.

12 Ramsay, T. M., Personal notes.

13 Wikipedia, 2012.

14 *Sun News Pictorial*, 27, 28 March 1942.

15 *Herald*, 11 December 1941.

16 *Examiner*, 7 February 1944.

CHAPTER 9
THE ROAMING RAMSAYS

1 Letter to Tom Ramsay, 5 October 1933.

2 Tom Ramsay, History notes, 6 July 1946.

3 Letter translated from French, 27 March 1945.

4 'Kiwi Polish Short History of Operations in France', 29 September 1969.

5 Letter to Fred Whitney, 11 April 1945.

6 Interview, Anne Folk, 7 December 2011.

7 Interview, Michael Burnett, 11 November 2011.

8 Letter to Fred Whitney, 19 March 1947.

9 Ramsay, T. M., Personal notes, 18 November 1947.

10 Tom Ramsay, Letter to John Ramsay, 24 July 1946.

11 *Daily News*, Perth, 17 January 1948.

12 Ramsay, T. M., Personal notes, 8 May 1952.

CHAPTER 10
THE SINCEREST FORM OF FLATTERY

1 Interview, Jennifer Jeffries, 8 May 2012.

2 Ramsay, T. M., Personal notes, 28 March 1955.

3 Hill, Alan, *Bill Edrich: A Biography*, A. Deutsch, London, 1994.

4 'Kiwi Polish Short History Operations in France', 29 September 1969.

5 Advertisements in *Philadelphia Inquirer*, *Chicago Tribune*, *Los Angeles Examiner*, *New York Daily News*, *New York Daily Mirror*, 23–24 March 1949.

6 *Kiwi International Review*, July 1979.

7 *New Zealand Review*, January 1951.

8 Interview, Fergus Ramsay, 2 April 2012.

9 *Storecraft*, 28 February 1952; Cozzolino, Mimmo, *Symbols of Australia*, Cozbook, Melbourne, 1980.

10 *Argus*, 2 March 1953.

11 T. M. Ramsay, Letter to Bert Bulling, 25 July 1949.

CHAPTER 11
POLISHING THE WORLD

1 *Storecraft*, 28 March 1952.

2 'Kiwi International Conference: Report of Proceedings', March 1963.

3 Ramsay, T. M., Personal notes, 24 March 1953.

4 Interview, Alf Anderson, 19 January 2012.

5 Interview, Cam Smith, 12 August 2012.

6 *Financial Review*, 7 June 1962.

7 *Sun Herald*, Sydney, 10 June 1962.

8 Yule, Peter, *Ian Potter: A Biography*, Miegunyah Press, Melbourne, 2006.

9 *Sun News Pictorial*, 1 July 1967.

10 Interview, Simon Ramsay, 17 May 2012.

11 Calder, Winty, *Mount Martha Lands and People*, Jimaringle Publications, Mount Martha, 2002.

12 Interview, Peter Hunt, 25 May 2012.

13 'Confidential Report on Eastern and Southern Africa', Ivan McLaws, 31 January 1973.

14 Interview, Dennis Shelley, 13 February 2012.

CHAPTER 12
CHANGING TIMES

1 *Wall Street Journal*, 13 January 1964.

2 Letter from Royal Warrant Holders Association, 1 August 1973.

3 Interview, Russell Martin, 22 January 2012.

4 *The Journal*, Traralgon, 11 July 1960.

5 Interview, Fergus Ramsay, 2 April 2012.

6 Ramsay, T. M., Personal notes, 12 April 1976.

7 *National Times*, 24 July 1972.

8 *Age*, 27 July 1972.

9 *Sun News Pictorial*, 27 July 1972.

10 *Age*, 8 February 1973.

11 *Age*, 16 May 1975.

12 *National Times*, 27 May 1975.

13 Interview, Lee Barr and Moreli McDougall, 4 February 2013.

14 Ramsay, T. M., Personal notes, 29 March 1974.

15 Interview, Moreli McDougall, 21 November 2012.

16 Interview, Michael Burnett & Malcolm Daubney, 11 November 2011.

17 Sir Thomas Ramsay to J. W. Ramsay, 23 October 1974.

18 J. W. Ramsay to Sir Thomas Ramsay, 4 November 1974.

19 J. O. Wicking to Sir Thomas Ramsay, 11 February 1975.

20 Interview, Jan-Willem Taminiau, 27 August 2012.

21 Letter from Jan-Willem Taminiau to J. O. Wicking; Interview, Jan-Willem Taminiau, 27 August 2012.

22 *Financial Review*, 24 March 1976.

CHAPTER 13
TOM RAMSAY RETIRES – KIWI MERGES

1 *Weekend Australian*, 12 January 1980.

2 Interview, Anne Folk, 7 December 2011.

3 Interview, Malcolm Daubney, 8 December 2011.

4 T. M. Ramsay, Personal notes.

5 Interview, Michael Burnett, 11 November 2011.

6 T. M. Ramsay, Personal notes.

7 Interview, Ivan McLaws, 24 July 2012.

8 Interview, Anne Folk, 7 December 2011.

9 T. M. Ramsay, address to friends of Baillieu Library, 10 December 1967.

10 Letter to T. M. Ramsay, 24 September 1988.

11 Interview, Liz Cooper, 23 April 2012.

12 Smith, R. Grenville and Barrie, Alexander, *Aspro: How a Family Business Grew Up*, Nicholas International Limited, Melbourne, 1976.

13 Interview, Tony Nicholas, 30 July 2012.

14 ibid.

15 Nicholas Kiwi Annual Report, 1983.

16 ibid.

17 Interview, Lindsay Cumming, 11 July 2012.

18 Interview, Anne Folk, 7 December 2011.

19 Interview, Lindsay Cuming, 11 July 2012.

20 Archival records supplied by Greg Campbell, Church of the Resurrection.

CHAPTER 15
THE CHALLENGING FUTURE

1 *Kiwi: The Future Report*, 1980.

2 ibid.

3 ibid.

4 Interview, John Murphy, 25 October 2012.

5 *Martha Gardener's Book: Everyone's Household Help*, Martha Gardener Publishing, Melbourne, 1983.

6 *The Kiwi Scrapbook*, 1978.

7 ibid.

8 Interview, Simon Israel, 29 April 2013.

CHAPTER 16
THE AUCTION

1 Interview, Brian Healey, 12 May 2012.

2 *Australian Financial Review*, 6 July 1984.

3 *Australian Business*, 24 October 1984.

4 *Age*, 6 July 1984.

5 *Business Review Weekly*, 28 July 1984.

6 *Australian Financial Review*, 6 September 1984.

7 *Herald*, 3 October 1984.

8 ibid.

9 *Age*, 18 October 1984.

10 *Australian*, 26 October 1984.

11 *Sun News Pictorial*, 28 September 1984.

12 *Australian Financial Review*, 1 November 1984.

13 In conversation with Patricia Fullerton, 2012.

14 *Age*, 1 November 1984.

15 *Age*, 20 August 1986.

16 Interview, Malcolm Daubney, 11 November 2011.

CHAPTER 17
BRINGING A SHINE TO THE WORLD

1 Dame Elisabeth Murdoch, Letter to Lady Ramsay, 5 February 1995.

2 Betty Radford, Letter to Lady Ramsay, 30 January 1995.

3 Frank Newman, Eulogy read by Peter Cooper, 17 June 2002.

4 Cadzow, Jane, *Good Weekend*, 15 March 2003.

5 *Sara Lee Annual Report*, 1989.

6 Interview, John Murphy, 6 December 2012.

INDEX

PICTURE CREDITS

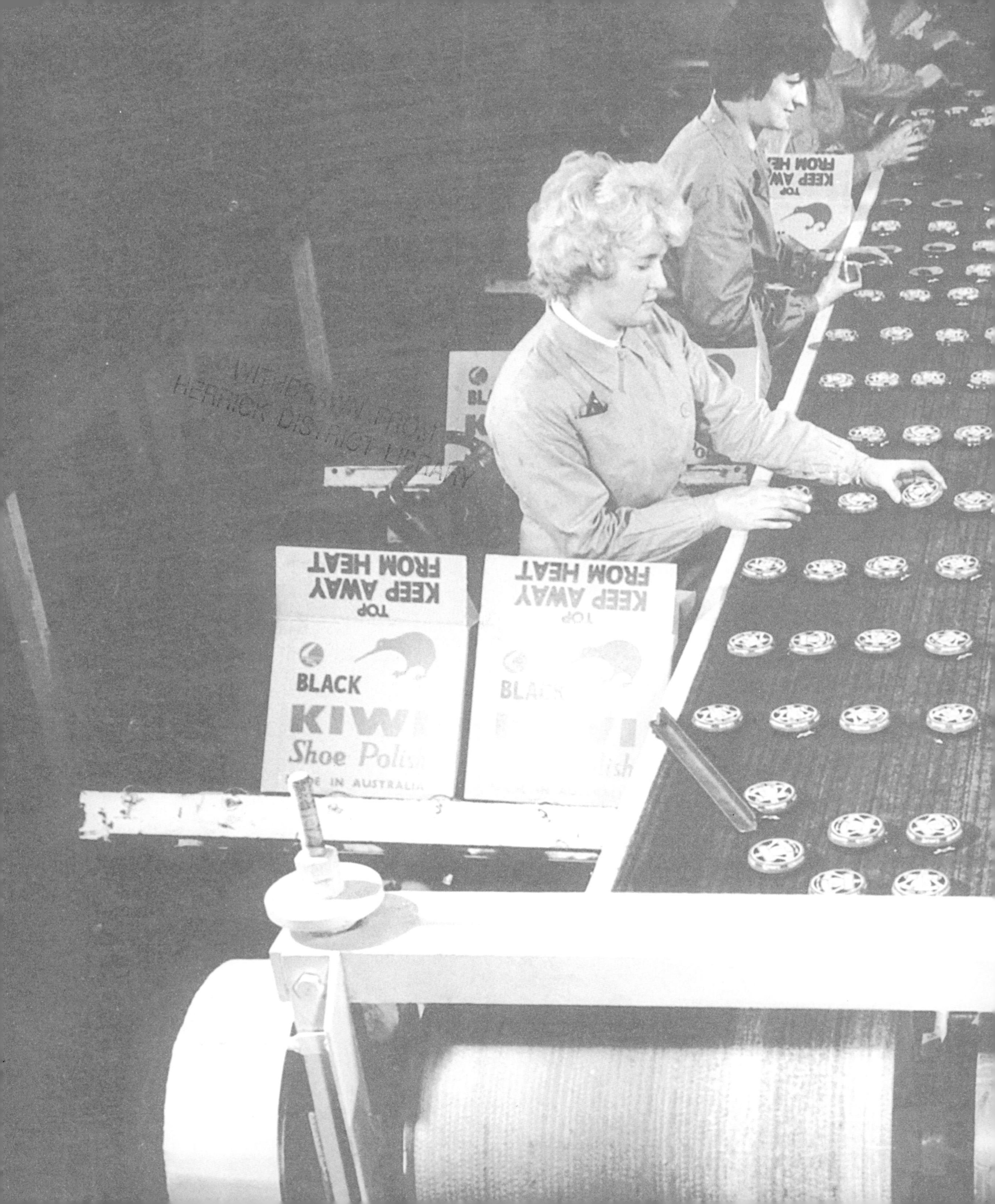
TOP
KEEP AWAY
FROM HEAT
BLACK
KIWI
Shoe Polish